D0518176

CHINA-
THE SURPRISING
COUNTRY

Myra Roper

CHINA—
THE SURPRISING
COUNTRY

DOUBLEDAY & COMPANY, INC.
GARDEN CITY, NEW YORK
1966

CONTENTS

ACKNOWLEDGEMENTS

My warm thanks are due to Professor C. P. Fitzgerald, of the Australian National University, not only for his books but for his reading of my manuscript, which saved me from some errors of fact and of interpretation. Dymphna Cusack's comments on the first draft were most valuable.

In China the senior members and interpreters of the National Federation of Women and the Association for Cultural Relations with Foreign Countries gave me unstintingly of their time and energies; without these my journeys and film could not have been made. I express my gratitude to them and to the dozens of acquaintances and strangers throughout the country who were as keen to answer my questions as I was anxious to ask them. If this book adds one iota to its readers' understanding of the Chinese people today part of my debt will be paid.

LIST OF ILLUSTRATIONS

PROLOGUE
Three Times to China

> Amanda: 'China must be very interesting!'
> Elyot: 'Very big, China.'
> Noël Coward, *Private Lives*

Like Coward's hero, I knew that China was very big; I had learned something of his country and his people from Lin Yutang; I had read Waley's translations of Chinese poetry and the Analects and seen some of the world's best collections of Chinese art. Because of my interest in international affairs I had, over the years, read enough to have a fair idea of the problems involved in establishing relations between the West and the Communist régime in China; but I could hardly have regarded myself as particularly well-informed on the contemporary Chinese scene, when one morning in June 1958, I picked up my telephone to hear a voice asking me if I would like to go to China!

The Women's Federation of the People's Republic of China each year entertains guests from various countries. That year it was Australia's turn and the Federation had asked the Australia–China Society to invite, on its behalf, four women connected in some way with women's affairs; here, out of the blue, was an invitation for me from the Secretary of the Society.

Surprised and rather excited, I said yes at once, subject to further information and professional commitments – a month's break with interesting things to see was a pleasant prospect! I did not realize then that the telephone call was to destroy my political equanimity and involve me in so many reappraisals, arguments, explanations, visions and revisions that there have been times when I wished I had never received it. For my subsequent visit to China destroyed once and for all the neat stereotype, the newspaper headline division, of the Free World and the Rest – the 'goodies' in white hats – Western, democratic and free; the 'baddies' in black (or red) hats – Chinese, Communist and enslaved.

After an intensive reading-course and talks with some of Australia's Chinese scholars, I left in mid-September with three other Australian women. No attention had been paid to political affiliations and, I believe, none of us had any.

The Federation is undoubtedly the biggest women's organization in the world since about 350 million women are in some way connected with it. Among its honorary officers are some extremely able and dedicated women, most notable of all being its President, Soong Ching-ling, widow of the revered founder of the first Chinese Republic, Western-educated, Methodist Dr Sun Yat-sen. Born Soong Ching-ling, one of the three beautiful and brilliant sisters of the fabulously wealthy financier, T. V. Soong, at the age of nineteen she married China's first great revolutionary leader, whilst her sister, Mei-ling, became the wife of its leading counter-revolutionary, Chiang Kai-shek. (It is, incidentally, one of the ironies of history that these two remarkable women should find themselves at the very poles of Chinese life.) Vice-Presidents of the Federation include the Ministers of Justice and of Health, both women.

It has immense authority and prestige, and its guests, I was to find, can visit places and meet many people inaccessible to the ordinary visitor.

The prime purpose of the visit was to show us what the new régime had done 'to liberate' women in China and at the same time to show us developments in any fields of special interest to us. I asked in advance to see as much as possible of higher education and the theatre, my two major interests.

I left for China with no illusions that I was to 'find out the truth about Communism'. My friends and critics assured me, almost to a man, that I would be shown only 'set pieces', see only what they wanted me to see and be beguiled by Chinese charm and subtlety into accepting the essentially unacceptable and seeing the specially-prepared as the usual. Nobody could have been more determined than I to do no such thing; I would look round every corner, under every bed, sift every statement, check every claim.

This, exhaustingly, I tried to do, but, rather disconcertingly, the necessity for it was never dramatically apparent; indeed, one of the least expected features of a remarkable month was a kind of relaxed, take-it-or-leave-it air about what we were shown and told. Triumphant statistics poured over us (the love of these is at least one thing that Americans share with the Chinese). Visible national achievements were laid out daily and out-of-sight ones recorded; but the steady hammer-hammer of Communist propaganda as such was absent; there was no hard-sell by the fanatic proselytizer; I found a tacit acceptance of the régime's past achievements, its present wisdom and future successes, but not the doctrinal ear-bashing for which I had prepared myself. There was less underlining, fewer capital letters in the book of words, numerous as its pages were, than I had expected. Through politeness, policy or lack of interest, nobody ever asked us for our own political opinions or suggested that we should accept theirs. But on my first visit to a Communist country I was most anxious to find out all I could about what Marxism meant to its people, so I initiated political discussions and found that the Chinese never lost their patience, gave as good as they got, and seemed to like me the better for having a go at them from time to time.

Daylong and nightlong we moved around the country and the cities; Canton, Shanghai, Hangchow, and, above all, Peking, to whose spell I succumbed completely. Unforgettable are the glowing splendours of the ancient buildings – the Summer Palace, the Temple of Heaven and, above all, the Imperial Palace with its vast courtyards, Throne Halls, marble steps and terraces, its vistas of multiple overlapping roofs, shining with amber, turquoise and sapphire tiles; remarkable the wide, treelined boulevards and modern buildings, some as splendid as the old; and memorable so many of the people: the plump, black-button-eyed babies, in granny's arms or in the kinder-garten pedicabs, the old man in the park teaching shadow-boxing in the early morning sun, the young students proudly showing off their skills in the Opera School or nervously trying out their English at the Teachers' College.

In spite of official anti-Western slogans and anti-Imperialist posters, China offered us the warmest welcome, and in spite of some irritating political jargon, and doctrinaire pronouncements, 3

I never ceased to feel that the Chinese are one of the world's more civilized people; not for nothing are they the inheritors of the world's oldest continuing cultural tradition.

1958 was a specially exciting year to visit China – the year of the Great Leap Forward, and the country was in a state of euphoria. A widely-circulated English language booklet with the Leap's symbol, a flying horse on its cover, was entitled *We Will Overtake Britain in Fifteen Years*. The first Chinese car had just come off the factory-lines, Chinese food rations were the highest ever. The People's Communes, we were assured, had made a promising start. China was buoyant.

Then, late in 1959, rumours began that the Leap was not the bounding success its symbol indicated; but the tenth anniversary was celebrated joyously enough, on 1 October 1959.

After this, China's public performances decreased in number and scope and in 1961 and 1962 the theatre went dark. There were fewer delegations; 'natural calamities', flood and drought, came and went and came again, with, we read, devastating effect on food supplies and on industrial development.

In the late 1950s, both in India and China, I had heard protestations of mutual regard; India's policy of non-alignment was accepted by China and her support of China's admission to the United Nations was welcomed. Then, with barely a warning rumble in September 1962, the India border dispute erupted into armed conflict (though China's refusal to advance beyond what she claimed was the true boundary did something to ease Western fears).

In August 1963, China broke with an even closer friend. Fascinated, the world watched like spectators at a tennis match, the back and forth of the dialectical ball hurtling between Eastern and Western Communist champions.

Then came the shock of China's denouncement of the Atomic Tripartite Treaty. 'A gigantic fraud,' they asserted, 'the atom bomb is a paper tiger.'

Trying to get at the Chinese points of view I turned to the prolix pages of the *Peking Review* – official English language weekly.

I read the more liberal Western papers but truth seemed at the bottom of a very deep well. I wondered increasingly what my Chinese acquaintances thought about all this. Had their attitudes changed? How severe were the shortages? All the people I had met – the interpreters, the students, the children – were they suffering severe deprivations?

I recalled an incident in a Canton street. I was focusing my camera on a nine-year-old girl with her baby sister strapped on her back. Madame Huang, the International Secretary of the Women's Federation, watched me. 'Take the picture,' she said gently, 'but please tell your Australian friends that we don't like that any more than they do. Come back in five years and it won't be so easy to take that sort of picture.'

I wondered if this promise would be fulfilled; were there more prams in China? Were the women still pushing heavily-laden handcarts of bricks or dung?

To go back was, clearly, the only way to find an answer – or at least the hint of an answer, for that is all the Westerner can hope for in a country as vast, as subtle and paradoxical as a China which has not only the world's oldest civilization but is also witnessing the most thoroughgoing social experiment in history.

In the lean years from 1960 to '62 visitors were not encouraged but in July 1963 the bulletin of the Australia–China Society carried an invitation to join the first Australian tourist party allowed to visit the mainland. Up to this time Australians had visited China only for business or as guests invited by some Government or professional body. This was most encouraging news, for it indicated that China had turned the corner, economically, or she would not be able to look after visitors. I decided to go.

There was great interest in my trip and I was asked by many friends and acquaintances to take full notes, make tape-recordings and bring back pictures. At the time I was doing some work with a small television production company and it struck me that the best way to make a record would be to shoot a television documentary on the tour. Apart from several journalists 5 well known to the Chinese (Edgar Snow, Felix Greene, and the Gelders), very few people had been given permission to make a film of everyday life in China.

I wrote to Madame Huang. Whilst waiting for her reply I optimistically planned the story-line, arranged to hire cameras and buy film. An experienced cameraman and producer, John Dixon was prepared to take the risk of joining me if China was prepared to co-operate.

There were quite a number of ancestral voices prophesying woe – we'd not get in or we'd not get out; we'd only be able to make a Communist propaganda film; it would do us no good; I'd lose all my money, etc., etc.!

Madame Huang wrote to say the Association for Cultural Relations with Foreign Countries would be glad to discuss my request with me when we got to Peking. It was rather non-committal, but I was convinced that we would not get to Peking with all our equipment only to receive no for an answer; my mind was made up.

I decided to raise the capital needed to make the film and set about fixing overdrafts and getting offers or loans from more affluent friends in case of urgent need. Interest in the venture was growing and I began to realize the potentialities of the film.

It was clear to us, of course, that we would get help because it suited the Chinese too, and it was in their interest to see that we did a good job. By good luck, my request must have come at a time when China had decided she needed more voices in the West and a small independent group, organized by someone known to the Women's Federation, apparently filled their bill. I tried to make it clear that we were not committing ourselves to make a 'propaganda' film, free of any kind of criticism. This would not represent our own beliefs, nor would it do China much good for we might not get a showing for it.

What we wanted was to make a fair and objective record of what life in the new China is like for the ordinary man and woman in town and country. We hoped to interpret China in human terms, getting beyond the ideological label, to show

what they ate, how they dressed and played, what they laughed at, what they thought of themselves, even what they thought of us.

We shot the film and, once the work of editing and scripting was finished, I began writing this book, only to find after several months that events in China were moving so fast that once again I was beginning to feel out of touch. China had exploded her first atom bomb, simultaneously suggesting a world nuclear disarmament conference; more and more American forces were massing near her southern border with Vietnam and, though Chou En-lai's March report on the state of the nation (and the United Nations report also) presented a cheerful economic picture, the Premier indicated that the situation in South-East Asia gave cause for the greatest unease. He said China absolutely would not stand idly by' if the war were escalated.

When I heard there was a tourist party leaving Australia for a month's visit in April–May 1965, I decided to postpone the finishing of the book until I had returned for another look. So back I went to try to catch up with history!

In the main, then, this book tells the story of how we made, late in 1963, one of the first documentary films about conemporary China and of what I learned about its people and its spirit during that time. The story is brought up to date in an occasional footnote and in six interchapters and appendices where I expand on aspects of the New China which seem specially valuable in any attempt to interpret China to the West.

1 · HONG KONG
The Waiting-Room

Our little party left Sydney airport, late in September 1963, for Hong Kong via Manila – a smooth journey of some nine hours only. China is Australia's very close neighbour.

Hong Kong has a singularly spectacular airport. A man-made landing-strip runs out into the harbour from the base of a steep mountain range and our incoming plane dived into a girdle of cloud before gliding down the precipitous hillside and shooting off, like a fairground coaster-car, into a harbour crowded with craft from warships down through ferries, sampans and cargo-steamers to junks and rowboats.

With ears popping after the flight and deafened by the street-din, we were shepherded into the neon-lit lounge of our hotel and informed that our Chinese visas had not come and would we please fill in new forms, in triplicate, just in case! At this stage we heard that the present whereabouts of the cameras were unknown. The lounge was stuffy, a television set with some blood-and-bashings serial blinked away – mercifully soundlessly – pens scraped on triplicate forms, luggage littered every inch of space; it was all most dispiriting and my bright visions of Ming palaces, Peking operas, wide green rice-paddies began to fade and ugly prospects of overdrafts, the failure of a mission, to take their place.

Suddenly, the folly of the whole enterprise seemed monumental. Here was I, with a few years' sporadic experience of television, a modest knowledge of China and a more modest one of Marxism, helping to promote – the verb had all the necessary pejorative overtones – a company to tackle a highly speculative and expensive job!

Gloom settled on my spirit. As I scrawled on the visa forms another doubt pierced me like an arrow. Even if our cameras turned up in time and we made the film, would we get it out?

To my surprise my gloom did not prevent my sleeping well, and next morning I woke to good news about the equipment, the arrival of the visas and an interesting invitation to dinner. I bounced up again, my image no longer that of a misguided female but an enterprising woman on an unusual venture.

Geographically, historically and politically Hong Kong is unique. The island itself, along with the city of Kowloon, was given to Great Britain by the treaty which ended the Opium War of 1842. At the same time the New Territories, stretching beyond Kowloon and used partly for dormitory-suburbs and partly for agriculture, were leased to Britain until 1997, when they revert to China. So today there are nearly four million people crowded into one of the few remaining Crown Colonies on the fringe of the world's largest Communist country. Depending quite considerably on territory which it must lose in a few decades, Hong Kong has no guarantee that China will not either try to take possession at the same time of both Kowloon and the Island – or, indeed, seize the whole area long before that.

This uncertainty seems to cause, on the face of it, singularly little immediate concern; it certainly heightens the pace of living, lends an air of excitement, whilst the very proximity to Communist China produces several valuable assets.

Hong Kong has become one of the world's major listening-posts, full of correspondents from all over the world and of intelligence agents, East and West, masquerading as travellers, students or businessmen all busily keeping an eye on one another and writing reports back home. The atmosphere is a blend of an Ian Fleming novel, a Susie Wong film, and a PhD thesis on East–West relations.

But, febrile as the news front is, both sides clearly regard the colony as a precious source of information. As an international *entrepôt* its value is equally high; European and Australian goods enter for sale in China which in turn sells about £200 million pounds' worth of manufactured goods a year to Asia and the West. The sky-scraper Bank of China thrives in its great stone building in the heart of the city (incongruously towering over the Hong Kong Cricket Club), and the mainland Government runs, very successfully, two large retail shops.

Americans cannot shop in these Communist stores in Hong Kong as, with all purchases, they must have a certificate of
10 origin in order to get the articles back into the United States.

The management of the Hong Kong Hilton Hotel may have forgotten this when they filled their new building with thousands of dollars worth of fine *chinoiseries* of every kind and had the usual glittering opening party, only to be informed by their consul that, since insufficient certificates of origin had been obtained, the *chinoiseries* must go. When I reached Hong Kong it was smiling over the Hilton's water supply. To relieve the severe and extremely uncomfortable water-shortage, the British Government had brought water from the mainland, and this, mingled with the local water, flowed through all Hong Kong's taps. What, then, should the Hilton management do? Should it ask its patrons not to wash and to take soda with their Scotch since no certificate of origin could be supplied to distinguish the Hong Kong – and British – water from the mainland – and Communist – water? Americans in Hong Kong were as much amused as the rest by this predicament (Hilton Hotel management excepted).

Being so valuable to East and West, Hong Kong is flourishing, and there is an air of great prosperity, at least in the centre of the city. Building is going on everywhere. Millions of pounds change hands in every sort of deal, with investors reckoning to get their capital back within six years. Trade figures for the first two months of 1965 showed an increase of seventy-seven million dollars over the same period in 1964.

There are beggars and filth and slums, but fewer than in most great Asian cities. The Hong Kong Government has done a remarkable job in extremely difficult circumstances. By the middle of 1963 well over half a million people had been provided with new homes, a resettlement programme costing nearly fourteen million pounds sterling. The average rent in a resettlement estate is about 17s. 6d. sterling a month.

Most of the big money is in Chinese hands and one expects, therefore, to find the strongest anti-Communist sentiments among the Chinese traders. They are there, of course, but not by any means always. A very successful refugee businessman, with a nephew in Melbourne, invited me to an excellent dinner in his big Kowloon flat. He produced a crop of anti-Communist 11 stories and warned me about the brain-washing that lay ahead of me on the mainland. But far more frank conversation with an even wealthier businessman showed me a different attitude. When I gave him my introduction from an English business colleague, he received me politely enough and asked if he could help with my shopping, but when I told him I was *en route* to the mainland he became immediately much interested and insisted that I have lunch with him so that he could ply me with questions about my past and coming visits. Every detail seemed grist to his mill.

'If you are so much interested, why don't you go yourself? Is it hard to get a visa?' I asked.

He looked at me quizzically for a moment, then:

'Frankly, it's what I'd like to do more than anything – to see my own country coming into its own in the world – but I must live, and I live mostly by trade with the United States, and so . . .' He shrugged, smiled and added, 'I can't get to Peking for National Day like you, but we'll have a little celebration here, just the same.'

As a wealthy capitalist, and a Christian, he seemed to stand for everything that the Communists clearly reject, but he was obviously proud of the progress he believed they were making. This was to me only one more illustration of a phenomenon I had noticed on other occasions, both in Hong Kong and Australia: Chinese national pride – belief in the glory of the Middle Kingdom – rises above political doctrine, even considerations of personal interest, for thousands of overseas Chinese (or mainland ones, for that matter).

A contribution to Hong Kong's commercial boom is, of course, the amount of cheap labour available because of the great expansion of its population in the last decades.

Ever since the Colony began to develop it has been, like any city, a magnet for the surrounding countryside where life in the villages used often to be 'nasty, brutish and short'. There is no steady stream, now, of refugees but a little trickle of people coming in daily and a similar one going into Communist China; for families frequently make visits between Hong Kong and the mainland. The *Hong Kong Standard*, 30 April 1964, reports a total of 143,000 re-entry permits given to Hong Kong citizens visiting China during the first quarter of the year.

This is not to deny that there are probably a number of people in South China who are tempted, as they always have been for one reason or another, to go to Hong Kong, which offers them, on the face of it, easier money than the country and has all the traditional pull of 'the bright lights'. I talked to a Shanghai 'refugee' who had established a small tailoring business in Hong Kong in the early 'fifties, which, by 1963, employed eighty tailoring hands. Certainly he could have had no such opportunity for business enterprise in the Shanghai of today.

It is estimated that, since the Communists took over in 1949, the refugees into Hong Kong have constituted about one hundredth of one per cent of China's 700 millions.

As a first glimpse of the Orient, Hong Kong is a colourful and fascinating place; but it is a polyglot city without much character of its own. For me, impatient to 'go in' (from Hong Kong nobody visits China – one 'goes in' and 'comes out' as to jail or an operating theatre!) the Crown Colony of Hong Kong was just a waiting-room.

2 · GOING IN

Only when the China Travel Service Guide met us at Kowloon railway station did I really believe that, cameras and all, we were 'going in'.

The train to the border chuffed cheerfully along through the suburbs of the New Territories, each station crowded with young Chinese men in lightweight Western suits moving confidently among older, peasantlike folk lugging clumsy bundles. In the streets was the same amalgam of East and West, with European and American commuters' cars glistening in the carparks or threading their way among rickshaws and handcarts on the narrow streets. It was odd to think that a few miles away, as if Aladdin were to rub his lamp, almost every trace of the West would disappear the moment we crossed the little iron bridge between the British New Territories and Communist China.

Shum Chun railway station is one of the world's more remarkable little places. One end of it is part of the colony of Hong Kong, and unmistakably British. Beneath the Union Jack, English soldiers and customs officers go about their business in leisurely fashion. Examining my passport, one of them addressed me in faultless 'Oxford', another answered a query in the broad accents of my native Yorkshire.

On the waiting-room tables were old copies of the *Tatler* and *Country Life* with pictures of Home Country debs and thatched cottages for sale in the Cotswolds; indeed, the whole atmosphere was so completely British that it was hard to believe that only a few yards away, beside the Union Jack, the flag of Communist China, with its five gold stars on a red field, was flying in the breeze. 'The East Wind will prevail over the West Wind,' said Mao in a memorable phrase. Today at Shum Chun the Union Jack flutters bravely enough though its days are numbered by the 1842 Treaty.

On the narrow iron bridge between the two countries lounged a few Chinese soldiers; a few peasants, carrying bundles or battered suitcases, were crossing into the Colony with the soldiers grinning amiably at the children trailing behind them.

Picking up our luggage, we walked across the famous bridge alongside the railway line. In two minutes we were on Communist soil being greeted with smiles and handshakes by two China Travel Service interpreters, Li and Liu, and one senior official of that Bureau, Ling. As we walked along the covered way leading to the Customs offices, I knew already that I was back in China, for all along the corridor were the brightly-coloured posters which are one of the most characteristic features of the country, unique in their range and quantity. Political, industrial and local exhortations abound, accompanied by simple often attractively-designed illustrations. There they were, mother getting daughter to clean her teeth, young girl swatting flies, groups of youngsters – black, brown, yellow and white – in attitudes of rather exaggerated friendship, and the Chinese militia, men and women alike, guarding the Motherland against giant-sized Imperialist aggressors; and these were only the first of the thousands more to come.

My fear of a change of attitude on the part of the Chinese towards foreigners was soon dispelled.

The Customs Officer, relaxed in spite of the sudden rush of passengers, smilingly passed our luggage with the most cursory examination and we changed our travellers' cheques with equal expedition. All officials spoke simple English.

We began to pick up our smaller suitcases to go upstairs to the restaurant for lunch, when Ling assured us they could be left where they were.

'Nothing is stolen in China now; your things will be quite safe here.'

If I had heard this on my first visit I should have been more than sceptical of what seemed a very crude piece of easily disproved propaganda. It wasn't, of course.

Many travellers have their special story about this honesty. In 1958, I, for example, left a pair of cheap straw slippers in our special compartment on the Shanghai train. At the end of a twenty-minute reception by the Women's Federation I emerged from the station reception-room to find a porter holding up the slippers for identification. Later, on a visit to a Peking mill, a weaver near us picked up a five-yuan note from the floor; we handed it to one of the supervisors since none of us claimed it. As we left the factory an hour later, it was returned to us; since, we were told, no worker had claimed it, it must have been dropped by one of the visitors. On my 1965 visit I was pursued by a used biro pen which was rescued from two hotel waste baskets; I finally got rid of it by burying it in a way-side bush!

So I left my luggage without a qualm and went upstairs to the restaurant, which had a faintly Victorian air, with lace curtains, a few easy chairs with lace antimacassars, plants in brass or porcelain pots, and large square tables with white cloths. Everything was spotlessly clean. The waitresses, in pigtails and blue cotton pants and white jackets, may have been any age from sixteen to thirty; rather incongruously it seems to us, some women retain pigtails well on into their twenties; they say it's easier to keep their hair tidy that way and leaves them more time to get on with the job.

For the same reason one rarely sees make-up, and certainly our station waitress would probably not own a skerrick of lipstick or rouge, though both are on sale in the towns. Life for women in China – peasants, workers, academics, politicians – is real and earnest, full of strenuous physical and moral endeavour and yet, by one of the country's many paradoxes, most of them are cheerful, even gay. Certainly, our plump young waitress was cheerful enough as she crowded bowl after bowl of food on to the table. There were only chopsticks available and, realizing her mistake, she promptly procured cutlery; but now, as on my previous visit, I was determined when in China to do, in this matter at least, as the Chinese do and use their weapons.

At first the pesky things crossed themselves wilfully of their own accord, like a beginner's skis, but after a time I got them under control and I was away, shovelling in my rice from my lip-high bowl with the best of them. The whole process was like relearning to ride a bicycle – after the initial wobbling, it all comes back!

With the meal we were offered soft drinks or Five Goats beer –
an oddly-named brew which was very good indeed.

On the wall was a portrait of Mao Tse-tung and his bust in
ghostly white plaster was in the foyer. The manufacture of these
busts and portraits must create a major industry for they are,
literally, in every public place and in nearly every home, I suspect; this means that millions of them have been produced
with the portraits showing Mao in his study, gathering flowers,
digging the Ming Tombs Reservoir, smiling at children, leading his comrades on the epic Long March but never, as far as I
could see, surrounded by the paraphernalia of war, although
it was his brilliance and patience as a guerrilla strategist that
gave the Party its final victory over Chiang Kai-shek.

I found train travel in China fascinating and revealing,
affording glimpses of the way of life in the countryside, on
stations and in wayside villages. We were *en route* to Canton for
our first stop-over in a rather old-fashioned steam train. Smuts
were not uncommon, but floors and windows and carriage seats
were very clean, as industrious young women dusted and
polished throughout the journey, while any passing attendant,
or even passenger, picked up the tiniest scrap of rubbish dropped
by an anti-social litter-lout.

As soon as the train drew out of Shum Chun on went the
public-address system. The announcer, a young woman, gave
passengers the latest figures in the current production drive, or
athletic and sporting achievements. There were also national
and international news bulletins (sometimes the latter, when
translated, had a sort of through-the-looking-glass quality).
There were exhortations to work hard, to keep the train clean,
and build socialism, as well as more immediately important
information about train arrival times and food facilities at certain stations. All this was punctuated by wistful little folk songs
or rousing patriotic choruses, strongly reminiscent of their
Russian counterparts. Only the classical opera solos, in their
high falsetto tones, were piercingly and unmistakably indigenous. Once our first interest wore off, we began to find the
system a first-class hindrance to reading or conversation, and 17

were relieved to discover a knob under each window to cut off the noise.

On the little table beneath the window of each private compartment were four mugs, one for each traveller, with small paper packets of green tea beside them. Soon after the departure of any train a girl, in the usual blue cotton garments and wearing a duster-like head-cover, appears with a large watering can, empties the contents of the packet into the mug, douses it with her off-the-boil water, puts on the lid, smiles and departs to return again every hour and refill the cup until the brew is barely coloured by the overworked leaves. But in the considerable heat of South China's early autumn, we found the tea, however pale, most refreshing. Incidentally, notwithstanding all the tea in China, it is a fairly expensive commodity and not yet taken for granted as an everyday drink by the peasants and workers.

On either side of the railway line lush, green rice-paddies stretched away to distant hills with a fringe of trees silhouetting their conical shapes against the sky. It was dreamily beautiful. Fields were unbroken by fences, crops were varied, and everywhere were copses of young trees planted in recent years. Houses and villages, though shabby, were clean and in fairly good condition. People on the platforms were simply dressed in blue cotton suits or floral dresses; no cheong sams with side-splits, no well-cut natty suits, not a stiletto heel in sight – and no commuters' cars at the barriers.

In the countryside the centuries-old way of life still existed, it seemed. Peasant women still wore the rather elegant lampshade hats, each with its frill of black cotton hanging from its broad brim to shelter eyes and head from the fierce sun; half-naked boys steered lumbering water buffalo or leaped laughingly up and down on the foot paddles of primitive irrigation 'systems'. And, just as much as ever, it seemed, the women were as hard at it as the men – threshing wheat, gathering rice or trotting along with that peculiar, swaying gait which is demanded by the long bamboo carrying-pole and its two heavy, swinging baskets.

18

China is a vast, unexploited country with its feudal age not far behind it and still so short of mechanized transport that it cannot make even the smallest leap forward without the toughest manual labour by millions of its citizens. But now Persuasion makes clear the reasonableness of this; it is necessary but not everlasting and at least handcarts have rubber tyres. So the men and women who now grunt and sweat under their burdens glimpse the end of it, if only in their children's day, and in the meantime they do not lack food, clothing or shelter of some kind. Nor, it would seem, do they lack an occasional chance to travel, for as soon as our train reached any platform dozens of passengers leaped out, to be greeted excitedly by friends awaiting their arrival and dozens of others leaped in, waving to friends watching their departure; platforms were a mass of jostling, mostly good-tempered, humanity and the station food-trolleys did brisk business.

Once, as the train was slowing down, we were able to watch for several minutes a traditional funeral-procession passing along the side of the track. Ten or so mourners in shabby, white cotton garments were straggling after the draped coffin, uttering disharmonious cries to the accompaniment of reverberating gongs and melancholy, high-piping flutes. They contrasted oddly with the Party slogan painted on the wall behind them. A little farther on we passed the burial-ground which was still available. Though Communism discourages ancestor worship and animist beliefs we understood that the local council can decide, without pressure, whether burial-grounds should be retained or ploughed up. It seems that the Government, in this as in many other matters, is prepared to wait until a new generation outgrows old beliefs under the influence of new teaching rather than force the issue and cause trouble. But as I watched the elderly men and women stumbling wailing along the track towards the graveyard, I could imagine the different generations among the peasant families struggling to reconcile age-old Taoist beliefs and some of the age-old Confucian concepts with the atheism of the Marxist doctrine taught in the schools.

Chinese cities rarely sprawl, chiefly because, in the past, 19 thousands of city-dwellers had no homes, sleeping in streets or at best in overcrowded tenements instead of building their own little suburban villas far out into the surrounding fields. The city buildings now being erected to provide a roof over every head take the form of great blocks of tiny flats in carefully-located satellite towns, or in so-called model villages, within the city confines. So, comparatively soon after seeing the fringes of Canton city, we drew into the main station.

The Chinese today are much given to official greetings and celebrations. In 1958 it was the Women's Federation who greeted us; in 1963 it was the China International Travel Service representatives and those of the Association for Cultural Relations with Foreign Countries who were helping with the filming. After speeches and handshakes and a bouquet for our unofficial 'leader' we set off in cars to our hotel.

INTERCHAPTER
Interpreters by the Hundred

China might well organize a Ministry of Visitors for it is now high Government policy to encourage these and on a less selective basis each year; visas get steadily easier to obtain.

For every May Day guests are bidden and probably several times the number for National Day on 1 October. All kinds of scientific and artistic congresses are held and foreign scholars are invited to lecture (four members of the Australian Academy of Science visited China in 1964). Forums, athletic meetings and student congresses are common and innumerable small groups are invited just to see what is going on.

The majority of visitors come from Afro–Asian or Communist countries but there is a sprinkling of non-political Western groups or individuals, often of fairly high national standing. For example, senior officials of Australian and Canadian national banks have negotiated quietly and successfully, as far as one can gather from the discreet statements issued on their return.

The President of the Bank of Canada spoke with unusual frankness on the stability of the Chinese economy. 'The growth in industry,' he said, 'the change in living standards, the feats of human effort, are truly stupendous.'

Not surprising, then, an increasing number of Western businessmen are cocking a snook at political differences and going to China to develop the potentialities of 700 million customers with a rising standard of living. The Canton Trade Fair, held twice a year, in spring and autumn, is increasing its business steadily. When I attended, with two thousand other guests, the dinner which marked the closing of the 1965 Spring Fair, the Director reported that there had been over 5,000 customers, 600 more than had attended in 1964. They had come from 120 countries. We saw many Asian – especially Japanese – visitors in Canton and Shanghai (where there is a permanent Industrial Exhibition) and, quite by chance, ran into several Australian businessmen buying shoes, textiles, toys and laboratory glassware. We found the French Ballet Classique touring the country.

We were told that China is planning a big development of tourism and is busy providing more hotels. We saw the beginnings of the 250-room extension to the old Aichun Hotel in Canton and stayed in a new and very well-run hotel in both Wusih and Soochow.

Of all these visitors barely one will speak or read a word of Chinese and even the few who may know enough Mandarin to get by in Peking would be tongue-tied in Shanghai or Wuhan. So China must find a veritable army of interpreters.

For example, our party of twenty-two had two, Li and Liu, and in addition our Travel Service official, Ling, spoke good English; for the filming we were given an extra interpreter. In addition, in each new city we had one or two local interpreters. For big business deals, and, even more, for specialist scientific consultations, the visitor may have his own interpreter throughout his stay.

The demand, then, for interpreters is great and so are the demands on them. From early morning to late-night theatres or banquets they must be on hand, for their wards are helpless without them in a country where even street names cannot be read or maps consulted. They have to answer queries about all the minutiae of daily living – where to buy stamps, to make a phone call, to shop, to find a doctor, dentist or a camera-repair shop. Certainly a special sort of bond is established between an interpreter and a visitor wholly dependent on him; he or she becomes the stranger's *alter ego*. Interpreters also have to supply a steady stream of information on political, topographical and economic questions. Non-communists like myself, of an argumentative turn, involve them, in addition, in protracted, often near-acrimonious arguments on Marxist beliefs; on long train-journeys, these used to go on amongst us for hours. Many of the impressions which visitors take back home depend on their interpreters.

Interpreters must, then, be carefully selected and trained. Clearly, they will be wholeheartedly loyal to their Government and the ideals of Communism; in addition they must be singularly patient and good-tempered; I have seen and heard of tourists getting very angry or demanding but have only once known an interpreter seriously provoked. This was at the end of

22

three and a half weeks of persistent needling and contradicting and demands for special treatment by one of our tourists. The rest of us had marvelled at the interpreters' patience and were not surprised or unsympathetic when one of them finally lost his patience momentarily and gave as good as he got. I knew the interpreter would be angry with himself for losing control, so when I met him shortly afterwards, though I felt I couldn't express my sympathy directly, I offered him a sugared cumquat from a bagful which I had just bought: 'This may help sweeten things.' 'If that is an implied criticism, I accept it,' he said with a rueful smile as he took the sweet. 'Not a criticism,' I replied, 'a little balm for your conscience.' Next day he gave our companion a handsome apology, which was as handsomely accepted, and a happier relationship was established. I always felt the young men and women interpreting for our parties on all my visits were honest; I never found one out in the hint of deliberate untruth, though occasionally they gave inaccurate information through a misconception. I noticed that if any of us expressed serious doubt about their answer they took the trouble to check their facts and report back, right or wrong. Considering the immense range of questions flung at them, the interpreters do very well indeed by their charges. Often inaccurate answers are caused by a misunderstanding of a badly-worded question.

The interpreters do not take final responsibility for decisions of any moment, for with every visiting group there is some senior member from the host body, the Women's Federation, the Association for Cultural Relations, the Academia Sinica, for example, and to him or her the interpreter refers any more involved or contentious matter. Also, this senior member clearly, but not obtrusively, accepts major responsibility for the visitor's welfare. Ling was thus a more influential person than either Li or Liu. Such officials are usually, I believe, members of the Communist Party whilst few of the younger interpreters are.

When I first went to China I was surprised to find so few of the interpreters Party members since, like most Westerners, I had vaguely believed every other person at least must be one. The error of this thinking was brought vividly home to me on a 23 long car-ride across Peking in 1958 with Tai, who had become my rather special friend among our three women interpreters. (Discovering that I taught English at the university, she had asked me, rather shyly, please to correct any of her mistakes; we had had some interesting discussions on pronunciation and finer shades of meaning.)

Tai was a handsome girl, married, more socially-sophisticated than most of her colleagues and with wealthier home-background. Though friendly, like all interpreters, she was reluctant to talk about her own affairs beyond telling us her husband's surname and job and the number and names of her children.

I asked Tai if she really wanted to be a member of the Party and was a trifle nonplussed when she said, with unexpected intensity of feeling, 'I want to very much indeed.'

'But why don't you join, then?'

'Because,' she replied, 'I am not yet worthy.'

So might a novice have spoken about her final vows. Such intensity from a rather detached-seeming Tai took me aback, so I asked, in a suitably awed voice, how she could become 'worthy'. There is something about the back of a dark, swiftly-moving car that seems to loosen tongues normally tied. For a quarter of an hour Tai explained to me her bourgeois background, her family prosperity, her narrow education, her complete lack of contact with the people until Liberation. Unless she learned to see the masses as equals, often her superiors, unless she learned to forget her inherited bourgeois prejudices and preconceptions and could work in all humility side by side with peasants and factory-hands, she would never be worthy. She had also to learn to demand fewer luxuries and comforts, cease to worry about higher salaries and financial rewards and work for the love of her country and her fellows. On paper all this sounds embarrassing and even pious, the Communist variant of a 'revivalist' conversion, but as told me by an intellectually and emotionally sophisticated woman whom I had come to know and trust, it rang true. Multiply Tai by tens of thousands and we begin to see one of the more powerful of the currents driving the New China dynamo.

24

Somewhere in the Party, we know from its own statements and the Press, there are bureaucrats and power-seekers who have to be disciplined. And we can fairly assume, human nature being what it is, that many must join for prestige and authority although not, it would at present seem, for material spoils. As a discipline, Party members' salaries, for example, are lower than those of non-party colleagues. Party members seem to live simply; the homes of the VIP's in Peking are said to be unostentatious.

Party members are undoubtedly a *corps d'élite*, for they comprised, in 1961, only about seventeen million out of a population of nearly seven hundred million. (I have not obtained later figures, but the proportion will not have varied substantially.)

Younger aspirants to membership, like our interpreters, seem to have, then, no chance of material gain, only the prestige and responsibility that membership brings with it.

From quite casual conversations with interpreters the visitor often gets an unexpected slant on national tastes and attitudes. I got a new one on East-West contact from Shu, an intelligent and sensitive young woman, when we went shopping in a State department store in Peking. A soapstone copy of a carved, jade lady was on display next to a Western-style lamp with a panda base and a lolly pink and green shade; the juxtaposition was so embarrassingly in the jade lady's favour that I rushed in to acknowledge it first:

'I'm sorry you are getting some of our worse Western styles. We have some very good ones and it's a pity you are copying things like that lamp.'

'But we like some Western things; they are very modern. What is wrong with the lamp.

I was too taken aback to explain that the lamp was not Western furnishing 'modernity' at its best and that I had expected Chinese good taste would have led manufacturers to copy our better not our worse styles.

Shu added, perhaps reading my mind, 'We cannot look backwards all the time; we must be modern, too. I think it is a nice lamp. Why do you not like it?' I gave up.

Li and Liu, the China Travel Service interpreters, were attractive men in their early thirties, resembling each other in face and manner as well as name. Both were university graduates with an auxiliary course in interpreting; both were married, one to a fellow-linguist, the other to a doctor; both were highly-intelligent, dedicated, but gentle people, most anxious to be helpful, and their kindness, for example, to a one-legged war veteran and to a seventy-year-old woman in our party was unfailing. I believe both aspire to Party membership, and, beneath their gentleness one occasionally glimpsed the tenacity, the singleness of purpose that a member of the Chinese Communist Party must have. They showed an unobtrusive but unmistakable belief in the basic rightness of their Government's policies, though they were flexible enough to admit some mistakes in carrying these out. In the course of political discussions, I thought they tended to overestimate their own strengths and underestimate those of the West about which they had their share of misconceptions. It is here that they can be valuable to their fellow countrymen, for they are too intelligent, I think, not to revise at least some opinions after contacts with their foreign guests. The more of these, then, the better for everyone.

Interpreters take a great pride in their work. An Australian scientist tells me that a foreign delegate at a Science Congress made a particularly unintelligent comment during discussion and was pounced on accordingly by his fellows. He then complained, hoping to dissociate himself from his *bêtise*, that he had been misinterpreted. Thereupon the senior interpreter rose to his feet, insisting, politely but very firmly, that no such misinterpretation had occurred and he wished to exonerate the member of his staff from such an unfair accusation; the translation, he said, had been scrupulously accurate.

Neither Li nor Liu ever introduced a political topic, but both were ready to follow up any that I introduced. Li, on the long train journey from Canton to Wuhan, proved more than willing to explain and justify, for him quite fiercely, the China line in the Sino–Soviet dispute.

26 Ling was a long-standing member of the Communist Party.

Short, plump, fortyish, Ling was the most vital of the three with a quick wit, a nicely-developed sense of the ridiculous, a ready laugh and great personal warmth. His English, self-taught in his spare time, was less fluent and accurate than the others' but he followed conversations with ease. He was clearly a man of authority easily and smoothly exercised. Well-informed on affairs, widely-read and avid for information, he, none the less, occasionally made comments on Western beliefs or habits that showed he had his share of Communist misconceptions about them, especially about the place of the workers.

Not the least valuable result of Western visitors must be the steady infiltration of facts of this kind, for just as I learned to respect the essential honesty of my Chinese acquaintances, so I believe they respected mine and that of my fellow-Australians so that the learning process went on for both of us. It is all the more a pity that there are not some sensible American visitors to dispel a few of the cruder misconceptions of the American way of life.

At least once a day, early in the morning or late at night, the three Ls got together and having, no doubt, pooled their findings on their visitors' idiosyncrasies, recalled the day's mistakes and planned the programme for the morrow.

This sort of discussion is one facet of the nationwide criticism-self-criticism apparatus which is an outstanding feature of the régime. Every office, factory or working-group in town and country periodically holds these sessions to discuss its own shortcomings and plan how to avoid them in the future in order to work better for the common good.

Though much time and nervous energy may be wasted, the basis of this is, of course, psychologically sound (and very much on the lines of group-therapy work being developed by Western psychologists, especially in the United States). In a country where not only the economy is planned, but also many aspects of everyday living, co-operation is essential and warring team-mates a liability.

Not only local but national policies are everywhere discussed and, in addition to the National People's Congress, there is also 27 the People's Political Consultative Committee (and 'consultative' is the operative word). Everyone is encouraged to feel that he or she has a part in what is going on.

In his *Flood Tide in China* C. P. Fitzgerald writes: 'To the great surprise of the Chinese people themselves and also of foreign observers the first, the dominant, the incessant technique of the Communist role turned out to be not violence but talk, unending talk.'

Certainly the interpreters and their colleagues in the Government agencies – the Women's Federation, the Travel Service, the Cultural Association – would have their 'criticism' sessions, for beneath the good-humour and the friendliness there was clearly a tightly-disciplined approach to their responsible job. They must remove not only the routine difficulties of the day's work, but also any 'contradictions' among themselves which might, in any way, hinder their ability to promote the well-being of their country's foreign guests.

3 · CANTON
The First Glimpses

The drive from Canton station to the hotel is a disappointing introduction to the visitor's first Chinese city. There is a certain faded grandeur about the long colonnaded streets and a shabby elegance in the curve of the terraces of houses. Yet all these are European and there is no trace of Chinese architecture. Paint seems scarce, and the courts and alleys opening off the route are dingy and colourless.

As we drove along, I was disheartened to notice that, though there were no rickshaws (these are forbidden), hundreds of Cantonese still earn their living driving pedicabs, the rickshaw's bicycle variant, and there is still an immense amount of human pushing and pulling of heavy loads – logs, building materials, vegetables, refuse – by women as well as men. (There is more in Canton, I was to discover, than in Peking or Shanghai.)

But my spirits lifted as we approached the Pearl River, for then the scene brightened as lawns and trees appeared and the white façade of China's biggest International Trade Exhibition Building gleamed handsomely on the waterfront.

We were to stay at the newly-completed Yang Cheng, which has all the highly characteristic insignia of modern hotel design throughout the country. Spacious to the point of bareness, it has an entrance hall the size of a ballroom; carpeted staircases and corridors, wide as roads, lead to large bedrooms whose polished floors are dotted with occasional islands of small mats, between which are yellow-brown chests of drawers, two bedside tables, a couple of arm-chairs and a desk; bed covers and curtains are usually of shiny silk. Each room has a well-equipped bathroom.

The Yang Cheng had so many wings, so many identical corridors, that one could wander lost for hours unless one was canny enough to note minor landmarks as guides. There are also many dining- and reception-rooms graded for differing numbers of guests. The echoing spaces, the general uncosiness, at first depressed me, but when the hotel staff appeared – they lived in oases on each floor, I discovered – I cheered up considerably, for Chinese servants not only realize they are there to serve, but actually seem to enjoy doing so – and the better they serve the more everyone will be pleased. With smiles cases are carried and morning tea and evening drinks brought at any hour. Other services also come easily and cheaply; I had a white linen, pleated dress laundered in two hours for fifty fen*. Tips are not expected and, if offered, refused; and there is no service charge on the bill.

Canton prides itself on providing the world's best cooking, and I found that the Yang Cheng sought to live up to this exhausting standard with its Chinese cuisine. The European menu which was offered for every meal was appetizing but, of course, less interesting, though I always had the European breakfast with good omelettes and coffee, strange butter and stranger preserve.

Like all other hotels, the Yang Cheng has its many stands for Foreign Language Press publications whose name is truly legion. Given away free – 'please take one' reads the notice in French, German, Russian, Japanese and English – are past and present numbers of booklets, leaflets, weeklies, closely-argued, quotation-filled treatises on doctrinal and practical aspects of the Communist way of life in China. These are often heavy-going, but a most valuable source of information for the serious student of Chinese affairs. More attractive and decidedly more readable are the beautiful, lavishly-illustrated magazines, *China Pictorial, China Reconstructs* and – for the young – *Evergreen*.

After an excellent lunch in the Chinese dining-room, we left on a tour of the city and I realized that, in spite of some drabness and poverty, there is neither despair nor lethargy in Canton, none of the hopeless resignation of, for example, some of the poorer city-dwellers of other Asian countries or the Middle East. The people know they are moving forward, and though some of their streets may be dingy, they are all very clean. The city has uniquely attractive litter-bins of dark blue and white pottery, made in a centuries-old ceramic factory, and the

* About 1s. 6d., there are 100 fen to the yuan, which is worth just under 3s., 45 American cents or 30 cents Australian.

Cantonese very conscientiously use them. We drove past many parks and gardens, a cultural park and an athletics stadium seating 50,000, which stands in a 200-acre park constructed on war-devastated ground by voluntary labour.

We made our first stop at the Martyrs' Memorial Park. The wide, shallow curve of its stone gateway is fronted by a great patio; on this children played, old people sunned themselves, and, surprisingly, a few street hawkers peddled their wares, including, even more surprisingly to me, 'icy-poles', a sort of water-ice on a stick; I had thought such things would be near-luxuries in China.

A revealing little incident occurred. I broke off a conversation with Ling, an officer of the Travel Service and the senior of our Chinese companions, to take a coloured 'still' of a picturesque old woman in vaguely traditional garb seated beside her baskets of fruit. As soon as she saw me focusing, she leaped to her feet, shook her fist at me and let loose such a flood of, presumably, Cantonese Billingsgate that I hastily retreated; an amused and interested, but not hostile, crowd gathered as I ostentatiously put my camera away. Ling, a generous soul who liked his guests to do as they wanted, looked embarrassed, apologized and explained that if that was how she felt – well, no picture. It was only later that I realized the significance of this incident. Ling was a senior Party man of some standing, yet he did not complain to the woman; he did not even try Persuasion; she had a right to object and he let her. I better understood the woman's attitude when, soon after, I tried to photograph an ancient peasant in the countryside; the local guide explained that it would be better if I did not take the picture for the old man probably believed I would have a malign hold on him if I possessed his likeness.

Back to the Memorial Park. It is well laid out with trees and flower-beds and some cunning vistas leading the eye to coloured pavilions and pagodas. I was walking along with Frank, an ebullient, middle-aged member of our party with all the socialist enthusiasms of the 'thirties still alive in his heart!

'Wonderful park, wonderful,' he said, literally rubbing his 31 hands. 'You Chinese certainly know how to do these things; we've nothing like this in Australia.'

I was nettled into a sharp reply because I thought a principle was involved.

'Ever seen the Melbourne Botanical Gardens, my Sydney friend – they are even better.'

What had stirred me was the 'internationalist's' tendency to try to establish good relations with a foreign country by praising its achievements at the expense of those of his own country. Such well-meaning attempts must have helped, unintentionally, to create some of the tragi-comic misconceptions about the West which obtain in both China and USSR False images of the country on the other side of the river, the people beyond the curtain, are built up assiduously enough by both sides' propaganda and reactionaries, so it is tiresome when sympathetic moderates cross the river and, with all the goodwill in the world, help to carry on the bad work.

Of course, this is precisely the kind of thing that makes a visit to China today so exhausting; the constant comparisons, the scrupulous weighing of pros and cons, the deciding when to admit our own weaknesses and when to tell our hosts quite bluntly that they are wrong about us; or, harder still, to tell them when, by our standards, they are wrong about themselves.

The Martyrs' Memorial is itself a simple circular mound of earth, contained by a low, stone wall whose only decoration is a few carved, stone, stylized lions. It was built in 1954 near the Red Flower Knoll where Chiang Kai-shek executed some five and a half thousand revolutionaries after the first Cantonese uprising in April 1927. The victims had been members of Chiang's own Kuomintang Party – itself pledged to reform – but Chiang turned against them when he decided to break with the Communists in his ranks. On this spot, it is said, 'Chiang Kai-shek first betrayed the Revolution' and it is sacred soil to the Communist Party of China.

Not far away, on the grass, a group of seven-and eight-year-old children were out with teacher for air and exercise; more cheerfully-dressed than adults, they wore bright cotton smocks or long pants with floral blouses, the girls sporting bright ribbons on the ends of pigtails or perched, butterfly-like, on the crown of the head. Even in Canton, with its Trade Fair visitors, Europeans are a source of excitement for the young and our arrival, with cameras, queries and head-pattings, produced shrieks of mirth. Two of the children seized hold of my hands at once and dragged me, proudly, as their captive, to their own little circle of friends; here Frank joined me and in his usual lively fashion started to sing 'Waltzing Matilda'. I sang, too, and there we stood surrounded by clapping, jigging youngsters, belting out a tuneless but very rhythmic version of Australia's best-known song.

Meanwhile, Li, the interpreter, had arranged for the whole group to sing for us; their behaviour was wholly characteristic of Chinese children today. At a sign from the teacher they became quiet, sat down on the grass, relaxed and unself-conscious, giggling softly; then a nine-year-old girl rose and took charge of the proceedings. With great solemnity and considerable authority, she conducted the first two songs, which, to some of the newcomers, came as a slight shock, for here was the first example of politics for beginners. The first song was 'Hail, Chairman Mao' followed by a local song 'We are Walking in the Martyrs' Steps'. After this there followed a breathless little speech of welcome from a six-year-old boy: 'On behalf of the children of China I give welcome to visitors from Australia.'

As we sat down the singing immediately began again with gusto.

'Red Star', we were told.

This struck me as going a bit far for babies, so I asked the teacher if the class sang only political songs like this; what about children's ditties and folk-songs? (I knew that these were officially encouraged.)

'Oh, yes,' she explained, 'they know many of these, too; but we thought you would find the others more interesting.'. Then, very sweetly, the class struck up, 'The moon is rising, a gentle breeze is blowing; we are sitting under a tree listening to Mother telling us a story – a story about the past.' It was most 33 attractive and we waited for another like it, but then up sprang a young man, and in a piercing soprano declared, 'I am a Negro boy from South Africa; exploitation and colonialism will come to an end. We want peace, freedom and independence.' Afro–Asian solidarity in the making!

The sentiments of the song were impeccable but as the fourth political item out of five, it depressed me; I longed for them to sing more about Mother's moonlight stories and less about national and international problems. How much they understood of them I hardly knew, for they followed in the martyrs' steps with some cheerfulness, and seemed unmoved by the catalogue of Africa's miseries.

As we left, my two young friends returned to take my hand with confident smiles, and as we all moved away, the children stood waving vigorously and shouting in chorus, 'Good-bye, Uncles and Aunties, come again, come again.'

On this and other occasions I expressed to the Chinese a certain unease about what seems to us an untowardly early start of political instruction. I was told that it was not only political, but moral instruction, too. Children must learn to be good citizens, and make the best possible contribution to the community; they must love peace, help the oppressed nations and understand the necessity to defend their country against possible aggressors.

Canton is a key city in the history of the Chinese Revolution for it was here that Dr Sun Yat-sen planned the movement that led to the final overthrow of the Manchu Dynasty and the establishment of the first Chinese Republic in 1911. One of the national shrines is the Peasants' Movement Institute, which, after years of war and foreign occupation, has been restored as far as possible and given the appearance it had in its heyday. Originally a Confucian Temple, it was taken over as an educational institution in the early 'twenties.

It is built round courtyards filled with trees and flowering shrubs; the walls of its cloister-like terraces are lined with portraits, some faded and mildewed, of early patriots and revolu-
34 tionaries who worked or visited there.

Several of them, notably Chou En-lai, Mao himself and the scholar, Kuo Mo-jo, lived to triumph twenty-five years later; many others perished at the hands of the Kuomintang or during the rigours of the Long March.

Whether one looks at Mao Tse-tung from the Left or the Right, he is certainly one of the prime movers of history and so any place or person with which he was closely connected must be of world interest. In the Institute is a bare, cell-like room, with stone floor and high windows; ill-lit, it has a rough table, a couple of simple chairs and a narrow bed with a white cotton cover; in these Spartan conditions Mao Tse-tung lived when he gave his famous lectures on the state of China in the 'twenties, and on the same table, in 1926, he wrote his epoch-making treatise, 'An Analysis of the Classes in Chinese Society', charting the course which the Chinese Revolution must – and did – take. Rarely have prophecies proved so accurate and few rooms have witnessed such far-reaching revolutionary birth throes. The Institute poses one of the great 'ifs' of history.

It was the Cantonese, Western-educated Sun Yat-sen, 'that improbable medical revolutionary', as Professor Needham calls him, who planned a Western-style democracy for his country after toppling the Manchu Dynasty in 1911. If he had been a better soldier, a more ruthless administrator, less influenced by those aspects of the democratic ideal ill-suited to China's urgent needs; if, above all, the West had better understood the modifications which had to be made in China's political pattern to suit a hopelessly out-of-date economy; if, in spite of some doubts and pressures, it had supported him instead of the 'compradors' and warlords, then would there have been the need for Mao's treatises, the civil war, the bloodshed and the long agony of Japanese occupation? But when many Europeans ask if, with enlightened Western help and tutelage (not domination) China could have achieved its own peculiar variant of Western democracy, they must also ask if Western democracy is too much a product of slow growth and careful nurturing to be suited to a country emerging from feudalism and anarchy.

35

Sun Yat-sen died too soon and his young Moscow-trained successor, Chiang Kai-shek, took over his inheritance, but followed neither Western democracy nor Russian Communism, seeking instead to establish an old-style, near-imperialist oligarchy with himself at its head.

One can regret deeply Western depredations in China, but must admit that, when it comes to blood-letting, the Chinese at war with themselves have nothing to learn from us. When Chiang 'betrayed the Revolution' a second time by breaking the anti-Japanese pact with the Communists, he slew some 12,000 Shanghai workers in three weeks in 1946 (quoted by Felix Greene), and Edgar Snow reports that a senior Party member told him that of the 50,000 members they had in 1927, some 40,000 were killed by the Kuomintang. Stuart Gelder, quoting from the report, 'United States Relations with China', writes that 100,000 suspected Communist sympathizers were massacred in Kiangsi Province in 'indiscriminate slaughter'. Tens of thousands of villagers perished in the floods when Chiang Kai-shek breached the Yellow River dykes in 1936, to stop the Red Army's advance. The exact numbers killed by the Communists is hard to discover; it varies from the undocumented, unverified 'countless millions' of popular Western Press statements, to the 800,000 given by Edgar Faure, former Premier of France, in *The Serpent and the Tortoise*, and the 50,000 of Professor C. P. Fitzgerald in *Flood Tide in China*.

Between them all, modern China has seen more of the long agonies of death and destruction than any country; the toll of human life in establishing the New China has been horrifying; and along these now peaceful corridors, I thought, as I myself trod them, walked the men to whom Fate had given leading roles in this tremendous drama. I have rarely felt a building to be so nearly haunted or so uncannily surrounded by an aura of the past.

Since the China Travel Service takes it for granted that the visitor comes to China not only to holiday but to learn, every few days it draws up a list of carefully-planned visits to illustrate the glories of ancient China and the achievements of the new in as many fields as possible. This is by no means rigid and one can cut out or ask for alternatives.

On our Canton list was an example of a characteristic national phenomenon – what I call a 'home-made' factory, an industrial enterprise near the bottom of the industrial ladder whose top rungs are the great iron and steel combines of Wuhan and Anshan, and the bottom ones the neighbourhood factories or the occasional backyard smelter left over from the 1958 steel-drive. The Government, we were told, encourages the people to branch out for themselves. *Dare to think; Dare to speak; Dare to do* is the title of another Foreign Languages Press booklet, giving what the Westerner who has not visited China before may consider rather unexpected advice.

At the small electrical factory, next morning, we were met by the manager, neatly-dressed and, as so often, seeming very young for his responsible position. We drank tea in his office whilst he gave us one of the detailed briefings which await the visitor 'hot for certainty' in the New China.

On the face of it, the place had a hand-to-mouth appearance with its clean but untidy yard dotted with unpainted sheds of various sizes. Not much seemed to be going on, but we were told that the factory had 780 hands making, mostly, 5,000-kilowatt transformers and portable electric fans and pumps. Built before the Revolution, the place had gone out of business, but 'under the leadership of the Party', it had been successfully restarted at a minimum of cost and with staff trained by a minimum number of skilled technicians in 'crash' courses. It was a local success story.

Wages were low, an average of sixty-eight yuan a month* for a forty-eight-hour week, but housing was provided for young workers at only fifty fen a month, whilst food cost them only eight yuan a month; for married workers rents were about five per cent of their income; retirement-age was fifty-five for women, sixty for men. The place had an amiable, relaxed air.

An important part of China's persuasion-propaganda-criticism apparatus are the factory and office wallboards, called

---

ta tzebaos—'big character news'. They show production-target figures, with names of model workers and successful part-time students—and of the laggards who failed to reach their targets and must try to do better next time! Party encyclicals go up, too, and the local council's requests for workers to join in some community drive for cleanliness or mental or physical health.

Workers' complaints about 'the management' can be posted on these, too. A professor at Peking University told me that students could so criticize their teachers and he assured me—seeing I looked shaken!—that he did not mind because the students did it as nicely as possible, and with the best intentions in the world! Dymphna Cusack, the Australian novelist who lived for two years in Peking, and speaks Chinese, tells me that she saw a notice on the Board of the Foreign Languages Press in Peking which declared: 'Department Heads do not mingle enough with the workers.' On a Primary School 'big character news' I saw a drawing of Picasso's dove with a small child beside it saying, 'I want to be a bird of peace, too.'

Bitter outbursts against imperialist aggressors in Cuba, the South-East, Asia, Africa and Latin America often rub shoulders with moral exhortations—'Don't smoke too soon.' 'Don't be bourgeois.' It is characteristic that such businesslike and often uncomfortable statements are often surrounded by chalk or pen-and-ink sketches of flowers, landscapes or children, drawn by amateur artists. On this Canton board the bitterest anti-imperialist diatribe had a delicate border of chrysanthemums and butterflies!

As we walked around the grounds, the public address system was blaring forth with a girl's voice interspersed with music. I found myself humming 'Blue Skies...all the day long...nothing but blue skies from now on.'*

'That's a good old tune,' I said, turning to Li who was with me; then, watching him closely, 'It's American, you know.'

Li looked startled—'Oh no, it's Czech.'

'One hundred per cent American,' I said firmly, and added, dead-pan, 'You should get a certificate of origin with your music.'

What with trying to catch the reference and working out the implications of Communist workers listening to imperialist tunes, Li's imperturbability was shaken and he didn't smile.

'I'm only joking, Li,' I said, 'don't look so serious, even if it is a Yankee tune; I think it's rather funny.' Li did not. As we entered the next shed, he slipped away and a few minutes later 'Blue Skies' ended in mid-bar; two more minutes and there blazed forth the unmistakably non-imperialist rhythms of the 'Internationale'. Shades of the Hong Kong Hilton!

The same theme returned in the same serio-comic circumstances at the theatre we visited that night. It was a sort of variety show held in one of the many open-air theatres in the big Cultural Park where citizens can wander for hours watching classical and modern operas, puppet shows, films or TV. They can roller-skate on a large rink, visit an aquarium and a variety of exhibitions, sit in one of several cafés or tea-houses, or watch chess matches where the players' moves are marked off on a giant board for the crowd to follow each move. Entrance fee is ten fen for the lot*, though there is a small extra charge for seats at the operas and acrobatics. A bewilderingly clever conjurer concluded his act by producing from nowhere a stage-wide, scarlet banner with great golden characters; these, being translated, read 'Smash the Imperialist Aggressors'. Liu was the interpreter this time, and as ever, he saw nothing incongruous about translating this fierce injunction to a Western guest for whose happiness in his country he was, I know, genuinely concerned. I was not to take this to heart because I was one of the Western masses and it was not against me, then, that all this was directed but against our 'imperialist' leaders and grasping capitalists. This sounds perilously like double-think but, on balance, after meeting many examples of it, I am sure it is not. We were just not expected to be offended at anti-Western slogans, which were unself-consciously translated for us; if we

* About 3½d. See p. 30.

are in China it is because we wish to be friends with her people, and so criticism is not directed against us.

A British diplomat in Peking told me that he and his family, on holiday, had been invited by the local Mayor to a concert as honoured guests and received as such. Amongst the song and dance acts were scattered topical sketches, two of which dealt savagely with the behaviour of the British in the Middle East crises then obtaining; this was not in any way regarded as a deterrent to the good time being had by all, and none of the charming hosts expected offence to be taken.

Before the theatre visit we had a most satisfactory conference on the filming with the Canton officers of the Cultural Association, who told us they had found a good cameraman to help us during our stay in Canton, and were also providing a special interpreter and transport so that we could leave the main tourist group when we needed. We were most grateful and recognized this as a very favourable indication of the kind of help we were to receive throughout our visit.

INTERCHAPTER
The Communes

Among all Chinese myths and legends reaching the West the communes hold pride of place. They have been presented as quasi-concentration camps. We read of peasants herded into military-style barracks, separated from their families, always hungry after 'staggering food-production failures'.

Even to the more sensible Western reader it has appeared that the whole commune movement was imposed from Peking by the Party ukase. 'Let there be communes,' said Mao Tse-tung and, like it or not, the peasants had communes.

Having visited some eight communes, and spent several days in one of them, I could not find any foundation for all this. To begin with, far from being fenced in, a commune has no obvious boundaries. I had at first vaguely expected at least to pass through a gate and be aware that I was well and truly in such and such a commune; in fact, I was no more aware of moving from one to another than I am of crossing from Yorkshire into Lancashire or Victoria into New South Wales. Only the locals know which village is in which commune, for the term 'commune' is really an administrative and social one, referring to roughly the age-old division of the Chinese countryside into *hsiangs* or townships, each containing a number of villages. I noticed that, as for centuries, the village today counts its inhabitants by households rather than individuals; the family is still the important unit.

It struck me, too, that the commune as an administrative unit bore some resemblance to the English County Council, though its role is more inclusive and its control far wider. Not only is the commune responsible for agricultural production and organization, but also for primary and some secondary education, for shops, canteens, light industries, hospitals, clinics and sporting and entertainment facilities.

The short- and long-term needs of the country as a whole, for both agriculture and industry, are worked out in great detail by the various ministries and Government agencies in Peking. These, along with Government economists, set various targets; but they do this only after the most thorough consultation with relevant representatives at various levels of the community, from city or provincial councils down to the commune committees at grass-roots level. In this, as in many other things, the traffic is two-way – ideas are sent up as well as down (probably more now than in the early days).

Within the commune itself there seems to be much room for discussion, even argument; provided the general directives are observed and targets achieved, there is some opportunity for adaptation and alteration.

The finance of a commune is pretty much its own concern. It can market its produce either through Government purchasing agencies or, by arrangement, direct to local industries after deducting food and other products for its own needs. What these needs are the commune councils decide. The more they keep, of course, the less they earn in cash. Commune members pay no individual income tax, but each commune pays to the state six per cent of its earnings, and once this is paid a certain proportion of income is allocated to reserve funds or to capital expenditure on commune or regional developments. From the remainder wages are assessed on a system of work-points calculated with reference to the available labour and finance.

The size of communes varies greatly, both in area and population, not only according to the productivity of the land, but also to the traditional habits and occupations of the region, for, in communes, as elsewhere, the Communist Party does not use force or direction when discussion, persuasion, re-education will serve its purpose better. From the question of ancestor-worship and funeral customs down to the planting of the odd acres of land, the Government is usually prepared to wait for local decisions to be thrashed out. Of course, every village has long had its Communist cadres, its Peking-trained young men and women who have acted as a stimulus to modernization and Marxist–Leninist thinking, but after some initial mistakes they have worked as far as possible within the local traditions and with some of the local people.

The commune has a democratic structure. Its basic unit is the production-team, which, again, varies considerably in size

between wheat, rice and tea-producing districts, for example –

between the steppes of Inner Mongolia and, say, the rich fish and rice areas of the Taihu lakes, near Shanghai.

Ten to twenty teams are grouped into brigades, and I found that often the brigade is co-terminous with a village, so that the pre-revolution unit maintains its identity. As well as the commune itself, each team and each brigade has a leader who acts as chairman of the appropriate committee or council. Team committees elect members to the Brigade Council, which, in turn, has its elected representatives on the Commune Council. At least forty per cent of the Commune Council members must be women, and very often the Vice-Chairman of the Brigade and Commune Council is a woman. There are regional meetings of commune councillors to discuss joint projects for irrigation or large-scale mechanization.

The Commune Council usually meets two or three times a year; the Brigade Council once a month, whilst team committees meet whenever the need arises, often in the fields on the job. In addition, of course, every adult man and woman votes for the local member of the Regional and Provincial Congresses. Though commune and brigade leaders are responsible and important people, they are not very highly paid; they need not be members of the Communist Party, but I believe they usually are.

Wages are lower than in the cities and the general standard of living may, generally speaking, fall below its urban counterpart. But, even so, conditions are more than satisfactory compared with the miseries of the old days, when flood, drought and the depredations of war were endemic. And wages have increased tenfold since 1949. Members of the tea commune near Hangchow, where we shot our commune sequence for the film, had, in 1965, an average family wage of 920 yuan per annum, but I heard that one large, specially hardworking family earned as much as 2,300 yuan. In addition, today, most peasants have a house, or part of a house, of their own; they are allocated supplies of basic foods from the commune's stock and can augment these from the vegetable or animal produce of their own private plots which they cultivate assiduously. Education is 43 very nearly free, medical services free or very cheap, and sporting and entertainment facilities are increasing. There is every encouragement to the women to start their own co-operative ventures, for which the Commune Council may allocate loans or services to help them get off the ground; enterprising women can earn good money in this way. Because of the close-knit character of the whole life, few can be lonely and the old and the sick are cared for. Families temporarily without the bread-winner for any reason are supplied by the commune welfare fund. There will be no privacy on a commune, but no loneliness or neglect, either.

Village amenities are steadily improving and it is estimated that the majority of villages now have electric light. Certainly, I found it in all the dozen or so that I visited. Furniture, once very scanty indeed, is now becoming commonplace, radios are almost taken for granted, and most peasants have, or are saving up for, a bicycle and a wristlet watch. It is Government policy to do everything to ensure that the standard of living in the country shall approximate to that in the cities as far as possible.

This is not to say that the peasants have a particularly comfortable existence. In most of China modern production techniques as we know them are wholly inadequate. The shortage of chemical fertilizers is lamentable, and even the increased output of the new fertilizer factories, which have diverted labour and materials from certain heavy industrial plants, is still far from adequate. Even in the more prosperous communes I saw, as late as 1965, innumerable handcarts doing the job of a couple of trucks, and innumerable muscles straining to give the pushing, pulling or lifting-power of one tractor, crane or bulldozer. Every kind of mechanical aid is now being made in China, but each will have to be multiplied a thousandfold before manual labour is noticeably reduced. The variety of food is small and there is still some rationing of rice and certain articles of clothing.

In the communes there are still tensions and strains, resulting both from habits of mind retained by some former wealthy 44 peasants and landlords, who resent communization and the equality of all commune members, and from mishandling by Communist cadres or by impractical 'experts'. These are problems of which no casual visitor to however many communes can be more than dimly aware. But they are not wholly concealed by the Government. They appear – and, of course, with tacit official approval – as the theme of many stories, plays and films. A widely-acclaimed modern opera, in traditional Peking-style, called *The Seal*, recounts the efforts – defeated, of course – of old-guard reactionaries to undermine commune discipline and morale. Party writings, exhortations in the *People's Daily* and in local papers, reveal many wrong attitudes, 'contradictions among the people', some abuse of privilege, some lack of initiative, some fuddy-duddy fussing and sticking-in-the-mud, some considerable errors of planning. But all this does not invalidate the concept of the commune as a viable rural unit for China; it indicates weaknesses but not failure; it mainly indicates that people living in communes are human.

Small-scale, non-mechanized farming is as outmoded for China as for Australia, the United States or the United Kingdom; and far from being a curb on China's agricultural development, the communes have been its spur. Professor Joan Robinson of Cambridge, the well-known economist, has paid some six visits to China since the revolution. In a talk on the BBC, reprinted in *The Listener* of 30 January 1964, she said:

> Even the slightest first-hand impressions dispel the fog of propaganda about the communes, recently coming from Russia as well as the West. It has been said that they aim at destroying family life. On the contrary, the commune system fosters and protects the family.
>
> Did the communes break down in the bad years? Anyone in China will tell you that the opposite is the case. It was the communes that made it possible for the authorities to see the country through without the famines and massive deaths from starvation that were commonplace in the old days, and to keep the prices of foodstuffs steady.

It now seems clear that the account of the origin of the 45

communes given by official sources in 1958 is substantially correct, though it was turned down out of hand by most Western writers at the time. The steps in their development were logical. Long-overdue land-reform was started by the Communist Party in the 'thirties whenever they took over any province. This revealed the Party's genuine determination to carry out the reforms promised repeatedly by the KMT but never widely-implemented. Land to the tiller seemed fine at first when the old days of landlord and money-lender were still vividly recalled. But it soon became obvious that small peasant-plots were uneconomical. Mutual-aid teams appeared, helped by the Party and trained cadres; these in turn became agricultural co-operatives in which several mutual-aid teams joined together to buy seed and equipment and rationalize labour. In each village there were peasants who contracted out, rejoicing in having their very own land and not wishing to give labour or support to the co-operatives. But soon the majority of these found that they were less prosperous than their fellows and gradually they joined in. A good deal of experience and technical skill was interchanged between neighbouring co-operatives during the 'fifties and this, amongst other things, revealed a need for even wider joint efforts and consultation. News of a few experimental communes spread with extraordinary rapidity until by mid 1958 almost the whole of China was communizing itself with greater or less expedition.

This is an over-simplified account, but the pattern is clear enough and has by now been documented in detail by several impartial observers. I was given a first-hand account of it by Pam Keys, a young Australian–Chinese woman whom I met in 1963. Born in Australia of Chinese parents, she was educated in Melbourne until she was twenty-one, when she went back to China to see her grandparents near Canton. She became so absorbed by the developments in China that she decided to stay on there. Pam gave me her own eye-witness account of how the communes had come to Kwangtung Province between 1952 and 1958.

She arrived when the mutual-aid teams had become aware of

their limitations and were starting co-operatives. She heard all the discussions on the need for bigger holdings and more mechanization which, because of her knowledge of Australian agriculture, made a great deal of sense to her. News came of commune developments in a neighbouring area and several co-operative members, including one of her relatives, went off to investigate. On receipt of their report, a commune was decided on by mutual consent. She believed there had been no directive from above though, when asked, the Party sent cadres and advisers. She pointed out that one great obstacle in the way of rural development had been the widespread illiteracy that prevented training in modern methods of farming. Literacy classes had had to receive the highest priority and crash courses were started in every village. Attendance was not compulsory, but very few had to be pressed into attending; all except the dullest and oldest had been keen to learn.

Pam Keys's account matched that given to me by the brigade leader in the Hangchow commune.

An intensive inquiry into the development and functioning of the communes was made by Jan Myrdal, a Swede of country stock, who spent several months living in the closest contact with the peasants of a commune in North Shensi. With great patience he collected from the villagers themselves the story of the coming of Communism and the communes into their lives. Their simple, unvarnished accounts, recorded almost verbatim, have the ring of truth and are most revealing – often unconsciously so. Myrdal has told the story of his Shensi researches in his *Report from a Chinese Village* (Heinemann 1965). It is mandatory reading for anyone seeking more of the truth about Chinese communes.

4 · TRIP TO TA LIH

Ta Lih, the People's Commune in Nantai County, Canton Province, looked like any other rural district going about its business in a very normal, everyday fashion when we arrived there on a sunny September morning. There was time to see only one of its villages, for the whole commune covered some fourteen square kilometres and included over twenty villages and settlements. Its population of some 80,000 are all members of the commune, and when of age can vote in the elections of brigade and commune representatives. Ta Lih has nineteen brigades which, in turn, comprise three hundred and ten teams working together within the commune plan.

We were met at the village hall by the young manager; twenty-nine-year-old Mr Oh looked barely twenty. He had a most responsible job for one so young, for running a commune with its many activities requires a knowledge of agriculture, accountancy and, certainly, a marked ability to deal with personal problems and situations. Mr Oh seemed cheerful enough as he undertook the usual briefing over the usual cups of tea. As the statistics poured over us, I caught Ling's eye, and with him our little filming group slipped away to have our first taste of peasant reaction to Western cameras.

As we were later to do an 'in depth' study of a commune, this morning's filming was by way of a try-out.

We wandered along the village street receiving interested glances and creating the usual excitement among the children. There were few new houses but the old ones had been whitewashed or cleaned up, and everywhere possible young trees had been planted. One of the most frequently reiterated slogans in the régime's early days, 'Plant a tree and watch it grow', had been widely heeded here as everywhere; even schools had tree-planting and tree-watering sessions so that all China is an afforestation area. My main impression of the commune village was of greenness – the brilliant sunlit green of the rice-paddies; the duller green of the great vegetable gardens; the lily-like leaves of the taro, and the acid-green, mossy mantle of the village pond.

Our first shots were of a team of rice-gatherers who turned

out to be high-school students in a research-group carefully selecting the best ears for seeding; they were amused to be the centre of attention and co-operated well. We went on to the men hacking the resistant roots of the taro crop, to boys leading black buffaloes and an aged crone, standing knee-deep in the stream, splashing handfuls of water over great piles of cabbages waiting on the bank for collection and transport to Canton market. As usual, everybody was busy but nobody in a hurry; we dawdled along under the blazing sun, towards a group of houses where we were to visit a team-leader in his home. Having read of the much-publicized barracks we had asked especially to film living conditions, especially any communal facilities. We were told that the only 'communal' dwellings were some miles away and that these were hostels for unmarried men and girls; everyone else, we were assured, lived in their own home or lodged in somebody else's.

It was a collection of poor, little, rather tumbledown stone houses that we finally reached and where we met the team-leader. About sixty years old, he was a short, bent, wrinkled, but brisk and communicative peasant. Once illiterate and desperately poor, he had seen little in his early life but war and famine as Communist, anti-Communist and Japanese armies fought their way backwards and forwards across the country.

'Now,' he said proudly, 'I can even eat meat several times a week and rice every day. My children go to school – imagine a peasant's child being educated.'

He told us he had a good, well-paid, regular job and some responsibility as head of a team of one hundred and fifty workers – people depended on him, and his team always reached its target.

As he led us to his house we passed five or six middle-aged women sitting on the grass by the roadside making what turned out to be simple fireworks; this was a women's co-operative venture and they kept what they earned.

The leader's house was a fraction larger than the rest; it had a small courtyard of unbonded stones on to which the 49 sitting-room opened. This, spotlessly clean, had a polished tile floor, two beautifully carved teak chairs and a few pieces of cheap furniture. On the mantelpiece there was a clock, and on the dresser an old-fashioned radio set; the wall carried pictures of Mao Tse-tung, of children chasing butterflies and one of a fierce, inhuman-looking being, which, we learned afterwards, was 'an old god'.

'Some people still worship him,' Mrs Ho, our local interpreter, told us. 'Nobody minds that, they are all old people.' The funeral mourners, I recalled, had been similarly described to me – 'all old people'; their children will know better!

The team-leader saw my roving glance and my note-taking and asked Mrs Ho to be sure to tell me to make a note of his radio and his clock; he was very proud to have these as, apparently, the final symbols of his material prosperity. He also wanted it made clear that he and his fellows now had their own garden-plots whose produce they could eat or sell and that his wife did very well out of her share in the firework co-operative – above all, please let it be noted, his was one of the best teams in the commune. There was nothing boastful about the old man; his pride and pleasure in his possessions and his team were very touching. All the time we talked village children peeped in the courtyard gate, so that my tape-recordings have a background of children's laughter and conversation; to them our visit was almost Martian in its novelty.

When we rejoined the party Mr Oh was keen for us to see the transmitting station and hospital, about which he spoke so proudly that we were sorry we had to disappoint him and return to the cars. His enthusiasm was infectious and, as so often in China, I found myself getting carried away by it, caught up in this national excitement, this transformation scene; but the sight of two women pushing a dung-cart in the fierce heat reminded me that to reach even the minimal standards of the good life, China's hardworking millions had struggling years ahead.

On the way home Jack, one of our party, and I shared a car
50 with Mrs Ho; married, a mother, in her late thirties and with a

badly-fitting cotton dress and a scraped back hairdo, she was very gentle but nobody's fool. Jack, with great good humour, began teasing her.

'You Chinese women – most of you have marvellous figures – film-star standard in our degenerate West – look at that one, and that one,' pointing out of the window. 'If only they made the most of them. Why don't they use make-up, Ho? And why those everlasting pigtails! Don't Chinese men believe that pretty women make life so much pleasanter?'

Though she knew Jack was teasing her, Mrs Ho took him seriously and her forehead wrinkled with the sincerity of her reply.

'It is not our habit to use make-up; we are too busy.'

'Building the New China?' I said with a laugh, meaning to keep the tone light.

'Yes, Miss Roper, building up our country.' The answer wasn't meant to squash me but it did, and, seeing this, she relaxed a little. 'We do use make-up occasionally – for holidays and festivals; and we even put up our pigtails – or cut them off.'

'Do you have parties, Ho? For birthdays or the New Year?' – this was my question.

'Not often for birthdays; before the Liberation life was so short nobody liked to celebrate another year gone by; so few might be left – even for children – that, in a way, we often preferred not to notice a birthday.'

Here, in simple everyday conversation, I had come up against what has been called 'cultural shock', a double dose of it, actually. I had to try to make a far-reaching adjustment of long-accepted values in a land where starvation, war, epidemic disease had so long been natural hazards that a child's birthday was regarded a triumph of keeping alive rather than as an earnest of dozens more to follow, automatically. At the same time, here was serious little Mrs Ho sincerely forswearing pretty clothes and adornments the better to serve her country. She should have seemed unbearably pious – but she didn't.

That night we were asked to attend a hail-and-farewell banquet given jointly by the International Travel and the 51

Cultural Association representatives in one of Canton's best restaurants.

These banquets, like factory-briefings and station-greetings, are part of the pattern for welcoming and entertaining foreigners. Having attended many of them, my heart sank a little; I had been looking forward to a visit to a classical opera that night. (I am an addict.) But these functions are a *spécialité de la maison chinoise*; no other country takes so much trouble over its guests and one realizes that through them one learns a good deal about Chinese attitudes; and, of course, they do make the visitor feel important and wanted, a matter of concern to everybody, and that is a comfortable experience. Almost all the time the speeches, public and private, are inevitably at the superficial level, but every so often in conversation with one's Chinese neighbour one penetrates a little deeper, establishes a fractionally closer contact, on human, if non-political, terms, so that the labels 'Communist' 'non-Communist' seem no longer to mark such a yawning gulf of separation. And the food is invariably excellent.

The dinner party was held in the private dining-room of one of the famous park restaurants of Canton, the Pei Yuan, which lay beyond a central courtyard with trees and flowers and fountains. On the walls were great silken scrolls and traditional paintings; there were tables and chairs of elaborately carved teak and beautiful porcelain vases stood on shelves and on stands in corners. There was a reception-line, headed by the Mayor and the representative senior citizens, and carefully planned seating arrangements ensuring that each guest was near enough to a local interpreter to enjoy easy conversation.

Both chopsticks and cutlery were there, and two glasses: a larger one for the local, rather sweet, red wine and a smaller for *mao-tai*, the innocent-looking, colourless spirit that makes vodka seem like mother's milk!

The first course was a culinary *tour de force*. Our eyes as well as our appetites were regaled by *hors d'oeuvres* beautifully arranged in the form of a peacock, head and beak moulded in rice-paste

and the multi-coloured tail fashioned from thin slices of meat, eggs, fish and vegetables, some of them delicately chopped to a fine semblance of feathers. Along the edge of the dish were exquisitely-moulded flowers and fruit of coloured rice-paste.

One by one the waiters brought in bowls of the delicacies for which the restaurant was especially famous, until each table was crowded; steamed chicken with *hua-tiao* wine, fried shrimp paste and chicken liver barbecues, followed by rural-style fried fish-head with a truly Lucullan sweet-and-sour sauce. Then came the soup, bird's nest with shredded chicken, after which the smiling waiters cleared away the debris leaving the tables empty only for a few seconds before bringing in hot pastries, some like our patties, others like small steamed dumplings with a translucent skin. As one of the sweets they brought my especial delight, bitter-sweet lotus seeds in syrup with their unique chestnut-like texture so pleasing to bite into and savour on the tongue. To finish – tea, of course, green or black of varying flavours.

In China speeches start early in the meal, between courses, so that one can eat and listen – which is better than staring at empty coffee-cups whilst orators run over time. The Mayor spoke first.

Australian visitors were welcome, he said. China wished to be friendly with the whole world, especially her nearer neighbours; she wished them to see how she had progressed under the rule of the Communist Party and the guidance of Chairman Mao. He hoped that the visitors would see as much as possible of the achievements of their great and growing city. His first toast was to the friendship of the peoples of the whole world. The speech was brief, but seemed protracted because it was delivered two sentences at a time and rather hesitantly translated.

We selected one of our group to reply, and her speech was much as expected; what else can such speeches comprise but thanks for the welcome, praise for the city and congratulations on the food? More speeches, then, from the Travel Service representatives; then, from the Cultural Association, a special welcome for the Television team, one of the first to come to China. They would give all possible help because the film 53 should help to increase friendship and understanding between Australia and China. Warned beforehand, I knew this was my cue.

Now that we were over our first hurdle and in China with our cameras we had the second one to encounter – we had to make it clear that, although we were concerned to record their achievements and help remove some of the mountains of ignorance and prejudice that hinder East–West understanding, we were none the less Westerners from the outside looking in.

It was easy for me to begin my speech by recalling my previous visit, to express my pleasure at my return; easy, too, to express positive delight at permission to make one of the first films of life in China today. Then I took a deep breath – 'But we are British, and we have,' I continued, 'a different outlook, different political traditions. And though we wish to be friends we must look at your new world with eyes made critical, inevitably, by our democratic inheritance, and with our hearts and minds tuned to this rather than the Marxism–Leninism by which your achievements are inspired. We truly wish your country to "walk on two legs", to be free from foreign exploitation, but we are not members of the Communist Party and cannot accept its creed as the sole world-saviour. Even so, we believe that the British Commonwealth, the United States and the Communist nations, along with the neutralist countries, can live together in peace if they learn to understand one another better, and this they will do if they know more of one another's way of life. But understanding cannot be reached by routine handouts. In our film we want to show not only what China has done but what it still has to do, not only where it has succeeded but where it has failed as yet: back streets as well as boulevards, doubts as well as certainties – for this sort of film will be accepted by thousands in the West who would reject a picture of Communist perfection; such a one would do a disservice to you and us. Our film will show some great successes and foreshadow others to come; but, above all, it will try to 54 show an essentially friendly people – something which the West,

thanks to possible misinterpretation of some of your official pronunciations and slogans, finds hard to believe.'

Then, after compliments on Canton's cooking and an acknowledgement of their warm welcome, I sat down and waited in some apprehension; but from the applause and whispered comments of my neighbours in my ear, I realized with relief that the point had been made and well taken, both by Australians and Chinese. I prayed that the Western audiences would be equally generous at the film's receiving end!

Mercifully, Chinese reception banquets end briskly with the last course the officials must have a good many of them to get through and so are wisely reluctant to protract them – and after just ten minutes to sip the final cup of tea our hosts rose, bade us good night and *bon voyage*, and departed with admirable expedition, leaving us time to get a good night's sleep before the early start by train for Wuhan on the next day.

5 · CITY ON THE YANGTSE
Bridges and Temples

Wuhan, six hundred miles from the mouth of the great Yangtse River, is really three towns in one, Hankow, Wuchang and Hanyang, the whole group comprising one of the rising industrial centres of the country and possessing one of the first great achievements of the régime, the Yangtse River Bridge.

We stayed at the Victory Hotel, not new like the vast Yang Cheng, but a pre-revolutionary, Western-style hotel. Built for Western business-visitors and a few wealthy Chinese, it stands in the old concession quarter and its architecture is wholly European. The local interpreter explained, with what I imagined was a deliberate and professionally-induced lack of heat, that most of the older high buildings in Wuhan had been built for their British, German or Japanese owners by Chinese labourers who themselves lived in hovels or on the streets. All the new buildings we would see had, of course, gone up 'since the Liberation' and more were being built every month as the city expanded – built by the Chinese for the Chinese this time. Already the population had reached the two million mark; industries, notably ship-building, chemicals and textiles, were expanding fast alongside the great iron and steel corporation for which Wuhan is especially famed.

After an excellent dinner in a dining-room that reminded me of the Midland Hotel, Manchester, we were shown a special screening of the latest Chinese musical film. *Ars longa, vita brevis est* might well be a Chinese proverb, for, as also in India, films and plays tend to move much more slowly than ours with more talk and less action; but *Five Golden Flowers* moved at a fair pace and lasted only one and a half hours or so.

Officially the arts in a Communist country should be didactic, point a moral and adorn a tale; but *Five Golden Flowers* wore its moral with a difference. Set in the remoter parts of the province of Honan, the film told a simple love-story of five pretty village-girls. Mountains and meadows, a village fair, a dance festival, moonlight love scenes by fountains and pagodas, daring tests of horsemanship between rival lovers, practical jokes played on the boys by the girls, picturesque local costumes, periodic outbursts of song, solo and chorus, all in gorgeous technicolor, provided a musical as lavish in sound and spectacle as any from Hollywood.

There were, though, major differences of approach. In the love-scenes only adoring glances and affectionate smiles or, at most, an exchange of handclasps were seen, not a close-up, not a hint of décolletage or a trace of leg above the calf, for any more intimate glimpses of sexual relations are wholly taboo by Chinese standards, which make the American movies' Hayes Code look lax!

Equally important, equally different, the moral was driven home – that all must work together to serve the state and help build the new China by co-operation with their neighbour and under the guidance of the Party.

The total amount and exact nature of the didactic content could, of course, not be judged without a knowledge of the language, but, visually, the film was a delight, the storyline clear and well developed; any Western audience would enjoy its beauty, novelty and high spirits. The Chinese film industry is expanding fast and becoming increasingly interested in export.

At least there was no moral in the film version of a classical Peking Opera we saw some three weeks later in Hangchow; in this magicians, demons, man-to-beast-and-back-again transmogrifications, magic potions, fierce battles between men and supernatural powers, all with colour and sound to match, out-Disneyed Disney. This film is extremely popular.

Next morning we left for the Bridge at 8.30. Even when viewed through a thin drizzle against a lowering sky it is impressive. It is about 1,280 yards long and has eight spans of approximately 240 yards each. It is a 'double decker' carrying a highway on the top deck and a double railway line on the lower. We were shepherded beneath the structure to a palatial chamber, all marble floors and pillars, easy chairs and pot plants, where a senior engineer gave us the history of its construction. As we listened to statistics and anecdotes we heard overhead the dull rumble of trains moving across the old river 57 boundary that had once divided China into a North and South which too rarely met.

'Before Liberation,' we heard between the rumbles, 'few people crossed the river, because only ferries could cope with the treacherous currents and for the people the ferries were too dear; in any case they were often delayed by floods or bad weather. Now a train crosses in two minutes and vital trade between the North and South has already multiplied many times.' He spoke with affection and enthusiasm; it was his bridge, dearly-loved and a theme of heroic proportions! 'Once,' he continued, 'an American engineer came out as consultant – that was before Liberation – (I found the parenthesis hardly necessary) he declared the river was unbridgeable because the bottom of it was too shifting, the currents too treacherous to take safe foundations. But' – a dramatic pause – 'the Chinese engineers, inspired by the Party, proved the American wrong and laid foundations twenty yards below the surface.' I asked about the Soviet engineers (their help had been mentioned to me in 1958). 'Yes,' he admitted a little grudgingly, 'there were some Soviet technicians.' We were then given, in meticulous detail, facts and figures about every aspect of the achievement, including the number of volunteer working-hours put in by citizens of every age and background.

There is, I should say, no major building or planning project of national importance, and many of local importance only, that has not attracted its share of voluntary labour. The only pressure to join working-parties is that of public opinion, which is, admittedly, very strong indeed in China; but the young people I spoke to about it, students, interpreters, told me they usually enjoyed the community effort and often had great fun in the work camps or weekend working-parties. All who had taken part in major projects received a small badge of which they were proud. I saw Yangtse Bridge, Ming Tombs Reservoir and Great Hall of the People badges, in the form of small enamelled brooches or lapel pins.

After the briefing, a long walk over the great structure with its rail and roadways finished at the tall, commemorative pillar on the north bank. On this, faithfully reproduced in the calligraphy of the writer, China's most revered living poet, was a short poem answering an old rhyme:

'A bridge can never be built; the river can never be crossed.'

With Chairman Mao's famous answer beneath it:

'A bridge flies across the river from North to South; a deep chasm becomes a thoroughfare.'

Mao Tse-tung is admired not only as a war-leader, a party-chief but as a poet, philosopher and calligraphist.

With no sense of dramatic contrast, I am sure, but merely because of proximity, Ling took us straight from the mechanical marvels of the bridge to an ancient Buddhist temple. Restored by the Government as a national monument, the temple is again in use. A small building with an elaborately-painted facade, it stood on the top of a wide flight of shallow stone steps hollowed by the feet of thousands of faithful worshippers. At the top of these we were met by a shaven-pated monk in grey – not saffron – robes; plump, serious, bespectacled, he led us through the scented darkness of an entrance hall to the main temple, glowing with the light of red crystal lamps hanging from the ceiling. Incense was burning, the slow parabolas of smoke touched to grotesque life by shafts of the ruby glow. Above eye-level, on wide shelves, were great wooden *lohans*, or effigies of disciples, in five hundred different moods. Painted a rich red-gold, these rows of sitting, standing, kneeling, bending, stretching, striding, leaping figures looked in mirrors, read books, sang songs, carved wood, cleaned their nails, patted their bellies, yawned, scratched their heads; five hundred different creations, the tallest more than twenty feet from tip to toe. Along the walls were ancient carved chests, faded scrolls of silk and parchment; in a small adjoining room the monk showed us, laconically, a great carved screen which had taken several men three years to complete. It showed the local welcome given to the Chief Monk on his visit to this monastery 1,300 years ago, and soldiers, horses, flags, flowers and worshippers crowded on to it. The 59 monastery also possessed, he told us, one of the three sacred teeth of the Buddha, one other being in Peking and the third in Ceylon.

As he talked I glimpsed the mighty bulk of the Bridge from the narrow windows and it seemed more unreal to me, such was the magic of the place, then the religio-mystic, incense-perfumed, time-haunted atmosphere of the temple in which I stood listening to the quiet flow of the priest's voice and the lilting, Chinese-inflected antiphony of the interpreter's translation. Could this be Communist China? Yes!

'The monk,' we heard, 'the monk tells us that the Government has given funds for the restoration of his temple after its damage during the Japanese occupation and the wars of liberation. He is very grateful.'

We moved across the lawns to the adjoining Temple of Lute-playing, also restored and glowing with jewel colours, the carved beasts on the upward sweep of its eaves silhouetted clear against the sky. More interesting than the one-room interior was the marble pillar in the little walled garden with carved figures and characters on its four faces. Li translated these, telling the story with as much enthusiasm as he had shown translating the slogans in the Canton factory. For Li and his generation there is no contradiction in this equal and simultaneous affection for the old and new. Both are national versions, one ancient, one modern, of the good and the beautiful in the Chinese way of life.

The two figures were musicians of olden days who lived far apart. The first musician had to make a long journey down the river by boat. Overtaken by a storm he drew his frail craft to the shore, where, feeling lonely, he began to play his lute, thinking as he did so of running streams and high mountains. Amazingly, he was in the riverside garden of another musician, who, opening his casement after the storm, heard the exquisite notes of the master below. He listened entranced. When it ended he rushed outside to find his fellow-lutanist and tell him that the music had brought him a vision of running streams and high mountains. They became firm friends, made music together and parted, vowing to meet the next year at the same time and place. But, though the first musician made the long journey at the appointed time, he arrived only to find his friend on the point of death; there was just time enough for a brief farewell before the body was buried by the riverside where they had met. The dead man's friend composed an epitaph, set it to music and played it at the tomb; then he broke his lute and threw it into the waves, for none again could appreciate its music as had the dead musician.

6 · CITY ON THE YANGTSE
Medicine and Steel

On the following day I was dismayed to find the programme contained a visit to a machine-tools factory in the morning and the Iron and Steel Works in the afternoon; this seemed very heavy industry indeed! The women in the party agreed; so we pointed out to our hosts that a school or hospital would be more in our line, though I was rather shamefacedly aware that, by admitting Western women's interest in basic industry was pretty cool, I was letting the side down! It was, indeed, quite characteristic of the Communist belief in the essential identity of the interests of the sexes that our hosts had not considered the programme at all unfeminine! But we were humoured, and at short notice a visit was arranged to the Second Hospital attached to the Medical College of Wuhan, where the Director was a distinguished pediatrician, Professor Lu Hshiu.

Gambling was forbidden by the Communists in 1949, so all racecourses went begging. The Wuhan City Council took over theirs, planted a few thousand trees, and dotted among them several three- and four-storey buildings as hospital-wards and lecture-rooms. Used as we are to sky-scraper hospitals, we found it unexpected to be driving up a treelined drive, glimpsing what looked like a number of English cottage hospitals through the greenery.

The main unit was four storeys high, shaped like an aeroplane with two wings and two tail-fins, all placed at an angle to ensure, we were told, a maximum amount of sunshine for each room.

Professor Lu, the Director, was at the door to greet us. Feminist that I am, I was delighted to find the Professor was a woman! In her late fifties with a slight, straight-up-and-down figure, grey hair drawn tightly back, with steel-rimmed glasses and the workers' blue coat and trousers, she was not a striking figure at first meeting and her diffident manner towards us and the Cultural Relations officials gave little impression of the authority one expects from the head of a seven-hundred-bed hospital. I was not put off or surprised by this, for, generally speaking, throwing one's official weight about is not approved of in China and the workers' clothes worn by the Professor were a symbol of her identity with the people.

After tea and briefing, a girl arrived with a white coat for each of us to wear during the tour of the wards. Once her coat was on, there was no more diffidence about Professor Lu; she was quietly and completely in charge from then on.

In the children's ward the Director explained that as much as possible was done to keep the mother and child together during the child's illness, and that simple living-quarters were provided for mothers coming from a distance.

'China must walk on two legs' is an oft-repeated slogan with innumerable applications; in medicine it refers to the study and practice of both Western and traditional medicine. A student can choose to specialize in one or the other, but has to have some knowledge of the alternative discipline.

Most older peasants and workers have a suspicion of Western-style doctors and a lingering preference for their own. Australian Dymphna Cusack's elderly housekeeper, in Peking, was taken ill and a Western-trained doctor was called, but as soon as she was fit to leave the house she sneaked off on the quiet for a consultation with her Chinese herbalist just to be sure!

The Wuhan school offered European medicine to selected students entering at the age of eighteen for a six-year course. It very much resembled, as far as I could tell, a similar British one, except it contained more public health subjects and, of course, a proportion of 'political philosophy.'

We asked to see something of the two aspects of Chinese medicine most interesting—and suspect—to Westerners: herbal medicine and acupuncture. The hospital's Chinese pharmacy certainly lived up to its almost necromantic reputation. The room was smallish and darkish—I was reminded of Romeo's visit to his Mantuan apothecary—mingled odours, sweet, bitter, mouldy, astringent, assailed the nostrils. On the walls hung bundles of herbs, large and small, some almost fresh, others dried to complete brittleness. On the table, dishes with samples of leaves, roots and fungi, dried, shrunken and villainous-looking, were the basis, Professor Lu said, of some interesting new research into their healing properties. There are eight hundred varieties of herbs in the traditional pharmocopaeia.

Next door, the European drugs were stored and I was surprised to hear that China now produced enough antibiotics to be able to export a good many.

We wandered along the corridors in and out of wards; everything was clean and in good repair, but there was nothing lush or shiny, only the essentials were provided and extras like private rooms, expensively-furnished VIP offices and elaborate kitchen equipment or fancy menus, were all absent; China simply cannot afford them and, indeed, its austere philosophy would not recognize the necessity for them.

We had time for only a brief glimpse at a simple acupuncture operation on a young man's knee. The doctor, a graduate in traditional Chinese medicine, with considerable training also in Western medical subjects, carefully selected the needles with which the treatment is given. Each consists of three parts, a handle, a neck and a point whose thickness varies.

Apprehensively I watched him, gently but without hesitation, thrust them into the flesh to various depths; some of them he gently turned once they were in place.

At first I felt slightly sickened at the sight of the needles going in and then standing out from the quiescent flesh 'like quills upon the fretful porpentine', but when I saw the patient looking almost cheerful and uttering no cry of pain, I relaxed and watched with admiration the insertions of the remaining few needles.

In China acupuncture has a long history. Its basic concept is the division of human illnesses into the *yang* type, which calls for the toning down of the body's vital force and the *yin*, which demands its stimulation. There is a voluminous ancient literature on this two-fold division and on the fourteen main nerve-routes and the three hundred and sixty-five sensitive spots with which they are punctuated.

This literature is now being augmented considerably with the establishment of well-equipped 'traditional' medical research institutes which are using 'Western' as well as 'traditional' doctors and scientists for their investigations.

So we returned to the sitting-room for more tea and a question-and-answer session. The Director spoke enthusiastically about the hospital's function as a health-education centre.

'We believe that preventing illness is more important than curing it, so we conduct health "drives" in our own area of the city by lecturing to schools, arranging exhibitions, and publishing and distributing leaflets. We are always available to advise street committees on all hygiene matters.'

When I inquired about the hospital's administration and its relations with the City Council and the Communist Party, Professor Lu explained that they had a democratically-elected committee. (I was still sufficiently conditioned by my Western upbringing to find it strange to hear Communists talking about their democratic system.) She herself was the Chairman of the Hospital Committee, under the leadership of the Communist Party, she added; other members consisted of representatives of the doctors, technicians, and working staff, who brought recommendations to the committee for discussion. At this stage I asked her if she would record a message on my tape-recorder, mentioning, perhaps, the hospital's greatest successes to date as she saw them, and her strongest hopes for its future. Like most sensible people, she recoiled visibly at the first mention of going on tape, but, seeing my disappointment, agreed, with all of her earlier diffidence, to do so.

'Students will be trained to be medical workers,' she said, 'with high social consciousness. Our hospital has made great strides under the Communist Party and the leadership of Chairman Mao. There is better health for the workers in a socialist country.'

My immediate reaction to this comment was one of mingled irritation and surprise, for I had expected that a highly-intelligent professional woman with a middle-class background would leave the beaten political track and speak freely, on her own subject at least. Trying to get what I regarded as an unfortunate incident into focus, I visualized an English or American doctor being 'taped' by a Communist commentator for broadcast in China, and told myself that she, too, would go on record only with platitudes; even so, I could not see any British 65 or American doctors going out of their way to offer tribute to Parliament or Congress, Queen or President, to make their patriotic allegiance clear.

But, then, Queens and Presidents are heads of long-established, firmly-founded businesses, the 'Old Firms'. China, for all its size, has a government only fifteen years old, which sees itself, understandably, surrounded by enemies, ignored and reviled by the West and containing, still, within itself, some subversive elements. And, in addition, one had only to look at the grim decades when the attainment and practice of a profession were alike hazardous, especially for women, to realize that today's gratitude and natural pride are so considerable that, whatever occasional honest doubts may be held by professional people, these would not, out of genuine loyalty, even be hinted at to a Western visitor in public.

Iron and steel do not loom very large in the life of most Western citizens; to the Chinese they are omnipresent, though the ardours of the steel-drive of the Great Leap Forward have cooled a little. In 1958 there appeared everywhere, on posters, banners, wallboards and even in a floral design in the West Lake Park at Hangchow the solitary figures '10·6', which everybody knew referred to the 10·6 million tons steel-target, and the progress towards it was listened to daily with as much fervour as some of us listen to football or baseball results. On the strenuous urging of Party cadres every local deposit of ore was worked and every available bit of scrap melted down in crudely-constructed smelters in fields and backyards; I remember small furnaces blazing through the night in the park opposite the beautiful Nanking Hotel.

My visit to the Summer Palace in that year had included a boating trip on the lake for which we hired a newly-painted, little red and green boat with a white sail. As we sped gently over the lake, I looked in delight at the blue water, the bright pagodas atop of the Dowager Empress's artificial hill, at the handsome, nineteen-arch bridge she had had constructed to 66 link shore and island. Our boatman struck up a slow, sweet song in a fine tenor; it suited the mood and scenery to perfection.

I turned to Madame Huang, Director of the International Division of the Women's Federation, and said, with a laugh, 'What a charming tune! Surely, in this setting it must be a love song. Do tell me he is singing about love.' (In the New China love songs are rare, I had discovered.)

Madame Huang laughed back at me and said, mischievously, 'No, Miss Roper, it is not about love.'

'Not – not, surely, about . . . steel?'

'Yes, about steel. You see, in China we cannot have love without steel!'

We laughed together until the boat rocked. Sometimes the Chinese can make fun of themselves.

By 1963 the fires no longer shone in Nanking Park and by the railway-side we saw dismantled smelters and abandoned hearths. The great drive had not been the hoped-for success but, Edgar Snow reports, it was certainly not the dead loss reported in the Western Press.

Today, the focus is on the big steel units. So we were prepared for a long, hard session at the Wuhan Iron and Steel Works – and we got it! After a long drive to the far edge of the city, we found the mills on waste land with numbers of buildings scattered about, many still in process of construction. The Assistant Manager, Mr Chou, again youthful, met us with tea and statistics. The main plants occupy five square kilometres of land. The biggest building under construction he explained immediately, was the new rolling mill, which would be different from all the others because it would be the very first designed and constructed wholly by the Chinese themselves. The rest had been begun in 1955 in what he called a 'neglected wilderness' and 'in poor and blank economic circumstances'; in 1957 a second instalment had begun. (He did not inform us that Russian engineers were then advisers and consultants. An official 1960 guide book states, 'The plant was designed by thirty-eight Soviet institutes, headed by the Leningrad Ferrous Metallurgical Design Institute.')

'Since then,' our guide went on, 'thanks to the General Line of the Communist Party, our progress has been quicker and quicker. Our first big plant was completed two years ahead of schedule.' He concluded triumphantly, 'One hundred thousand workers took part in the construction.'

Then there really flowed forth facts and figures, about the mill, the equipment, the products, the workers; outside, the massive machinery boomed away and the near-by clink of iron upon iron beat through my head, already buzzing with Mr Chou's information. Despairingly, I asked myself, 'How can one TELL? How can one tell, if all this be true? So many tons, houses, shops, schools, roads, amenities.'

'Five thousand people here in 1949, quarter of a million now,' I heard clearly through the din, and there followed an impressive account of the building of the largest chimney in China, with the numbers of bricks, tons of cement, hours of voluntary labour.

He was approaching his peroration, 'All this has been done through the inspiration of the Three Red Banners – first, the General Line of the Communist Party, second, the Great Leap Forward, and third, the People's Communes. Throughout the whole construction period we have carried out the mass line; we have obeyed Chairman Mao's advice: "Mobilize the masses and rely on them." Let us now go and see all this.'

Again I was suffering from cultural shock. I was impressed by Mr Chou's story, but his last remarks, with their seeming jargon, the near-caricature of the Party Line, the parrot-like repetition of certain phrases; at first hearing all these irritated me. 'Can they really think we accept all this? Can they really believe the workers can accept much of it either? Doesn't it just wash over them?' Such an approach by Public Relations Officers at home, fatuous as they often are, would have seemed pretty unconvincing. Yet, in the end, I decided I had to believe a good deal of it. Already I had seen many examples of 'working for the people' – the voluntary labour, the willing feminine sacrifice of pretty clothes and make-up, the interpreters' devo-

tion to their work well beyond the call of duty, the scrupulous

care of property in parks and public places, the widespread
honesty, even the occasionally expressed disregard for financial
reward, all these were actualities, not PR chatter.

In the West the Renaissance ideal of the individual splendour,
of the long struggle for self-discovery and self-fulfilment is
almost unquestioned; our poets sing of it, philosophers expatiate
upon it. Man is 'the master of his fate, the captain of his soul':
'to thine own self be true' – so we quote and accept; and
psychologists have put their seal upon these sacred claims of the
individual, uninhibited, unthwarted. All this taken-for-granted
philosophy has to be agonizingly reappraised in a country
where the individual's worth is measured by his value to the community, where his personality has to be developed so that it
can the better contribute to the whole which is more important
than any of the parts.

When we hear, in the West, that the individual must not live
for himself but for the State then all the overtones of the 'brave
new world' emerge; Orwellian nightmares haunt us and with a
shudder we turn away. But the idea of the individual developing merely as an individual for his own sake in splendid isolation, *in vacuo*, is utterly alien to Chinese Communism, which
teaches that the individual can develop fully only if he is part of
his community; he must serve the masses and thereby find his
true place among them and his true worth as a man. It is alien,
too, to the long Confucian tradition which also saw man as a
member of his family, his class, not as an isolated unit.

So I was tempted to believe some at least of Mr Chou's seeming jargon, and the temptation became a little stronger when, a
few minutes later, I asked Ling to translate a slogan painted
across the whole length of a wall in the rolling mill.

'When you are humble you will learn and progress; when
you are proud you will . . .' he paused for the correct word.
'What do you say when you mean you cannot walk with the
others?'

'Keep up with,' I hazarded.

'Yes, you will not keep up with; you will be behind all the
time,' went on Ling.   69

'I know what it means. If you are proud you will LAG behind. Lag is the word, Ling.'

Ling called Li and I heard the words 'fall behind', 'keep up with', 'lag'. Then Ling, his plump face wreathed in smiles, came back to me.

'Li says lag behind is very good.'

'That is admirable, Ling,' I said. 'But does it really mean anything? Do the workers take notice of all those slogans? They must get so used to them they hardly see them.'

Ling was serious in a moment.

'Of course it means something to them; they know they have much to learn and all have something to teach. We must all be ready to learn and teach. Nobody must be proud.' He meant it. This was in line with the Chinese tradition. I remembered that Confucius had said, 'We must teach others without weariness . . . and must not feel ashamed to learn and ask from the people below us.' (An even more significant link between Mao Tsetung and Confucius is a statement in the Analects – 'to govern is to rectify'.)

Reappraisals are exhausting, I thought, as I crossed the floor to talk to a young woman just emerging from the driving-seat of a great crane which had been manœuvring cauldrons of molten metal. She told me that she liked her job – she looked cheerful enough – that she had been trained for it along with the men and did not find it physically tiring; she went to evening classes in Chinese language and lived with her family in a worker's flat a mile away. Of course, many girls did the same work as men. 'Why not?' She took the equality of the sexes wholly for granted and her final query was puzzled, not defiant. She swung her crane round with a shy smile and left me to my note-taking.

I forget the speeches at that night's banquet, but I clearly remember a conversation with the local interpreter, whom, I was pleased to find, I had met in 1956 when he was in Melbourne on the first Peking Opera Company's visit to Australia.

He mentioned that the Hotel Victory had been used, before

their precipitate departure, by Soviet Union engineers and technical advisers.

'Were you sorry to see them go or had they become too difficult to deal with?'

My question moved him considerably.

'Of course, they were not difficult; we were very sorry when they went and so were they; we worked together like good friends. We had their farewell dinner in this very room; many of them had tears in their eyes. They did not want to go and they certainly did not wish to take their plans with them, but Krushchev made them go. He did not even give them time to help us to carry on after they had gone. It was all done in a great hurry.'

Here were the headlines, 'Big Sino–Soviet Split' in human terms; and clearly, in Wuhan at least, the Ministry of Propaganda did not need to flog anti-Krushchev feeling!

'But an Australian friend,' I continued, 'who knows China well, visited the Soviet recently and she heard that some Russians were glad to leave China because they had been treated as outsiders and made to feel inferior to the more cultivated Chinese. They said you were rather grand in your treatment of foreign experts and often ignored their advice.'

As he started on a hot denial of such behaviour, the call came for a toast. I drank it meditatively, realizing what an interesting and important point had been raised.

Throughout her history China has been the most self-contained of Empires, the Middle Kingdom, holding aloof from close contact with the 'barbarians' beyond her borders; absorbing even her own conquerors. This near-complete isolation continued well into the last century.

The new China declares her concern for international understanding, for an open-door trade policy and, incidentally, a steady increase of tourism; yet many people wonder if something of the old habits of mind linger on. The industrial self-dependency now stressed, United States military pressures, exclusion from the United Nations, continued non-recognition by many countries, all these must tend to reinforce the 71 age-long isolationist tradition even against China's own better judgement and her own and the world's best interests.

My thoughts were interrupted by the waitresses bringing round to each of us a little memento of our visit, as was the custom at all these functions – sometimes we were given a little embroidered mat, sometimes a painted fan or a set of paper cuts or one of the woven pictures of famous beauty spots which the Chinese, to my surprise, are very fond of (to me they are one of the least attractive things they produce). The gifts and the grace with which they were given dispelled my brief misgivings and my slight ennui at the speeches. The Chinese have this habit, at once infuriating and disarming, of producing a little gift, a joke, an act of unselfish generosity just when they have unwittingly exasperated or disturbed you by some argument which you want to follow up with a heat that their niceness has already annoyingly dispersed.

7 · 'PEKING DAY'
Leading Lady at the Cotton Mill

We were to leave Wuhan for Peking by train, a journey of some seven hundred and fifty miles; preferring the two extra days in Peking, we asked if we could go by air – we would gladly pay extra. In spite of the short notice, the Travel Service found a Russian Ilyushin – rather like a DC3 – and no mention was made of extra payment. The plane had little, white cottagey curtains and lace antimacassars over the seatbacks; it was not pressurized and bumped a good deal nearing Peking, so that I landed feeling too limp and dizzy to do justice to the surprise greeting of Madame Huang and Tai, my 1958 interpreter, who had broken into a heavy day's work to drive out and meet me.

Madame Huang is definitely a woman of the New China. Happily married with children and grandchildren, she is immensely able, handling with an air of imperturbability a complicated and responsible job at the Women's Federation.* She usually wears the common dark-blue cotton suit but sees that it is well-cut and, with a bright scarf and embroidered blouse to relieve its sombre hue, she manages to look inconspicuously chic. I was much touched by her kindness in coming to meet me when she had many other foreign visitors to cope with and I wished my efforts at fighting down periodic waves of nausea had not prevented my saying so adequately.

Peking Airport, opened since my first visit, is planned on the grand manner and is certainly an impressive starting point for airborne visitors with its spacious halls, lawns, trees and flowers, and its scrolls, ceramics and paintings.

China, moving straight from the feudal to the jet age, is developing transport by air quicker than by rail or road, and Chinese planners must regard airport architecture much as our English forefathers regarded the Doric splendours of Euston or the neo-Gothic turrets and curlicues of St Pancras station.

We travelled to the city along the new, broad avenue lined on both sides by young trees with farmlands stretching beyond for the first couple of miles, an unusually verdant approach to a great city. A post-feudal country has one advantage, at least, it

* In 1965 she was elected as a representative to the National People's Congress.

can start almost from scratch in its town-planning, since there are no out-of-date factories too expensive to be scrapped, no red rash of suburban villas or corner service-stations, no ribbon development properties – only a few good buildings and thousands of hovels and lean-tos, easily removed to make room for carefully-sited urban centres.

We drove straight to our hotel, the Chien Men (Front Gate), a replica of the Yang Cheng at Canton and just as vast, with the same smiling excellent service but rather less appetizing food.

On the train from Canton to Wuhan I had worked out, in general terms, what we wished to do to give a fair survey of the Chinese scene. 'TV is people', and political theories can only be expressed on the screen through human actions, so we planned to interpret Chinese life today by recording an average day in the life of a city and a country worker and had worked out a programme which the ever-helpful Ling had sent on ahead of us. In Peking we wanted a young couple, both working, with a child at school and preferably with a parent living with them (to give a glimpse of older people's life). We wanted to film them at their jobs, in their home, visiting recreational centres, in their factory, in public parks and theatres, visiting a clinic, a committee meeting or a political gathering. This would obviously have to be a composite day since no actual day would fall quite neatly enough into place to cover all these activities, but this was a telescoping demanded by filming exigencies.

In the country we sought a similar couple on a commune, and for convenience we called our two programmes 'Peking Day' and 'Commune Day'.

We wanted time to get to know these couples, talk with them freely, move about with them for a day or so beforehand so that we could see fairly well how their day ran, understand a little of what they thought and film them as real young men and women, not just prototypes of 'the Chinese worker', 'the Chinese peasant'. Our second intention was to try to record as many as possible of those aspects of the Chinese scene controversially presented to the West in order visually to prove or

74 disprove Western ideas on Chinese art, religion, education and

industry. We also asked to have an interview with the most senior member of the Government or Party that could spare time for us.

All the papers, we assumed, along with Ling's comments on them – and us – had been sent from Wuhan to the Cultural Relations Association in Peking, and on the evening of our arrival the verdict was delivered. To our immense relief it was more than favourable.

After dinner we went to meet the Vice-President of the Association, Wen Peng-chiu, who had been a teacher of German in Peking University. He introduced us to Feng Pei-lu, middle-aged, plump and twinkle-eyed, an experienced film producer, who was to advise John, the producer-cameraman, when needed and generally help with production arrangements. With him was youthful Cheng Kai-shu, tall and handsome, who was to be an assistant cameraman, and Yang Shi-hwa, a young woman interpreter. Shi-hwa was short and smiling, with a gamin face and wind-blown hair and a very simple cotton dress. This was to be our team and with them we could move where we wished, though it was considered desirable that we should make moves from one town to another with the tourist party for reasons of transport and accommodation. Yes, we could see the back streets, the remaining 'slums', photograph where we would and when; they trusted us to play fair, they said. We assured them, in turn, that we wished always to have Feng and Cheng with us, as we trusted them to help us fully. This was in part enlightened self-interest, as we did not wish to run the risk of our film being confiscated for an unintentional breach of security regulations or any filming unacceptable to our hosts. And so the team was formed; we seemed all to like the looks of one another and drank to our success in a light red wine.

Already Feng had found us our factory and our typical couple, he said, and we were to go next morning to State Cotton Mill Number Two to meet them and plan our two days' shooting there.

It was a successful but exhausting interview because, for both us and the Chinese, the situation was wholly novel and 75

fraught with some risks of misunderstanding on either side –
nobody can handle a film on Communist China, the most controversial topic on the international scene, with complete
equanimity.

'It is just as hard for them,' I said to John. 'They've got to
cope with two friendly, interested but known non-Communist
eager beavers poking around with cameras and tape-recorders,
collecting material to exhibit to millions of known anti-Com-
munists in the West. Both of us are walking a tightrope – we've
got to give a fair go to the Chinese Marxist apologists and they
ditto to Western democratic critics. We've really bought into
something here!'

In two cars, a Polish Warszawa and a British Humber, our
filming party left next morning; it now included Harold Carter,
a Melbourne lawyer, a member of the tourist party who had
enthusiastically volunteered to help me with note-taking and
tape-recording. Little Shi-hwa was full of life and obviously excited about her new and different assignment. It was a sunny,
crisp autumn morning and our spirits lifted as we drove
through Peking's wide treelined streets towards the western
suburbs to our cotton mill. As in Wuhan, the streets were litter-
free and almost car-free, but there was more public transport;
Peking's trolley buses are frequent, smooth-running and cheap.

Started in 1954 and completed the following year, the mill
employs five and a half thousand workers, of which seventy per
cent are women (none under sixteen years of age). Virtually all
workers live 'on campus', where every facility is provided; the
mill is a town in itself.

Like every other building, the mill was being given its
National Day trimmings. Enormous, fringed scarlet lanterns
hung along the entrance portico, and banners, flags and posters
were everywhere hailing the day and the success of the workers
under Party leadership. A wide drive led to the pillared entrance and on either side of this were garden-beds with gay
flowers and shrubs, beyond these lawns and young trees; this
was a garden factory, we were told, as were most in the New
76 China.

We were fidgeting to meet our 'star' couple. Though the Chinese are efficient they don't like to hurry things; it is one of many paradoxes that, though the most senior executives and politicians give a sense of there being all the time in the world, so many of China's overseas-propaganda statements have an almost febrile tone: 'We must catch up with the West in fifteen years'; 'We must do in one day the work of twenty years' – which give foreigners a sense of national haste and scramble.

At last we met the couple who were to be our typical city workers. Mrs Hsu-lin, a plump smiling woman in her thirties, was pleasantly, if not startlingly, telegenic; her husband, likeable, alert, was not, for he had an anxious look and a large, mobile Adam's apple! Clearly, we must get another couple or, temporarily, a new spouse for Mrs Hsu! It was an embarrassing situation but fortunately Feng himself realized the problem, took me aside and explained that he would deal with it by the time shooting started next day.

We spent the whole day visiting all parts of the great factory 'campus', planning the storyline and selecting subjects. Everyone was interested and helpful and we went where we would; all we needed was a good leading lady and husband.

As soon as we met Chang Mei-lang next morning we knew we had the leading lady all right. How they found such an ideal young woman in less than half a day we did not ask, but there she was, perfect for our purpose. Pretty but not distractingly so, friendly but not gushing, enthusiastic but not excitable, Mei-lang was to prove, in this her first glimpse of filming, 'a natural'. She never fussed or giggled, was conscious of the camera only enough to do herself justice in front of it and, though she was happy doing the job, never took herself so seriously as to put on airs or lose her good humour. What would her husband be like? Could he possibly match Mei-lang. Chin Chung-yi very nearly did. Tall, thoughtful, quick-witted – he never had to be given an instruction twice – he worked as well and quietly as his wife. (It is interesting to note that all married women in China keep their maiden name.)

We met Mei-lang in the spinning shed where she watched 77

expertly over her many spindles. After a few trial runs up and down her alley Mei-lang, in slacks, blouse and headscarf, smiling broadly but concentrating well, was shot at work, with long shots thereafter to give an idea of the size of the shed and the type of its machinery.

On the walls the slogans were moral, rather than political.

'If there are difficulties I will try to solve them; if there is convenience I will pass it on to others,' translated Shi-hwa a little quaintly.

'Unite and take care of one another.'

Two others were exhortatory: 'Work to fulfil your quota' and 'Pay more attention to quality'.

There was not even time for a cup of tea before moving with Mei-lang and Chung-yi to their home, a flat on the third floor of one of the red-brick blocks standing amid grass and young trees across the road.

Like lightning the news of our arrival got round and I don't believe there was a child within cooee who failed to come rushing to see the exciting spectacle, not only of long-nosed foreigners, but of cameras and sound recorders as well, so that by the time we got to the stairway we were pushing our way through hordes of laughing, shouting youngsters with older men and women bringing up the rear.

To our joy, we found that Chung-yi's mother lived with them. Fifty-five years old, with short grey hair and a drawn, sensitive face, Grandma wore a traditional black high-collared tunic with trousers and black cotton shoes.

Before they came to Peking she and her son had lived in a village in the province of Hopei, about one hundred miles from the city, so I calculated that for the first forty years of her life she must have known little rest from war and its attendant miseries.

Proudly Mei-lang and Chung-yi led us up the stone staircase with its shabby walls and peeling paint, kicked by children's active little feet (paint seems still to be scarce in China), into their home on the third floor; here the three of them lived, along with Jen-bao, Mei-lang and Chung-yi's year-old little boy. The flat consisted of a bedsitting-room, small bedroom, tiny kitchen and shared bathroom and lavatory.

Some ten feet square, the larger room was crowded with cameras and lights but I managed to squeeze in and note every detail whilst the shooting went on. There was a rush mat on the stone floor, a table and four chairs under the window. A double bed with a shiny silk cover occupied most of one wall with Baby Jen-bao's cot fitting endwise at its foot; this left another wall free for a glass-fronted cupboard and a sewing-machine. In pride of place on top of the cupboard were a radio, an alarm clock and one of the giant-sized Thermos flasks dearly loved by the Chinese. This one was bright green with a sprawling floral pattern whose tastelessness seemed to me more out of place in China than most countries. These three are signs of prosperity – and this family also had a sewing-machine, which is rather more costly and much sought after. (I once saw an exhibition of these machines at a Trade Fair with a pleasing sign along the stand reading, 'We make these to save our women from drudgery'.)

Among the pictures and posters on the walls was a coloured photograph of Mei-lang and her husband, Mei-lang in pigtails, smiling broadly and both displaying some half a dozen medals pinned to their best non-working clothes. Shi-hwa, ever-watchful, slipped over to explain. (Shi-hwa, I had found already, was not only a highly competent interpreter, but sensitive, full of fun and quite unselfish.)

Apparently Mei-lang and Chung-yi were model workers, which meant that they had not only fulfilled their own work quotas, month after month, but had helped others to do so and also given much time to voluntary work for the good of the mill community.

'Do they get anything besides medals?' I asked, maybe fractionally sarcastic.

'Oh, yes; they get a cash bonus; they bought their sewing-machine with it.'

We were keen to show a family meal, knowing the world-wide interest in food. Whilst we were shooting inside the flat, 79

Cheng, the assistant cameraman, was at the market photographing Grandma buying pork, vegetables, and fish for the meal that she, as family cook, was to prepare. The vegetables and fruit were especially plentiful that year and very cheap. It is a pity that China cannot yet afford to build enough canning and freezing factories to preserve all her surpluses for winter use.

We were trying to take an average family at an average meal and here was Granny, with very natural human pride, putting on a real party-spread. She was clearly a very fine cook, and she prepared the meal in record time in conditions that would have daunted any Western chef. The kitchen was dark; it had a sink with cold, running water and a solitary gas-ring. 'We are very glad to have running water,' Grandma assured us. After a lifetime of drawing water from a well she would be the last person to complain about the absence of a hot water service. (Once before I had talked to an old lady in her worker's flat and she had three times switched on and off the light to show me how well it worked; her daughter explained that mother had only used small oil lamps or candles before she moved into the flat and still could not get over the thrill of 'switching on'.) Now I realized once again that it is only against the background of previous deprivations that one must judge today's living conditions in China.

We filmed Grandma deftly slicing her pork with the small razor-sharp chopper known to all old China hands, cooking the fish whole, and sending it in floating in a *cordon-bleu* sweet-and-sour sauce with three lots of vegetables.

Then Grandma joined the others and all set to. Fat, button-eyed Jen-bao jumped chuckling up and down in his cot, clutching a great bun of North China's much-loved steamed bread in his eager fist.

Leaving them at their meal, we went off to the canteen to film the workers eating their lunch there. Certainly nothing here was specially laid on, for all was just as it had been on our previous day's reconnaissance visit.

80   The main room, with a stone floor and bare forms and tables,

was full of workers, either eating or queueing at service hatches where they selected dishes from a menu on a blackboard: rice, noodles, steamed bread, chicken, pigs' feet, stuffed melon, dumpling, each costing a few pennies. Getting a dumpling was fun: I collected a warm, flat, bread-pancake (rather like what Australians call a 'damper') and took it to a side-table where there were some six savoury concoctions in bowls, from one of which I scooped up a dollop of minced meat, plomped it on the bread, folded over the edges and returned to the table to devour it. A selection of five or six dishes followed. This was one of seven canteens where workers could 'eat in' or buy and take away.

I soon began to feel that I knew Mei-lang quite well and she seemed at ease with me; indeed, nobody knowing Mei-lang could fail to be won over by her unaffected charm, gaiety and transparent honesty. She and I and Shi-hwa were so interested in all that was going on and in one another's opinions about it that the two-language conversation with its back and forth translation seemed surprisingly easy and we almost forgot our different races and creeds as I tried to get, and Mei-lang to give, a fair picture of her life.

She had been born near Hangchow on the east coast, about one hundred and fifty miles from Shanghai, where she had gone to work in a cotton mill on leaving school. When the Peking factory wanted skilled workers in 1956 she had been offered a job, her fare and accommodation in the hostel, and had decided to accept. At some factory function she had met Chung-yi and they had been married in a simple, civil ceremony.

Though she had stayed at school until sixteen, she was not so well educated as her husband; already he had mastered some three thousand characters of the Chinese language and passed examinations in three subjects of his textile engineer's diploma-course, for which he studied three nights a week at the mill classes.

She worked eight hours a day, six days a week, earning about sixty-two yuan a month;* her husband's wages were eighty-five

* About £9 – see note on p. 30.

yuan; their flat cost four-and-a-half yuan a month, food and clothing about one hundred yuan, with very little for extras; so they reckoned to save about 40 yuan a month, more if they got good bonuses. They had saved up for the radio, Chung-yi had just achieved a bicycle he had been longing for and next month Mei-lang would have her wristwatch – her eyes sparkled with anticipatory pleasure as she told me this and I found myself clapping my hands quite spontaneously to indicate, wordlessly, my own delight at her achievement. She went on, almost breathless with extra excitement, to explain that this was not all – they had even saved up nearly enough to take them back to Hangchow to visit her parents on their next holiday!

When I asked her about other living costs Mei-lang explained that there weren't many because all medical services were free for her and Chung-yi and only half fees were charged for Jen-bao and Grandma. When she was expecting Jen-bao she had fifty-five days' maternity leave on full pay.

'What about your spare time; what sort of amusements have you and how much do they cost?' I asked.

They could get into the city, she said, for a few pennies and a half-day in the Peihai Park or the Summer Palace was very cheap; even theatre seats cost very little; but there was so much going on at the mill that they did not often need to seek amusement in the city. There were television sets in the public rooms and films or theatrical performances in the mill theatres three times a week as well as indoor and outdoor sports; table tennis she especially enjoyed. She explained, too, that she wanted time to take part in factory affairs and attend meetings where local and national problems were discussed as well as methods of increasing the mill's production. In addition, each block of flats had a Family Committee working along with the Street Committee, and this met regularly to help all the women with child-care – 'and husband-care', she added with a grin.

'Well, Chung-yi doesn't look in need of much more care; he looks extremely well and cheerful,' I said, and asked Shi-hwa to translate for me.

Mei-lang blushed with pleasure and laughed again – we all did, suddenly very happy to be together, the three of us.

'Really, Shi-hwa,' I said, 'what a silly world we live in. Everywhere I go I see your "Smash Imperialism" and "Down with colonial powers". At home we are urged to defend ourselves against the encroaching menace of Communism; it may be hard to overcome prejudice to get our film shown on Australian screens – even harder on American ones. We wear our official labels and we are supposed to be afraid of one another – yet here we are, we three women, talking together, and we get along well.'

Shi-hwa translated, Mei-lang nodded, and Shi-hwa added immediately, 'But please remember we don't hate the people in imperialist countries – we love the people wherever they live but we hate the militarist leaders; the capitalists who exploit the poor.'

'Yes, I know you always say there is this distinction but the snag is, you see, they're our Government; we put them there; we vote them in, so you really can't distinguish so easily between the masses and their Government – and all so-called capitalists don't exploit their workers, who are often well-paid and protected by all sorts of legislation.'

I was relieved to be interrupted at this stage by the camera team, coming to do the baby-feeding sequence with Mei-lang at the crèche. My explanation had, of course, opened up a whole series of doubts about what I was saying. Obviously I could not assert with complete confidence that the freely-elected Government which we laud so highly always represents the voters who put them in office. Nor could I explain to Mei-lang and Shi-hwa what sanctions made our politicians keep their electoral promises. (I recalled Whitman's remark about 'the unending audacity of elected persons'.) Nor could I assure them that the free enterprise system with its monopolies and combines unfailingly did right by its workers or the national economy.

When one has to analyse the democratic process for someone who had only the vaguest concept of how it is supposed to work 83 one's own statements give cause for unease. Can we keep our smug belief in its inevitable rightness for all people, in all times and places? Yet these obstinate questionings, these blank misgivings, this hacking away at the very roots of our belief, I said, reassuring myself, are surely all part of the same democratic process, which I had inescapably inherited.

In their Communist tradition Shi-hwa and Mei-lang could criticize here and there; they could question details, personalities, even tactics, in long 'criticism-and-self-criticism sessions' at street and factory committees; but it is doubtful if the main strategy could be questioned, and the political lines of belief are firmly laid; both women were safely anchored on the great rock of Marxism–Leninism as expounded by Chairman Mao. And why should they not accept this? For these two women Communism had meant work and security; it had produced the goods. I doubt if either feel any limitation on their 'freedom'.

As I had done on my previous visit, I vividly saw the whole situation symbolized by a great circle drawn by Authority; within this the millions of Chinese could move to and fro, free within the wide circumference, but they must not go beyond it and question its existence or the rightness of those who drew it. There was far more latitude within that circle than Westerners, misinformed consistently for years, could ever credit, but even so could human reason, aspirations, move just within that circle? As food, clothing, education became taken for granted, as in the West, would not the Shi-hwas and Chung-yis everywhere want to go off exploring? Would not the artists, the thinkers, the scholars, discouraged, some of them, at the time of the 'hundred flowers' want to speak up again? Maybe the older ones would but maybe the new generation were well-fed, well-taught Communist 'organization men' to whom obstinate questionings and blank misgivings were either unknown or deeply suspect. Or, on the other hand, will the tremendous expansion of all levels of education ensure, in the future, a less doctrinaire attitude, a demand by an educated people for truth at any price? Moreover, one obviously has to ask if these dedicated young, like the unselfish and lovable Mei-lang and Shi-hwa, may be creating a world in which the community really matters more than the individual, in which the individual develops all his potentialities not only to be a more successful, more fulfilled person in himself but a better member of a better society? Shi-hwa and good old Ling, Madame Huang, little Mrs Ho in Canton, all accepted the Party line, accepted Chairman Mao and his vision of the good life for China and the world – yet they were not the zombies, the robots, the rigid doctrinaire creatures of the Western stereotype of Communists.

Here I was again in the philosophical rat-race, getting no-where fast, and I abandoned my speculations to go off, with a sigh of relief and my notebook, to the factory crèche, where we were to take what proved to be one of our most attractive sequences of Mei-lang breast-feeding a hungry Jen-bao along with three other young mothers.

Grandma was at the clinic consulting one of its nine doctors about her chest congestion; I rushed up at the end of the session to be told that there were not only nine doctors but also ten medical assistants, five chemists, twenty-one nurses, fifty-three beds.

'Miss Roper,' it was Shi-hwa's anxious voice, 'have you put down that they deliver sixty babies a month?' I hadn't, but I did, though I forgot to note the number of physiotherapists that the conscientious Shi-hwa discovered for me!

After the crèche it was natural to go on talking about babies and I asked Mei-lang if she wanted a large family. 'Not too large,' she explained, 'but certainly more than one.' Advice on family planning was available at the clinic and contraceptives were cheap. Shi-hwa frankly admitted that she didn't want a family at all, or certainly not yet, and her husband agreed with her.

They discussed all this quite unself-consciously and I was once again struck by certain marked characteristics of the Chinese attitude to sex, in its various manifestations.

INTERCHAPTER
Sex in China

One knows there is sex in China because there are so many children, otherwise one would be tempted to suspect that it had ceased to be, so rarely is there any other manifestation of, or reference to, it. Almost wholly absent are the innumerable public sources of titillation that we in the sex-alerted West expect or, at least, accept.

In plays and films not a décolletage, not an amorous clinch and only the most chaste of kisses – on the brow. Love and marriage are presented but sexual intercourse, as such, is not even hinted at and studies of sex psychoses or perversions are unthinkable outside the clinic or text-book. Even classical opera has been, we read, purged of any innuendoes or suggestive gestures. Funny men in variety shows, of which there are hundreds, have no scintilla of smut in their repertoires.

Women's clothes are wholly unprovocative, often almost indistinguishable from those of the men; it is, indeed, a commonplace of visitors to comment on the androgynous quality of Chinese dress. Certainly Hong Kong's dearly-loved, skin-tight, split-to-the-thigh cheong-sam is out.

I never once saw young people indulging in anything more passionate than handholding in streets or parks. Adultery, free love, unnatural vice are not merely reprehensible – they are criminal; divorce, though permitted, is discouraged.

I was told of a brilliant young student who was a bit of a Romeo – apparently an occasional gay dog still crops up – who made a modest pass at a young hairdresser who posted a complaint on the wallboard – 'wrote a *dazi bao*'. Four other local girls promptly did the same and the unfortunate young man with the wandering eye found himself briefly in jail instead of in the examination-room! The judge had explained to him that women had been so badly treated by men in the Old China they had to be given especial respect today.

Early on my first visit I spent a day at the Peking Drama School. After seeing and hearing about dramatized versions of social problems in field and factory, I asked, 'Are all themes social ones? What about the perennial "boy meets girl, boy loses girl, boy gets girl" formulae? Your audiences demand romantic conflicts sometimes, surely?'

'No, our audiences would not be interested in them.'

I resisted the temptation to raise my eyebrows, being at that stage sceptical. Later I was much less so. Whether or not there is a demand, there is certainly no supply of sex problem-dramas in the Western sense.

It sounds excessively Puritan, yet China is not, strictly, a Puritan country, because sex is not the simultaneously horri-fying-fascinating topic that it is to the real Puritan in the Cromwellian or Victorian sense of the word; sex is not a near-obsession to brood over in private and condemn in public. It is, rather, that in China sex, though important, is not allowed to occupy too much time and attention; it has to be taken in the stride, kept in its place, and its place is the marital couch, over which the veils of privacy have to be decently drawn.

Girls and boys, men and women, mix freely, as all schools, sporting-clubs, and volunteer working-parties on public pro-jects are 'mixed'. But male and female together, even alone, does not mean 'sex', and it is my impression that most Chinese, young or old, would be shocked at any implication that it did.

I met several examples of this attitude. One of the women interpreters was married, so were her three male colleagues; they all shared a four-berth compartment on our long train-journeys. This was all in the day's work! Planning train sleep-ing-arrangements for our Australian party, we once found numbers recalcitrant, and when the Chinese suggested solving the problem by putting two married couples together, it was we who were embarrassed to point out Western coyness about such 'mixed' sleeping arrangements.

In 1958 two members of our visiting women's group were social-workers who asked to see the birth-control film made the previous year and widely distributed during the great family planning drive. We had a private showing of the film. A simple physiological explanation of intercourse and pro-creation, with diagrams, was followed by equally frank advice 87 on contraceptive methods, distinguishing between viewers who had access to one of the many clinics established by the Government and those who had to depend mostly on 'home-made' contraceptives because of their isolation. It was, of course, quite unsalacious, but I can think of very few, if any, countries where such a film could have had nationwide public showing.

Our interpreter, unmarried, rather shy and reticent, would have been shocked by Lolita and bikinis but had no worry about translating; without a hint of self-consciousness, she gave us, loud and clear, every word of the script. (It was a little comic at times to hear those very literal translations of sexual intimacies, and I was glad the darkness hid my occasional wide smile.) This was a subject important to her country and to women; it was wrong for a family to have an unwanted child. We gathered that even prosperous couples were discouraged from having a large family as the country was not able to give, as yet, all facilities to these.

Although the great family planning drive of the mid 'fifties is over, contraceptive advice is widely available. Not surprisingly there are some indications of resistance to birth control among the peasants, to whom a large family still means more farm-workers, more security for parents' old-age.

On my visit to the Canton Cultural Park in 1965 I saw a Family Planning Exhibition. Diagrams and pictures were similar to those in the film. There was a series of posters and cartoons showing the advantages of spacing children so that the house was not overcrowded, mothers not overworked and father not overanxious. Too many babies were a bad thing for everybody, it was clear! One series dealt with sterilization, which was recommended for the father rather than the mother on health grounds. It was made pictorially clear that he would not suffer mentally or physically by the simple operation involved.

There seemed to be no reference to abortion. The Women's Federation had told me it was discouraged, but was permitted on medical advice. They discounted it as a means of population-control. In Canton I inquired of the interpreters what would 88 happen if an unmarried girl asked for such an operation.

'This is not one of our problems,' I was told firmly.

'But with seven hundred million people it must happen now and again,' I insisted, incredulously.

'We don't know of it,' came the answer. 'Our young people just don't behave in that way.'

Though not exactly embarrassed, they did not wish to pursue the subject.

I recollected that I had been told previously by the Women's Federation that an illegitimate child could be brought up by either parent and that no stigma was attached to the child, who had the same rights as others.

Certainly it is clear that illegitimate births do not constitute the same social problem as in the West.

This is the more remarkable when we consider that the marriage age is very much higher than ours. When I asked a couple of senior girl students in the University of Canton if many of them married during their courses, they burst out laughing, assuring me that it just never happened. None of them, boys or girls, ever thought of it; they hadn't time! They did not expect to marry until twenty-six or twenty-seven years of age.

One of our 1965 party was an Australian–Chinese who had a brother in Peking. He invited the brother's son and a friend to have dinner with us and I joined them to hear their story. The uncle acted as interpreter. The young man was twenty-one and in the third year of a five-year course at the Petroleum Institute. He had spent two years working in the country before he began it. He was living on his Government scholarship, which, he said, was small but quite adequate for his simple needs. He was receiving his education from the State and could not expect it to pay for elaborate clothes or entertainment, he explained. When we asked him how he managed to entertain his girl-friends, he assured us quite seriously that he was too busy studying to have time to go out with girls. He met them sometimes at social functions, but, since there were only a few at the Petroleum Institute, he certainly did not see one girl often enough to acquire 'a steady'. His friend told us that 'going steady' just did not feature as part of their lives at that stage. They both 89 told us that marriage would have to wait until they had started work and settled down; they would be twenty-nine or thirty then.

With us that night was a 'new Australian' member of our group. Born in Hungary, widely travelled, sophisticated, more than a little cynical, Otto was fascinated by all this.

'I simply can't believe it,' he said cheerfully. 'You must ask them how they cope with natural physiological urges. They surely must "sublimate" somehow at their age.'

But Uncle refused to translate because, he said, he knew his nephew would be shocked and embarrassed by such an intimate inquiry and it would be quite unfair to impute any irregularity of behaviour to either of the young men.

To hear more of the woman's attitude I broached the question next morning when I had an appointment with a Vice-President of the Women's Federation. With her were two secretaries, both newly-graduated from the Foreign Language Institute of Peking. They fully endorsed the young men's attitude, assuring me that love affairs would have interfered with their studies at university and with their work for the Federation. Both were very pretty young women!

Women-interpreters often accompany their men 'charges' for days at a time, looking after them quite sedulously; they are mostly unself-consciously friendly and expect visitors to be the same. But any hint of making passes comes, I know, as a shock to them, and is officially strongly deplored, of course. I was told of occasions when men's visas had been withdrawn and their visit hastily terminated as a result of their amorous advances to an interpreter. The Party has a most protective attitude towards women and I observed an interesting example of this.

The senior officer of the Travel Service and the senior interpreter came to me after breakfast one day looking serious. They wanted my help, they said. We sat down and they began by a longish disquisition on the necessity for looking after women; before Liberation women had been down-trodden and often abused and ill-treated, the second sex with a vengeance. Now
90 they were free and equal; but in some men there were still the

remnants of the old attitude which made them think they could take liberties.

Wondering what on earth all this was leading up to – and knowing, at least, it was not any experience of mine that was in question – I waited, full of curiosity, realizing by now that the Chinese nearly always approached the particular via the general.

It transpired that Otto, the ebullient Otto, had put his arm round the waist of a girl-worker in the narrow alley of the factory we had visited the previous day. The girl, they told me, did not say anything at the time as she did not wish to embarrass a guest, but she had afterwards complained to the manager as she had been much distressed. I knew Otto, they explained; could I please have a word with him, tactfully, in case he upset more young women!

I looked at their kind, concerned faces and asked them to forgive me for smiling. 'That's just Otto's way; he means no harm at all; he puts his arms round quite a lot of waists without giving it a thought. But I'll ask him not to do it again to a strange girl; I'm sure he won't even remember the occasion.'

And sure enough he didn't.

'Which girl? What factory? I can't remember!' he responded to my slightly embarrassed inquiry.

I reported back to my Chinese friends with an 'I-told-you-so' but with, at the same time, my own assurance that I, as a woman, certainly appreciated very much their sincere concern for the women and girls of the New China.

The whole temper of the Republic today is so strongly against sexual freedom that very few couples would think it worth making a stand for any kind of irregular liaison. The Party, the Women's Federation, the Street Committees, all education institutions have a firm attitude and their basic assumption is that nobody wants it. And most young people seem to share this view.

This general attitude to relations between the sexes is, I am told, very much in line with the traditional attitude of all but a very few Chinese. The great majority of them have always 91 deplored sexual laxity and even disapproval of any too obvious show of affection in public. This was certainly true of the rich peasant class into which Mao Tse-tung was born, which must have regarded the concubines and sensual excesses of the aristocracy and the Westernized millionaires with all the disapproval of decent French provincials for goings-on in Paris!

Allowing for an occasional primness, even naïveté, and the possible overestimating of human self-control, the Chinese are pretty adult about sex. It is open to neo-Freudians to argue that sex will catch up on them in a generation; that, human nature being what it is, greater freedom will have to come. But present attitudes seem healthy enough and it is certainly refreshing to spend several months in a country free of the more adolescent aspects of the sex-paraphernalia of Western stage, screen and billboard.

8 · 'PEKING DAY'
Young Dancers and the Summer Palace

The excitement of the five-year-olds was almost too great to be borne, and even the teacher was stuttering with nerves when, next morning, we arrived with cameras and sound equipment and improvised lighting to shoot the mill kindergarten class doing its song and dance acts for us.

The building was bare and simply furnished, but the class suffered not a whit from this – they were raring to go. The boys were in long, gaily-coloured pants and the girls, clearly expecting us, had been decked out in specially bright hair ribbons and flowered blouses; they were excited but biddable and, at a sign from the teacher, they ceased squealing and sat, tense, on the edge of their chairs waiting for instructions. They began by singing the catchiest of Communist pops, 'Socialism is Good' and then, with Chinese words, we heard, unmistakably, the old familiar 'Frère Jacques'! It seemed most incongruous, this old French nursery rhyme, following Communism's song of faith – but they all loved it so I hadn't the heart this time to tell them it came from the imperialist West.

The five boys and five girls sorted themselves out and, after a brief instruction from the teacher, the rest of the class began rhythmically clapping as the ten dancers gave their performance. Two of the girls were identical twins in bright, tartan trews with long, beribboned pigtails and, *mirabile dictu*, spots of rouge and lipstick produced by some proud parent for her daughters' camera début. The dance was one of their usual class-studies and was no mere children's romp. These children were born dancers; serious, absorbed, unself-conscious, they undulated arms and fingers, swaying from side to side, then down to the ground, where, with hands above their heads, they circled lithely from the waist, fingers delicately posed and poised in characteristic Asian dance fashion. One of them had that indefinable but unmistakable extra grace and flow which marks 'star quality'. The next dance had a sung chorus. It was a folk dance from Mongolia and, as they sang, each line was mimed by the dancers. Shi-hwa translated the chorus: 'Mongolia is a good land. We have a bumper harvest of corn; we have many sheep and cattle too. The people and the children are very busy and very happy.' And as the class sang the dancers milked cows, drove sheep, cut and stacked corn and then fell gently to sleep, head on hand.

The third dance, and the last that we had time for, unfortunately, was a gay folk romp. The moment they had finished, Harold, without a word to any of us, began to play back the whole sequence on the tape-recorder. For a few seconds the children sat silent, taken aback by the new noise; then the truth dawned – it was their singing and shouting coming from the magic box! Even their teacher could not control them as they rushed in a body to see it and marvel at what they heard, shrieking and giggling and jumping up and down in wild excitement; cameramen and technicians joined in the laughter; it was the most delightful pandemonium imaginable, and will, I suppose, never be forgotten by the class – or by us.

The din echoed cheerfully in our ears as we did a hurried tour of the building, which had all the insignia of Australian and American kindergartens: percussion bands, rest-cots, finger painting, sand-trays and the right kind of instructive toys of the simpler sort.

I remembered, before leaving, to find out the name of the little dancer who had so charmed me – Wang Ming-hua. When I next go to Peking I hope I shall remember to ask if she has joined some of the opera or drama schools to develop her talent.

The cameras went off to film the Primary School and I went wandering away alone, seeking any scene or incident outside our main theme which was so simple in itself that it could be taken for granted by our hosts and would yet throw light, for the Western viewer, on some unexpected aspect of everyday life. I found it just round the corner. There, on a worn grass-plot beneath the young trees, was 'our' Grandma with the *Renmin Ribao*, 'People's Daily', in her hand slowly reading the day's news to some half-dozen elderly men and women grouped round her. Grandma, unusual for her class and generation, was literate enough to be able to read at least the 1,500 simplified

characters required to keep her illiterate neighbours informed

of what was going on in the world and what their country expected of them.

It was a very moving little scene; an old man in his late
seventies leaned forward, hand cupped over ear, face tense with
the effort to hear and understand, his neighbour, maybe his
wife, sat more relaxed but equally attentive; a third had her
eyes closed, presumably to eliminate distractions in the street.
Shut out by their illiteracy from the world of the printed word
on which now so much of their country's life depended, they
followed closely as the reader spelled out the news of Vice-
Chairman Liu Shao-chi's recently-concluded visit to North
Korea.

The scene must have been typical of hundreds throughout the
country, for the Government depends on the spread of the Word
in such form that even the humblest citizen may understand it.
One of the Party's first great tasks was to reduce the eighty-five
per cent illiteracy rate that it inherited; so anyone who could
read or write was charged to teach family or neighbours in
home, field or evening classes. I was told of children going from
school into the fields and holding up cards with ideographs on
them for the peasants to pause in their labours and learn; every
factory and office had its literacy classes and the radio devoted
hours a week to teaching. The latest estimates give twenty per
cent as 'incorrigible' illiterates, that is, those who cannot learn
the minimal 1,500 characters needed to be reckoned 'literate'.
It is likely that the great majority of under-twenties now read
and write. This is a stupendous achievement in a mere fifteen
years.

As I dawdled along at my leisure I acquired the usual
retinue of children, interested, friendly, always well-behaved. I
watched housewives shopping at the open stalls; no more chaf-
fering about prices but much argument, often heated, about
size, quality or ripeness of the fruit or tenderness of the meat.
There were no paper bags or wrappings of any kind, each
shopper bringing her own bag or basket; the grocer's stall had
only the simplest basic packaging for its goods.

A tinker, with the thin hair and beard and the tight-drawn 95

skin of the old figures of classical art, sat unconcernedly mend-
ing pots and pans at his brazier; as a side-line he was repairing
shoes, judging by the little pile of them at his feet. Across the
road I saw young workers with drawing instruments and paint
brushes sketching in and colouring National Day greetings on
two great hoardings erected specially in the main entrance
drive of the factory and, in an open shed, half a dozen others
taking time off to make great piles of the paper flowers which
the workers were to wave, literally, in their tens of thousands, in
greeting to Chairman Mao on the 1 October procession. A few
boys were practising the widely popular basket-ball on a dusty
court and one lad of eight or nine was unconcernedly drifting
on his way, wooden flute to his lips, picking out a tune – maybe
'Socialism is Good' or even 'Frère Jacques'.

It was an enjoyable stroll for me and I was greeted with
smiles, but not encouraged to interrupt anybody's labours;
again I felt that, though everybody was busy, nobody was in a
scramble.

Mei-lang was not too carried away by her starring role to
remember to make tea for us at the end of the afternoon's shooting and she did the honours in their little sitting-room with her
usual unaffected grace and warmth.

'Dear Mei-lang,' I said impulsively, 'you've helped to give
us such a happy day, please take this as a souvenir,' and I took
off my near Woolworthian pearls and tried to fasten them round
her neck. As I expected, she refused firmly at first; it is tiresomely hard to give anything to the Chinese: tips are not expected or accepted and I found it difficult in 1958, at the end of
my month's acquaintance, to persuade my hardworking, devoted interpreters to accept even the simplest present as a
memento. On this trip I did manage to give away three pairs of
nylon stockings and a tablet of Elizabeth Arden's Blue Grass
Soap – unique in the length and breadth of China, I imagine,
such a foreign luxury article. The whole trend of teaching in
classes and via the innumerable exhortatory moral slogans is
against the acquisitive society; Middle and Primary Schools
96 have a subject listed as 'Communist Morality' which stresses,

among other things, the anti-social effects of greed and money-grabbing. I recalled the slogans in the spinning-shed – 'If there is convenience I will pass it on to others.'

Anyway, Mei-lang was finally persuaded to accept my necklace, because she could see that I was prepared to be hurt by her refusal – as indeed I was – and as she waved good-bye, with Jen-bao in her arms, he was plucking happily at the new bauble around his mother's neck. We climbed into our cars, packed our traps and left with half the Cotton Mill workers and their families clapping and waving good-bye, it seemed.

Feng and John were obviously pleased with the two days' work and relieved at the absence of any kind of incident at this our first major assignment on location. We told ourselves that maybe we need not worry any longer about 'incidents', but we knew that the ideological gulf always yawned between us and them – not as people but as representatives of East and West – so that some degree of tension was inevitably present; years of misunderstanding, misinformation, suspicion and mutual disapproval could not, with all the goodwill in the world, be forgotten in a couple of days' successful work together.

The last scene of the 'Peking Day' sequence was shot at the Summer Palace, where, on the Sunday following, we met our family again. Probably for the first time in their lives, Mei-lang and Chung-yi and Grandma had travelled into the city by car. Mei-lang wore a flowered cotton blouse with her slacks, Grandma her black tunic outfit and Chung-yi a well-cut Chinese suit. Young Jen-bao was dressed to kill with a red velveteen jacket and matching peaked cap; round his neck, just for fun, was a silver-painted, tasselled, cardboard dragon. All of us were quite excited to be working together again and smilingly Mei-lang showed me she was wearing my pearls.

The Summer Palace, one of the world's most beautiful and romantic parks, covers some eight hundred acres with more than a hundred buildings – halls, pagodas, pavilions, temples – scattered among them. Even this is less than the whole site of the original Summer Palace, Yuan Ming Yuan, which was rebuilt and much enlarged by the Ming Emperor, K'ang Hsi (1662–

1723) from a smaller Ming palace of which the most substantial remains are part of the Jade Fountain Park. Emperor Ch'ien Lung added the 'foreign style' buildings which the Jesuits designed for him. Yuan Ming Yuan bade fair to outshine even the Forbidden City itself.

When I asked Ling the date of the Palace and he told me about 1900 I forgot my Chinese history and incautiously exclaimed, 'Oh, I thought it was much older than that.' Only then did he point out what I had temporarily, and embarrassingly, forgotten, that the British and French forces burned and looted the original palace in 1860. (I was reminded of a similar moment when I asked a friend in Washington what had happened to part of the Capitol there. 'The English army burnt it down in 1812,' I was told, a little grimly. One can't help feeling some slight sense of guilt about the arson of one's forebears!)

The glories of the old Palace haunted the Empress Dowager and she determined to rebuild it in equal splendour, unblushingly expropriating a naval grant to do so. The old lady might have done worse. The Manchu Dynasty's pathetic little navy would be at the bottom of the sea now, but the Palace, restored in part to its pristine splendour, gives pleasure to thousands.

Neglected, falling to pieces, its pagodas rotting away, its hilltop temple leaking rain, its famous painted corridor fading and peeling, the Summer Palace languished throughout the civil wars and Japanese occupation. Now all is new, glowing. The autocratic old dowager, if she returned today, would abominate most of what the régime stood for but she could not fail to approve of the way it has looked after her palace.

The Buddhist 'Sea of Wisdom' Temple at the top of the great artificial hill, overlooking the wide artificial lake, is splendid with its amber-tiled roof and scarlet and emerald timbers sharp against the sky; the detailed landscapes on the roof and lintels of the famous Painted Gallery have been meticulously redelineated and the elegance of each charmingly-named pavilion has been restored – Hall of Listening to the Birds, Hall of Delight in Longevity, Hall of Virtuous Harmony.

98   In the Empress's gardens waterfalls tinkle down artificial

rocks and fountains play into great basins supported on the backs of dragons and lions; a quiet lake, full of lotus, reflects between the blossoms the shape and glimmer of yet more bright pavilions and, world-famous, in the shallows of the lake lies the Empress's marble barge, its white deck and high poop glowing opalescent in the sun. At least this one vessel materialized to justify that embezzled naval grant.

We photographed Mei-lang and her family wandering round the parks; they took out one of the painted boats, like the one I sailed in with Madame Huang and my steel-conscious tenor. But, unfortunately, a stiff wind had blown up and rowing was too difficult, so they returned quickly and joined us at one of the several tea-houses, where we drank not tea but the popular orangeade and North China's beer – very good, but not the equal of Five Goats down south.

The orangeade party was our farewell scene; the wind, strengthening all afternoon, was by then blowing hard, dishevelling Mei-lang's neat plaits, whisking away Jen-bao's handsome headgear, and making so much noise in the high fir trees by the lake that our four-way English–Chinese conversation was almost inaudible. So we had to say our rather melancholy goodbyes in the cars at the entrance gates. After three days' hard work together, in novel conditions of some strain and tension, we had established bonds of understanding, and we parted, as always on such occasions, trying to lessen the sadness by assertions that we would meet again one day.

'See you soon, little Jen-bao, dear Mei-lang.'

'See that you pass your exams, Chung-yi, by the time we're back.' Then '*Tsai chien*,' said John and Harold and Myra.

'Good-bye,' replied Mei-lang, Chung-yi and Grandma; Jen-bao was asleep. His Peking day, like ours, was ended.

9 · PEKING PANORAMA

With 'Peking Day' successfully completed we could turn with a quiet mind to the delightful task of filming the sights of the city.

I found that Peking had changed far more, for instance, than Canton since my first visit. The Government has clearly determined to make its capital one of the most beautiful, well-designed cities in the world where the past and present glories of the Middle Kingdom will be reflected. And it has harder tasks, for all the means are to hand: ancient imperial buildings, fantastically conceived and constructed with a disregard of labour, cost and time; parks and pleasances laid out with all the arboricultural and horticultural genius of the race; ancient walls rising dramatically above twisting streets; ancient court-yard-style stone houses with moss-patinaed tiles on their steep roofs; Buddhist temples, Muslim mosques, Christian churches, and, alongside all these, Authority has been able to clear the ground for its own splendours in the twentieth-century idiom.

We climbed to the top of Coal Hill near the centre of the city, so-called, according to one of several legends, because an Emperor stored thousands of tons of coal there to see him through a long siege. It provided the perfect eminence from which to obtain a panoramic view of the city's lay-out.

Immediately below us lay the almost incredible Imperial Palace – the Forbidden City – forbidden once to all except the Imperial family, their entourage and visitors. Innumerable buildings clustered along its central north-south axis, which led the eye, straight as an arrow's flight, from the Drum Tower behind us across to the towers of the Front Gate in the walls of the Inner – or Northern – City some two and a half miles away, and beyond them, faint in the distance, the walls of the Outer – or Southern – City. Old Peking roughly resembles a fat inverted letter T with the Inner City the leg and the Outer the arm.

No city is richer in history and legend, more haunted by the ghosts of a crowded and bloodstained past. Founded nearly three thousand years ago, it has, under one name or another, been a capital since the Norman conquest of Britain. The Mongol conqueror, Genghis Khan, descended on it in 1211 and, fifty years later, his grandson, Kublai Khan, warrior, tyrant, artist and connoisseur, was fascinated by it and built, among other things, a great palace in the Peihai Park. The Palace is gone, but the park and its lake are still there in the heart of the city.

'To this city,' wrote Marco Polo, 'are brought articles of greater cost and rarity and in greater abundance than to any other in the world.' But the splendours of Peking as we know it began when the Ming Emperors,* having driven out the Mongol Dynasty, set about constructing the wonder city of their day.

Henry VIII planned Hampton Court and Louis XIV Versailles as monuments of brick and stone, with multi-storey façades; they are great, solid, self-contained blocks of immensely impressive, immensely elaborate masonry. The third Ming Emperor, who conceived the Imperial Palace, had a different dream of palatial glory: a dream of timber halls, jewel-coloured, one storey but lofty and elegant, grouped around spacious courtyards, connected by long pavements and sheltered corridors, approached by flights of steps and fronted by wide terraces.

At the entrance to the Palace grounds is the great Gate of Heavenly Peace, the very heart of the nation and the focal point of all mass rallies. It stands, solid, like the blockhouse it really is, with its massive eighty-feet deep, carmine-red walls pierced by five tunnel-like entrances and topped by a sort of pavilion and now flanked by stands for the thousands of spectators of the rallies in the vast square before it. Now the largest concourse in the world (one hundred acres), this square was completed, after the demolition of many streets and houses, in 1959, for the tenth anniversary celebration.

We entered the Forbidden City through the Gate and walked across a sort of courtyard-cum-walled garden to the Wu Men, or Meridian Gate and, passing through this, emerged into the great courtyard of the Taihotien, Supreme Harmony. There we had an immediate and breathtaking impression of space and colour. It is over two hundred yards square and is crossed by the

* **Ming** Dynasty 1368–1644.

Golden Water Stream which has five elaborately carved marble bridges, each with two flights of steps and, between them, a ramp up which the Imperial sedan chairs used to be carried.

Beyond this, on a raised stone foundation with triple marble terraces, we saw the long, golden-roofed splendour of the Hall of Supreme Harmony with its vividly painted façade. On the wide terrace in front of it stood a marble sundial and a bronze crane and tortoise, symbols of longevity. Inside, beneath a green and gold ceiling on a dais some thirty feet square, was one of the great Imperial thrones. Beyond it we moved into another great courtyard surrounding the Chunghotien, Hall of Complete Harmony, used by the Emperor as a resting place *en route* to the Throne Room: beyond this, in turn, we saw the courtyard of the Paohotien, the Hall of Preserving Harmony, the Room for Receiving Successful Scholars. Around the great central buildings is a confusing agglomeration of courtyards, halls and gardens, some with fascinating names such as the Hall of Mental Cultivation and the Hall of Earthly Tranquillity. Many of these were used as residences for members of the Imperial family, their courtiers and concubines.

Whilst the others were busy with the cameras, I happened to notice an old lady shuffling along on her tiny, bound feet; it was a pathetic sight, but it was China, so I interrupted the cameraman, who broke off to 'shoot' her as unobtrusively as possible. Feng stood uneasily by but did not check us. Over tea, an hour of two later, Shi-hwa came up to me and said Feng would be pleased if we would promise to cut out the shots of the old lady. 'But we will say this was the Old China,' I replied. Nevertheless, neither of them liked our keeping in the old lady; it reflected on China, even if the Old China. I understood and cut the sequence out, of course.

From the side walls of the main courtyards we looked down on the roofs, tilted at many angles, of the smaller buildings. Indeed, one of the fascinations of the place is the vista of multiple overlapping roofs. Shining with amber, turquoise and sapphire tiles, with their long, upturned eaves cutting graceful arabesques against the sky, they form an exquisitely-proportioned contrast to the firm, upright lines of the wooden pillars, the long, horizontal beams of the main façades. Scholars believe there is a connection between Chinese architecture and Chinese calligraphy with its interplay of rigid lines and curving forms. Of course, because this is China, there were bushes and flowers everywhere; in the courtyards, on the terraces and even up the centre of the marble ramps cyclamens, chrysanthemums and cannas were blooming gaily in pots and tubs.

Wandering off alone I found myself in a small, rectangular yard surrounded by high terra-cotta walls, weathered to mellowness by the centuries; over the top of these spread the dark-green layers of the branches of cypress trees in the adjoining garden; the line they traced against the wall, the proportions of the treetops seen above it, were so perfect that the whole scene looked more like a painting than reality. The smaller walls were pierced by studded double doors, flanked on either side by fire – new, gilded beasts with upstanding, serrated manes. It was very quiet, utterly deserted, very sultry, and I suppose I was a little *exaltée* by the Harmony Halls, the golden roofs and the whole exotic air; for as I stood there, looking at the doors, I found that, for a second or two, I was waiting for something to happen, waiting vaguely for the doors to open of themselves and emit some Ming or Manchu Princess and her maidens coming for their afternoon walk in the sunshine. Certainly had they come I would have been no more surprised than Miss Jourdain and Miss Moberley when they 'saw' Marie Antoinette and her train come through the trees across the lawns of Versailles. Nothing happened, of course, except that I came to my senses and within five minutes was back with the cameras, watching Cheng take, from several angles, shots of a particularly elaborate little pavilion, in one of the smaller gardens. It was circular with several tiers of amber roofs and pillars, doors and windows picked out in brightest primary colours; this was a Chinese gingerbread house in its fantasy and elaboration. Someone commented that it lacked restraint, but I was delighted by its baroque exuberance of line, all its twiddles and flutings and the gaiety of its shapes and colours; for, despite its exaggeration, the 103 pavilion had a kind of proportion and unity that showed its creator was an artist amusing himself.

Coming out of the Forbidden City we walked across the square to the Great Hall of the People, Communism's own Imperial Palace. Planned to celebrate the tenth anniversary (1 October 1959) of the régime, the Hall, with an area of 170,000 square metres, was completed after ten months' work on the tenth day of the tenth month. (I am told that the Chinese enjoy playing around with numbers in this way.) This speed of building seems pretty hard to believe, but after a little experience of my own I am prepared to do so.

Coming back to the hotel one night I stumbled over a pile of sand on the edge of a vacant block of land; near by I saw bricks and other building materials. Two nights later, at about 11 p.m., I returned the same way to find lights blazing and men working away at a wall already several feet high, clearly designed to enclose the plot of ground. The next day the wall was completely finished; like Wordsworth, 'I measured it from side to side.' It was about one hundred feet long and ten feet high and well built, this little wall of China!

At the main entrance of the Hall of the People stand twelve tall, grey, marble columns on reddish bases carved with floral designs; the roof has light green and gold glazed tiles and, high above them, glows the Red Star of China. The Grand Auditorium has a floor space of 3,600 square metres and seats 10,000 people. It has cantilevered balconies and no view-obstructing pillars. Great staircases, marble foyers, elaborately-painted ceilings are everywhere and even Kublai Khan could have imagined nothing more exotically splendid than the huge gilt and crystal chandeliers that hang in almost reckless profusion in each hall and corridor. I did not find it hard to believe that the architects, as we were told, had made 3,600 blueprints for the building.

Facing the Great Hall, and almost equally magnificent, is the Museum of Chinese History. To left and right of the elegant lofty foyer lies a museum wing. In the one are exhibits of China's history from the Peking Man to 1840. In the other, three thousand six hundred exhibits illustrate the history of the 'people's revolutionary struggle'. The first section of this, which is called the 'old-democratic revolution', covers the years 1840–1919 and the second, the 'new-democratic revolution', from 1919–49. The main events dealt with in Section I are the Opium Wars, 1840–60, the Taiping Revolution, 1851–68, the Sino–Japanese War, the Yi Ho Tuan (Boxer) 'Anti-Imperialist Movement' and Sun Yat-sen's Revolution of 1911. Section II covers, in great detail, the whole story of the Communist Party's struggle from its founding in 1921 to its final victory over the Kuomintang and Japanese forces in 1949. Whatever the Western visitor might think about some of the interpretations of Sino–Western relations, he could not fail to be stirred by the records, in paintings, models, narrative and photographs, of the epic Long March of 1934–5, when Mao Tse-tung led his ragged, hungry armies for 6,000 miles across mountains, rivers and swamps, fighting, hiding, fighting once more against superior KMT forces, finally establishing himself and his military government in the Caves of Yenan, where he planned his final victory strategy.

Certainly, China got its Communist Government the hard way, and it may well be that the continuing, almost unbroken, accord of the Party leaders is the result of the bonds woven between them during those years of sacrifice and suffering. It is a phenomenon of the Chinese revolution that the original leaders of the Communist Party still alive have remained in high office, Mao Tse-tung, Chou En-lai, Chen-yi, Chu-teh, Kuo Mo-jo and Liu Chao-shi being the best-known.

Isolated in the centre of the Square, a simple pillar, marked only with the words, 'To the Heroes of the Revolution', breaks the emptiness and focuses the eye. The calligraphy is Chairman Mao's.

Because the art of China's past is a reflection of the essential and continuing genius of the Chinese race, the Government is nurturing national pride by restoring architectural and art treasures everywhere. Indeed, the Party has identified itself with national achievements of any former age and probably some of the support for the régime is due to the image it has established of China as a former great power returning to full splendour after temporary eclipse, in the arts as in all else. So, not only are great buildings restored and ancient treasures exhibited in museum collections, in every branch of the arts national pride is to be fostered. Up and down the country there are innumerable small art studios, factories and workshops reproducing classical works. Near Canton, on our return visit, we saw round a ceramics factory founded centuries ago near a fine clay-pit and now making faithful copies of porcelain and jade figures, beautiful and cheap and good foreign-currency earners. (Quite characteristically the factory, as a side-line, produces sewage pipes!) In Shanghai, in the mansion of a former French millionaire merchant, is the Folk Art Studio where master craftsmen, selected from many provinces, practise and teach their skills in paper-cuts, wood-carving, basketry, embroidery and the fascinating art of making dough-dolls.

And in Peking there is the Liu Li Ch'ang. This famous little street is in an old part of the Southern City near the Front Gate. The name means, literally, 'glaze yard' because the glazed tiles used for the roofs of the Palace were made there in Ming times, long before it became a curio-market. Tidied up, but otherwise unchanged, today it gives the visitor some idea of pre-revolutionary Peking. Running off a main road, the lane is lined with narrow, one-storey wooden buildings on either side. The Studio of Glorious Treasure has three large windows, double doors of carved wood and glass, rickety on their hinges, and steps worn concave by generations of customers. It is a typical Pekingese courtyard-style building with the front room as a sale-room, where scrolls, carvings and every kind of ceramics from ashtrays to six-feet high vases are on display. 'Customers' and 'sale-room' seem inappropriate words, for I felt as if I were visiting a connoisseur's drawing-room whilst the blue-suited salesman – another misnomer – showed me round with grave courtesy and a few words of English, gently lifting figurines and unrolling scrolls for my delight; obviously he was enjoying my frankly-expressed pleasure and sharing it with me.

For a few pounds I bought two scrolls on silk and parchment, one a modern copy of a Ming period painting and the other an original painting of the late Manchu Dynasty, probably about sixty years old. (Any *objet d'art* over eighty years of age cannot be taken from the country without a licence.) One of the Government's numerous indictments of the Western 'imperialists' is their 'cultural aggression'. I am told that some Chinese museums carry notices stating that such and such a collection on show is incomplete because part of it is in the Kansas City Oriental Museum or in the British Museum's collection and that on ancient temple walls blank spaces amongst carvings or paintings arc similarly labelled, but I saw none of these anywhere.

The shop is State-owned and accounts are carefully kept for Government auditors, so, after wrapping up my purchases and working out the cost with tremendous speed on his abacus, the salesman filled in, I believe in quadruplicate, an elaborate sales receipt before taking me over to the studios.

Beyond the shop was a cool, stone-flagged courtyard with two workshops opening on to it. Inside, seated at narrow tables, in silence, three men and a couple of women shared the task of making the hand-blocked copies of old paintings. One man, wrinkled as a tortoise, impassive, motionless except for his hands, with pestle and mortar was slowly grinding the pigments to powder. None spoke, the dull sound of stone from the grinding, the occasional flick of the parchment by the woman, were the only sounds in the old, low-ceilinged room. China has nearly 700 million inhabitants; they work very hard. Yet often I was aware, as now near the heart of a great city, of quiet, of unhaste. The concentration of the workers' expressions, their quiet acceptance of my presence, the measured tempo of every movement, even the slow, soft shuffle of the salesman's shoes across the yard, all contributed to the atmosphere of a curious, busy calm to which the artist had given a local habitation in the long, oval face, the downcast eyes, the slender hands offering a plate of peaches, of the Manchu maiden on my newly-purchased scroll.

Back at the hotel I found Madame Huang waiting with an unexpected invitation to go with her for a special Peking duck banquet at the famous Peking Duck Restaurant. Thanking her warmly, I rushed off to dress. In the taxi, *en route,* she told us that two African and two Latin American guests of the Women's Federation were to join us there.

In a sudden spurt of disapproval I burst out: 'I'll bet you have no Europeans this year; in 1958 half of us were from the West, now you talk so much of Afro-Asian unity, of China-Latin American accord. Can't you see you are isolating yourself more and more from the West? Nourishing more illusions about it? We've got to understand each other. East-West understanding is more important for the world-peace than Afro-Asian unity.'

I knew Madame Huang well enough to know she'd give as good as she got and be less ruffled about it than I.

'Miss Roper,' with a patient smile as if to a bright but uninformed youngster, 'we have freed ourselves from Western exploitation and must help others to do so. You can't blame us for that. And because we do not have contacts with some Western countries we aren't necessarily isolated. China can never be isolated when she has friends among the masses of the whole world. Anyway, it is not we who close the door to Western visitors—many of them come to China; you're here, aren't you, and not for the first time!' We laughed together.

None the less, I think it noticeable that the last few years had brought a markedly increasing stress on China's relations with Latin America and the Afro-Asian bloc. On his much-publicized African tour Chou En-lai was at pains to make it clear that China had no wish to impose any ideology; there was no hard-sell of Communism. However, being, as a journalist once called him, 'the world's most formidable diplomat,' Chou was not slow to stress China's unique ability to understand African and Asian aspirations because of her own experiences with an inimical Western world. This inevitably gives an impression of ganging-up on colour lines, even though colour may not be the primary bond in the relationship, or the immediate cause.

This is scarcely a matter for shocked surprise. China wants to be self-sufficient but not isolated. I found the Chinese very touchy at any suggestion that they were out of contact with the rest of the world; so, officially ignored and vilified by the United States and half of Europe, half-heartedly recognized by a Great Britain that still keeps up some sort of official relations with the hated Nationalist China on Taiwan, and now at odds with the USSR, her only strong Western ally, the People's Republic inevitably turns for support and sympathy to the rest of the world, which happens to be mostly black or brown.

Madame Huang and I ranged fairly frankly over this aspect of Chinese policy and, though the discussion was friendly, I think both of us were relieved to have it ended, naturally, by our arrival at the restaurant.

In keen anticipation we sat at an almost empty table awaiting the dramatic arrival of the cook with the distended, shining, golden, infinitely tender anserine carcass in all its splendour on its great platter, swimming in honey sauce. After he had exhibited it long enough for our delighted eyes to feast upon it, he departed, only to return soon after with the massacred remains ready for us to pick up in small pieces, which we dipped into a special sauce before placing them, with a spring onion, in a sort of round rice pancake and eating from our fingers. The golden crisp skin, the gourmet's special joy, must be cooked to a hairsbreadth turn. Culinary acolytes appeared after the high priest bearing dishes made, with considerable ingenuity, from every possible part of the bird: even the tongue is not forgotten. The dish's reputation as one of the world's greatest delicacies is deserved, though its richness makes it one for special occasions only.

10 · VICE-PREMIER CHEN YI
A Star Performance

During our filming in Peking I had, from time to time, dropped hints to Feng that our VIP interview was not materializing and, although he and the Cultural Relations Association had arranged everything else very well, we feared that this might be beyond them. Then one morning, in the middle of breakfast, Feng arrived in some excitement; at 10 a.m. we were to see Chen Yi and could we please have our questions ready in advance?

After Mao Tse-tung and Chou En-lai, Chen Yi is the most colourful of Communist leaders. Born into a wealthy landlord family, Chen Yi yet saw the abyss into which his country had fallen through civil war and corruption. On his return from university study in France he started a newspaper urging reforms. This was not enough and he left for Canton where he joined the Kuomintang (KMT), becoming an instructor in its Military Academy. When Chiang broke with his left-wing colleagues Chen Yi fled with those who managed to escape the slaughter and began the Communist reforms in Kiangsi Province. When, in 1937, the Communists made a truce with the KMT to fight the Japanese, Chen Yi, a brilliant military leader, took command of the Fourth Army only to have it betrayed again by Chiang with a loss of some 10,000 men. In charge of the Communist Third Field Army he fought the KMT from 1946 to 1949, winning sweeping victories and seizing Shanghai in one of the most vigorous and well-planned campaigns of the long civil war. As Mayor of that city he directed the great 'clean-up' and the establishment of a steady administration. Like Mao and Chou En-lai, Chen Yi is fighter, scholar, writer and a man of great personal magnetism.

The whole party was invited. Television cameras were allowed but, to our disappointment, no sound-recording equipment: verbatim notes, yes; tape-recorded voice, no! We were to find this with every senior personality we met and it was to be one of the major disappointments of the filming, for there is an immediacy, a sense of contact with the speaker, if the actual voice is recorded even though the words have to be translated.

Chen Yi, wearing European-style suit and an oddly Western-looking, almost 'old-school' tie, received us in the comfort and elegance of one of the dozen or so reception-rooms in the great Hall of the People, each one named after a different province and furnished with its local arts and crafts. Net curtains with elaborately woven borders hung at the long windows, on the floor was a deep silky carpet, against the walls stood carved teak cabinets filled with jade and porcelain figures – the real thing this time, no copies – and, focal point of the room, a great twelve-foot-long lacquer screen in front of which sat Chen Yi on a deep-cushioned, Western-style settee.

Chen Yi's air of amiability sat aptly on his plump bejowled face and sturdy figure and was enhanced by his frequent, almost boyish grin and his lavish use of gesture. He had the relaxed air that comes from a consciousness of long-proved strength and complete control of the situation. Without effort he dominated his audience. This in part was because of the aura that always surrounds any man or woman who has helped make history.

He glanced at our written list of questions and asked for the first one, but only, it was clear, as a matter of politeness for it was at once obvious that he was ready to anticipate this and others by giving a survey of China's concept of her place in today's world, and, as outlined by him, it was certainly a concept free of fuzzy edges or loose threads.

On our first query, China's attitude to peaceful co-existence and its implications, he spoke for about half an hour without pause; it was a bravura performance revealing a subtle, fast-moving mind which perceived nuances, anticipated objections, and presented a complex situation with deceptive simplicity. There was a wit and pawky humour that even translation could not dim (his interpreter's performance was second only to his own in clarity and vigour). Cracking jokes against the United States, the USSR and even himself, quoting English proverbs, drawing homely analogies, indulging in occasional flights of rhetoric, looking before and after, he was building up, piece by piece, his picture of a nation worthy of its age-long culture, secure in itself, reasonable in the face of unreason, patient with misconceptions, tolerant of brash accusations, conceding 111 short-comings here, difficulties there, but always moving forward with unfailing confidence to great power status.

He dealt immediately, and more in sorrow than in anger, with the idea that China was warlike and encouraging others to be so; that this was a travesty, he said, was clearly shown by China's steadfast refusal to reclaim her alienated territories by force. Taiwan, Hong Kong and Macao were indubitably part of China, but none had been threatened by military attack and China had not attempted to reclaim its Indian border territories until Indian forces moved into them in the wake of British imperialist cartographic aggressors. (The phrase was not his but has often been used by the Chinese.) He assumed, without justifying, that these border territories were Chinese and expected us to do the same. He stressed that, even so, China always stood ready to treat with India on the boundary question as she had treated with Burma, Afghanistan and Pakistan, for example. As for encouraging revolutions in Asia or elsewhere, he stressed that China was the great friend of all oppressed people, that it gave support and encouragement to Afro–Asian and Latin American revolts, but that this was never armed support.

'We do not export revolution. We gave no armed help to Castro against Batista and most vigorously deplored Krushchev's "adventurism" in sending missiles to Cuba.'

Then came a passage of sustained sarcasm in the best Chen Yi vein.

'Why,' he demanded of us, 'why should China, a poor backward country with no bomb,* be considered so powerful that it can fan the flames of revolution with a gesture? You imply that all we have to do is put up our hand and say, "Stop that revolution". No, our power is not quite as great as that.'

We were not told what form non-military assistance was taking.

He went on to say that nothing was farther from China's intentions than overrunning neighbouring countries. This would be palpably illogical; China had hitherto failed to develop her own extensive resources because of feudal control and foreign

* Exactly one year later the first Chinese atom bomb test was reported.

exploitation but full development was now planned and would more than absorb her population. For example, western provinces which now carry some sixty million people could well carry two hundred million and still be less crowded than Hopei. Our written suggestion that China might spill over even as far as Australia produced a hearty laugh along with a reference to Australia's inhospitable desert; our 'yellow-peril' fears were completely dismissed, to Chen Yi's satisfaction, at least!

In short, he declared roundly, China needed peace for development after more years of war than any other country and all she wanted was to be left alone to get on with the job of reconstruction.

He moved on logically to what he called the great slander – that China was not afraid of the atomic bomb and would sacrifice untold millions of her people with equanimity. The Chinese feared the bomb as much as the next man, he argued, but they needed it themselves as a defence weapon. The West disliked and distrusted China so that she herself could never feel free from the fear of atomic attack, in the face of which she would have two alternatives: to surrender or resist. The Vice-Premier smiled benignly as he posed the question: 'What happened to Chiang Kai-shek when he did not resist the Japanese? He went out fast and we should do the same if we did not resist, so resist we must – bomb for bomb.'

He went on to assure us that nobody need fear the Chinese bomb, for it would never be used for attack. The nation was reluctant to waste valuable time and materials, having naturally little interest in the bomb as such, in fact China's policy had been decided, and always would be decided, on what was best for herself regardless of atom bombs. That China could build a bomb there was no doubt, he assured us. 'Are we more stupid than the Americans?' Another burst of laughter. Already China had begun to plan atomic tests. Surprisingly, he admitted that they would not be ready to use the bomb for some ten years – or more.

Then came the first blast against the Soviet Union. Chen Yi argued that it was the precipitate signing of the tripartite treaty without China's approval that hastened the need for a 113

Chinese bomb. The signing could have easily been delayed until China had been consulted but the USSR had been as guilty as the United States of big-power chauvinism. 'Krushchev waves his baton and we must play his tune,' Chen Yi said. Together the USSR and the United States were indulging in nuclear blackmail, strengthening their hands by encouraging nuclear hysteria. On examination of the world situation anyone could see that the bomb was a 'blackmail' weapon and would never be used; Korea, Vietnam, Hungary had all provided occasions but no hint of atomic weapons had been given. The treaty is, then, a political fraud, as the signatories themselves will soon discover, let alone the rest of the deceived world. The signatories are unlikely and uneasy bedfellows. The only way to peace is by cessation of testing followed by complete world disarmament, and this is what China strongly supports.

Chen Yi made it clear that China resents any implication by the Soviet Union or anyone else that she has a subordinate role in the Communist world; and indeed national pride is as important in the new China as it always was in the old. It is the prime motivating factor today, and though the breach with Russia was ostensibly caused by Krushchev's abandonment of Marxist–Leninist principles of international Communism, Chinese nationalism played a vital part. This was underlined when Chen Yi moved on to answer our question on China's seeming isolation after her break with both the USSR and India. As we expected, he denied any isolation. 'China has friends all over the world; diplomatic relations with forty countries will soon increase to sixty and it will be realized that those who isolate China isolate themselves, for China is a great power.'

Here Chen Yi paused to pose and answer his own question. Asking if China could fairly call herself a great power when she was still poor and, by Western standards, backward, he explained that she would not be backward for long for she had immense, untapped natural resources, a vast population ready to work hard and, above all, a policy which they all knew to be the correct one – 'our strength is in the rightness of the Party's policy'.

The exceptionally difficult years, 1959–62, he explained, had proved this beyond cavil. Natural disasters, the withdrawal of Soviet experts and all their technical data and equipment had proved in the end a source of strength to the régime, for all had suffered together and come through with an increased sense of national unity. China had depended on no strength but her own, no skills and finances but her own – she needed no protection. 'The hand of protection is the hand of control,' he said. 'If you protect me I am to some extent your slave. Nobody protects China and so she is nobody's servant.' He paused and asked with his wide grin, 'How do you put it? The Lord helps those who help themselves!'

Here again he anticipated our immediate query, for he went on to add that China did not regard herself as self-sufficient, she wanted to trade overseas, to encourage cultural exchanges, even encourage tourists; she had no use for a closed-door policy. And the minds of the Chinese people were not closed either, for everyone in China not only listened to but asked for criticism and advice and her leaders were well aware of the country's shortcomings.

He had some frank comments to make on Western statesmen. He had met Averill Harriman, who had conceded that the Chinese had great restraint, in his opinion. The Kennedy régime, Harriman had said, would not continue the Eisenhower policy towards China; yet, back at a conference in Geneva, he had cursed China as roundly as any Eisenhower man. Both sides needed restraint, Chen Yi argued, but if Harriman kicks China she will have no choice but to kick back! Roosevelt, the wisest man of them all, died, alas, too soon. Recently Mr Rusk had been having a go at China; how could he believe that this country would be bullied and vilified and not defend herself? 'How does the United States think that we can ease tension? Where do we start? By removing military bases which we haven't got? Have we one on Taiwan (Formosa) or in Hong Kong, or have we a blockade on the United States to lift?'

Some Americans had realized the truth of China's position; 115

General Stilwell, whom Chen Yi had met in 1945, was realistic and far-seeing and anti-Fascist as well as anti-Japanese but, he said, Ambassadors Hurley and Wiedemayer would not see the truth in front of their eyes!

'The trouble with the United States,' he commented, 'is that she will act the big boss, indulge in great power chauvinism and want to dictate where she assists. We don't receive her assistance and get by better than Taiwan which has it. But we do not wish to break off the Warsaw talks with the United States which have gone on eight years – some contact is better than none.' He then added, as a postscript, 'Let the tourists and the cameras have a look at the bad as well as the good things – take them wherever they want to go. We have nothing to hide.'

Chen Yi's concluding instructions, thrown out with amused ease, indicated as much as anything he had said the confidence that does not fear criticism. He seemed to say, 'We know we aren't perfect but we know we're making progress, so why worry about occasional criticisms; they cannot alter the facts of China's achievements.'

As he made these final comments I looked triumphantly at Feng and Ling, who must have been quite relieved at implied ministerial approval of our shooting less impressive sights. (But we would still keep our promise about the old lady's feet.)

I had the rather alarming responsibility of thanking the Vice-Premier. Though much in his speech begged questions, much ran counter to Western ideas, and the assumption that Marxism–Leninism is the basis of all right thinking was hardly acceptable to us, I could express with sincerity our thanks for such a wide-ranging survey, such a show-piece of intellectual and oratorical skill and for such a chance to be shown, at first hand, the shape of things to come in China's foreign policy, or at least the shape she asked the world to see (which is as much as can be expected from any diplomat).

Chen Yi moved to the door, where, like the vicar of the local church, he shook hands smilingly with us all. He paused to talk with one of our members, a war veteran who had lost a leg 116 in the First World War and moved on crutches. He asked him about the action in which he had been wounded, expressed horror of war and remarked that he had been wounded three times and that if another war came he would not be in it! It was a remarkable occasion by any standards and I was as stimulated as one always is after witnessing any exhibition of first-class professional skill.

'Well, Shi-hwa,' I said when we were outside the room, 'that was very valuable; I should think you feel your Foreign Minister is a remarkable man?' She agreed warmly and added even more warmly, 'His interpreter is magnificent. He didn't miss a thing; he had every shade of meaning – and what speed! If only I were half as good. Do you think his English was accurate, Miss Roper?'

I assured her it was far more than accurate, it was idiomatic, flexible and economical; and I sighed aloud for the missing tape-recorder.

I had dinner that night at the Fang Shan Restaurant in Peihai Park where we were served with the *spécialités de la maison* – dishes imitating those most enjoyed by the last Empress Dowager. I failed to make a full note of the menu but can recall with great pleasure a number of delicacies concocted from different kinds of chopped nuts. My host, Wen Peng-chiu of the Association for Cultural Relations, told me one of those little food anecdotes of which the Chinese are so fond. The Empress had fled from Peking to the city of Sian and *en route* was benighted. She became very hungry but no food could be found. One of her entourage managed to beg two pieces of bread from a poor peasant. This tasted so delicious to her that, on her return to her palace and safety, she demanded that her cook make her the same kind of bread. She rejected it scornfully, so he finally concocted these nut delicacies with the same appearance but a subtler flavour, which the old lady graciously condescended to approve and devour. I devoured them, too, with such evident approval that when I rose to go, the pigtailed waitress smilingly brought me an attractively-packed, beribboned box containing a dozen of them as a present from my host.

11 · THE GREATEST SHOW ON EARTH
Chinese Style

We all returned to the Square of the Gate of Heavenly Peace and, in the cool, clear autumn twilight, were driven to the Great Hall of the People to attend the annual banquet on 30 September, the eve of National Day. About five thousand people were there, over half of us foreigners, mostly Afro-Asian or Latin–American peoples with noticeably fewer Europeans.

This year there were many Pakistanis but no Indians. Certainly, the Asian and African guests did justice to the occasion and the wide flight of marble stairs leading to the great banqueting chamber was a-dazzle with the vivid fabrics of their costumes and the gleam of their ornaments. The brilliance of the chandeliers was rivalled by the continual flash-bulbs of the photographers, who were as numerous as at a Hollywood premiere, though less obstreperous. We Australians felt a pretty colourless lot as we trooped up the stairs alongside black-skinned African Chiefs and exotic Indonesian beauties.

The Banquet Hall was vast and its high, elaborately-painted ceiling was supported by a very few pillars so that the view of all guests was minimally obstructed. The few pillars there were had a metallic, iridescent glitter and were covered with conventional designs of great intricacy. The room held, easily, without any congestion, some five hundred tables for ten guests each, as well as one large one for the senior hosts and special guests.

Everywhere was colour and excitement and an atmosphere of goodwill and pleasant international camaraderie. This, thank goodness, never assumed the hearty back-slapping style that can make such occasions pretty tiresome.

At the door the usual organization quickly had us sorted out so that each of us was led away to represent Australia at a multi-nation table. Some care had been taken, apparently, to team up kindred spirits so far as possible and I was gratified to find myself at a literary-academic table with a well-known author, a university teacher of Chinese literature and a Finnish poet and poetess. The poet, fresh-faced, bright-eyed, with a Pan-like beard, discoursed in a fascinating variant of the English language on Finnish literature, life and thought, and dis-

This is an original paper-cut made for the author by the instructor in the Shanghai Folk Art Institute, using scissors only and taking about seven minutes.

closed an acquaintance with a couple of Australian novelists. As the drink flowed he expressed his concern at the Sino–Soviet split; on which side of the fence was he to come down, especially as the USSR was a very near neighbour?

'After all,' he said, 'I'm a poet first and a politician second.' And he called down a plague on both their houses as he tossed back his fourth *mao-tai*. There were two orchestras in the long gallery. One was in traditional Chinese style, with cymbals, three-stringed fiddles and the eminently respectable larger variant of the humble mouth-organ – the popular *Chang*. The other was a Western symphony orchestra, but they both believed in co-existence and took it in turns to play!

I had now come so completely to accept Chinese efficiency in mass management that I almost took for granted the smoothness of the service at each of the 500 tables as dish after dish was slid silently into place. The host was Chou En-lai and I craned my neck to watch him, smiling and joking as he helped his guests to servings from several dishes. I had seen him twice and met him briefly in 1958. Then, as now, I was impressed by the extraordinary personal, rather saturnine, charm which few public figures can equal and which apparently age cannot wither – he is now sixty-eight. But there is nothing facile about the charm, for it springs as much from an impression of strength as from his easy adjustment to the occasion, or the person; there is a withdrawnness, a sense of inner depths along with the intellectual brilliance and social aplomb that have helped to make him one of the world's formidable diplomats. But there was neither warmth nor charm when he delivered his speech! (An English translation was on the table.) 'We resolutely oppose the United States imperialist crime of obstructing the peaceful unification of Vietnam; we resolutely support the Cuban people in their struggle against the United States aggressors. We oppose all modern revisionists and dogmatists.'

In conclusion he commented, 'The working class and broad masses of Europe, Africa, Asia and Australia are experiencing a new awakening.'

I was far from sure what he could be referring to in Australia, 119 where the 'masses' seem, of late, to have been no more revolutionary than they ever were! These remarks were delivered in the almost impersonal, unemotional tone of most statements by Chinese leaders, who do not seem to depend upon mob oratory for their immense influence. It is likely, even so, that Chou meant what he said.

As our host Chou En-lai was to give the only speech, and it had been brief; we now sat down to eat and drink and talk undisturbed. Cheerfully we drank to the health of every country represented at our table. Down went the *mao-tai* and the local red; the orchestra struck up 'Swan Lake' then stopped in mid bar; at the end of the room a sense of excitement was generated, then the whisper went around, 'Chairman Mao'. This was an unscheduled visit, causing flurry but no disorganization, apparently. A way was unobtrusively cleared to the platform, where, amid pot-plants and to the rhythmic clapping of all the guests, now standing of course, he smiled, waved, and made the briefest speech of welcome with an air of gentle benevolence. Anything less like the fierce-fanged, bloody-handed caricatures of the Western yellow Press one could not imagine – he looked for all the world like the poet and philosopher, ex-university librarian that he happens to be, as well as the greatest revolutionary soldier of the age.

My Chinese companions were beaming with pleasure and pride, but their clapping was as decorous as ours. However Westerners may regard Mao Tse-tung and his régime, only the lunatic fringe could fail to admit him as one of the great figures of history, so that to see him across the room was an experience to remember. As he mounted the steps, some young, and maybe over-eager, official took his arm to help him up; cameras flashed, then Mao stood alone on the platform. A month later, in Australia, a diplomat asked me if it was true that Mao Tse-tung had had to be supported all through the National Day ceremonies owing to illness and old age – he had seen a photograph alleged to reveal this!

Nobody could doubt the warmth of his compatriots' admira-
120 tion, but as he left their applause showed only the careful re-

straint, the well-bred moderation of, say, a very English gathering greeting Winston Churchill! Soon after, and before we ran out of conversation, the signal came for us all to depart and without fuss and confusion we fairly briskly did so. There had been no military guards and very few police anywhere in sight. The velvet-smooth organization was also apparent in the speed with which guests' cars and buses arrived, filled up, and drove away with barely a hold-up.*

Next morning, the great procession. On 1 October 1949 the declaration of the People's Republic of China from the top of the great Gate of Heavenly Peace saw the end of long years of civil war and foreign occupation and the establishment of an authoritarian government dedicated to the restoration of China's national glory. On this same Gate every 1 October Mao Tse-tung and his colleagues stand in the clear autumn sunshine and watch the anniversary procession – 'the greatest show on earth' – for how else can one describe over half a million marchers, singers, dancers, athletes, acrobats, workers, peasants and militia, along with floats, bands, streamers, flags, pennants, balloons, lions and dragons, flowers and foliage, moving solidly for two hours in packed rows, past the great, watching crowds, the Government hierarchy and the 2,000 visitors – the outward and visible symbol of a national ideology, a national faith.

The celebration starts at crack of dawn when people begin moving to their meeting-points all over the city, singing, laughing and often accompanied by small, unofficial bands of pipes, three-stringed fiddles and the much-loved Chinese cymbals. After 5 a.m. sleep is impossible so we rose early, ate breakfast in the European dining-room and watched the streets filling as we waited for our cars. The main roads were blocked to traffic,

---

* On this and similar grand occasions, as well as on tours of factories and communes, China is making her case to the backward nations with scarcely a word spoken. The message is clear. 'We, too, were once like you, desperately poor, exploited and backward and look at us now; thanks to Marxism–Leninism we are leaping ahead. Even more so than the USSR we have a lesson for you because we, unlike Russians, are non-European, non-white.'

so we took a devious route to the official car-park in the back garden of the Forbidden City. Nobody seemed in a hurry and, at a leisurely pace, we mounted the steps to our stand from the rear. As we reached the top, the enormous breathtaking panorama of the great square, the Changan Boulevard and the distant towers and hills, burst upon us.

The Gate itself was festooned with enormous scarlet, bulbous Chinese lanterns.* Everywhere were vivid scarlet banners, flags and pennants, many borne aloft in the still air by great white hydrogen-filled balloons, so my first impression on coming to the stands was of space and colour.

The stands are literally such, for no seating is provided; but there is the advantage that one can move freely amongst the other foreign visitors. Harold and I, going to see how many foreigners we could persuade to talk on our tape-recorder, easily collected Indonesians, Mexicans, Algerians, Cubans (girl soldiers in uniforms, these), Japanese, Nepalese, West Africans and Pakistanis, plus a couple of Cockneys.

Chairman Mao and his entourage appeared from the rear to be greeted by a great burst of music from massed bands and enthusiastic, but far from hysterical, cheering and clapping from the crowd below us. He had no observable military escort. After a salute of guns, the procession started on the left with the first lines of marchers moving forward along the boulevard in front of the Gate, some eighty or ninety abreast in each line, the vanguard carrying flags, pink, yellow, red, green, bearing words of welcome. Behind them came row upon row of young people carrying large paper bouquets (I had seen these being made in schools and factories during the previous week). Throughout the march, colours were so blended and balanced that, as the marchers raised their floral burdens above their heads, one saw a sea of scarlet fading to palest rose-pink, followed by deep royal blue dwindling to sky-after-rain tinge, and reddish-orange slipping gradually into palest lemon.

Then came the equally numerous balloon-carriers with

* Red has always been the traditional Chinese colour for rejoicing and celebration.

similar colour schemes, each batch releasing its string of balloons just before it passed Chairman Mao so that the sky seemed full of the floating, airy spheres. Periodically, youngsters carried, or pushed along on little trucks, solid, three-dimensional Chinese characters which our interpreters spelt for us: 'Long Live Socialism', 'Welcome to our Friends' or 'We will Liberate Taiwan', 'Hail, Chairman Mao'. Thousands of participants danced their way along in groups of several hundred at a time: in 'Gather the Turnips', a couple of hundred giant-sized papiermâché turnips were propelled mysteriously along, surrounded by dancing and singing children in peasant dress; scarf-dancers passed by each with great silk snakes undulating around them; there were outlandishly dressed dancers from Tibet and Sinkiang, sword-dancers, including young girls, brandishing great scimitars across one another's heads and beneath one another's legs with split-second timing. Then came hundreds of girls with fluttering fans or twirling parasols in kimono-like robes; thousands more wore baggy pants and elaborately-embroidered blouses, again in colours carefully selected for mass effects (most of these were shades of acid-greens and yellows and shocking pinks and purples). Clearly, the New China had some competent showmen.

Next were the floats, great, slow-moving behemoths, showing industrial activities and agricultural successes, peasants at work in green paddies, weavers, miners and iron workers, each set against a cleverly painted background. On others, athletes and gymnasts balanced, jumped, wrestled and boxed; and all the time the bands played on and the big white balloons stirred gently with their trailing pennants like tails behind them.

We became gradually aware that the crowd in the square beyond the marchers in the boulevard was taking part too, for each of them was carrying a paper flower bouquet which he raised aloft at regular intervals until the whole area was an unbroken meadow of paper flowers, changing colour and pattern as the people shifted position at given signals; so that the meadow looked for all the world as if a light wind were blowing across it bending the flowers this way and that in little waves of shifting movement and colour. One of my most rousing memories of the 1958 procession was of hundreds of comic animals – dragons propelled by dozens of human legs or writhing in colourful coils, balloon-borne, in the air, and shaggy lions shaking enormous manes, comic replicas of the great, golden beasts in the Palace gardens. But in 1963 dragons were out – and so was the military. Last time, I had noted in my diary, there had not been a great deal of military display but even so there were marshals and admirals as well as an impressive display of human and mechanized units of several kinds. In view of what in generally regarded as China's much-increased talk of war, her angry reception of the tripartite atomic testing treaty and her ever-expressed concern about encircling US bases, the military hiatus was as unexpected as it was unexplained.

But very much present, in fine marching trim, was the militia, line upon line, rank upon rank of them, in blue cotton uniforms. To me they looked extremely efficient, as professional as any colonel could demand. There were girls, every bit as trim as the men, with rifle on shoulder, eyes fixed straight ahead, a look of dedication on each face.

'Your militia are pretty good,' I said, turning to Ling. 'Tell us something about them.'

'There are many millions of them throughout China; they are our home defence forces.'

'Defence against what?' we asked. 'US imperialists?'

'Well, not against the American people, the masses, but some of their leaders. They hate China, so we must be on the alert. Please remember the American Seventh Fleet is in our home waters.'

'But the West doesn't want to attack you – they are only there, well – frankly – to keep you from attacking others.'

'What others?'

'Well,' I said, very self-consciously, 'Burma and Vietnam and Thailand. Just spreading – sort of spilling over the borders.'

'But we have made a peace treaty with Burma and Pakistan. Thailand is our friend. We have no armies outside our own borders. Why should we wish to attack anyone? We have had

124

more war than any other country, why should we want any more of it? Have we attacked Hong Kong or Taiwan . . .'

'. . . or Macao?' laughingly I finished the sentence for him. 'I can put your case as well as you, Ling. But you just don't see how warlike some of your statements sound to us in the West. They hear that you are not afraid of the atom bomb – and that seems pretty silly to us. We're scared stiff of it!'

'We only have these arms to defend ourselves against imperialist aggressors. General MacArthur wanted to cross the Yalu River and attack us. Chiang Kai-shek says America will support his attack on the mainland. The American Congress said they would support armed uprisings in our country. We need our militia, don't we, Miss Roper?'

'At least, this year, Ling, you have no regular army battalions in the procession. Are they busy somewhere else; up on the Russian border, maybe, or down near Vietnam?'

Ling, imperturbable, refused to be drawn and merely said, with his impish smile, 'Maybe we'll have them back next year.'

'Like your dragons – you had some beauties last time. Why no dragons this year?'

'We like to have something different every year – not always the same.'

'So dragons may be back with the army next year?'

'Maybe next year.'

The militia went on; in the distance I could see vast quantities of workers approaching. I felt overwhelmed by the sheer weight of numbers and their orderly progress so I excused myself and went down to the cool and comfortable rest-rooms below the stands to refresh myself with tea and orangeade. I returned after ten minutes to find the workers still there, marching in huge concourse; Mao was still on the saluting stand, the crowds still waving flowers and shouting, 'Hail, Chairman Mao'; slogan after slogan was born past or released into the air on a balloon. It seemed all this might go on for ever; maybe it would!

When the militia and workers had passed, the last floats 125 and banners brought up the rear; suddenly, abruptly, there was a silence and a space below us. It was all over, almost anti-climactically, it seemed. Then there came a sudden flutter of wings, a chorus of twittering bird sounds, and the air was darkened by flock after flock of doves released into the air. Guns boomed out again, and at the same time the crowds in the Square began to move rhythmically forward into the boulevard in the rear of the departing procession until every scrap of ground within view was wholly filled with their raised, vividly-coloured paper flowers. Mao Tse-tung, waving gently, with Chou En-lai, Liu Shao-chi, the Mayor of Peking and a few others, moved from their seats into the shadows of the reception-room behind them, and cheering and clapping again burst forth below as ranks broke, flowers fell to sides, and people immediately began to disperse.

The whole mass performance had gone off without a hitch; it had been superb, but it left one bewildered by the sheer virtuosity of the whole spectacle, the colour, the exuberance, the variety, the sheer splendour of it all, the impact on eye and mind of such vast masses of humanity. It was, in one way, alarming because no other race could match it in numbers or dedication and the world is full of fear and rumours of wars. But, and this is almost a paradox of the New China, along with the formidable efficiency there was a sense of fun and leisure-liness. On our way home we noticed many people dawdling around, sitting on the kerbside or packing cheerfully into trucks and buses still waving flowers or flags or playing odd instruments. Many were just filling in time until the evening fire-works and dance in the Square. The streets were uncannily clean – no squashed ice-cream papers, no cigarette packets or bus tickets because a litter-lout is liable to public reprimand by passers-by, and no drunks because alcohol is scarce and drunkenness frowned on; no late racing-editions because gambling is out; no worry about parking because there are virtually no private cars, only well-organized public transport and guests' cars.

126 After dinner we all returned to the Square for the amazing

display of fireworks which zoomed about the sky for hours above a city *en fête*. Some shot up like rockets, one colour or multi-coloured, others lingered in the shape of flowers or fountains, some like stars floated down on parachutes, some crackled, popped and exploded and great exclamations of wonder went up from the thousands staring heavenwards.*

Many of the procession's dancers were back and performing in small groups joined by dozens of ordinary folk. Musicians with Western or Chinese instruments were playing away at the centre of singing, clapping and shouting citizens. It was really exhilarating to move among them.

I was lucky enough to have been invited to join Premier Chou En-lai's large party on the wide, windy top of Tien Ah Men, where several hundred guests from many countries watched an excellent variety performance with singers from many provinces, an army choir, dazzlingly skilful jugglers and tumblers, and graceful dancing-girls in folk costume. Between the items we moved over to look down on the equally colourful crowds filling the square and boulevard below us.

Chou En-lai and the Mayor of Peking moved about among their guests; the Mayor, tall, powerfully-built, was laughing and cracking jokes, radiating enormous jollity and bonhomie; Chou, more subdued and withdrawn, was showing, fractionally, the fatigue of the long day.

Sailing along, her generous figure comically enlarged by rugs and padded garments, was a large 'Western' woman; this I was told, was the self-exiled American writer and Kremlin-ologist, Anna Louise Strong. (She is revered now more than ever in China because of her book on the life of Stalin.)

It was all very interesting but, on the windy roof, it was also very cold and I was glad that hot tea was ready for us back at the hotel.

A remarkable day by any standard.

* A visiting Australian scientist reports he was told that the 1964 fire-works cost three million yuan. 'Expensive,' commented his informant, 'but worth it once a year!'

12 · TRAIN JOURNEY THROUGH THE FLOODS

The final Peking morning – 'Look thy last on all things lovely' – an early walk to see the first sunlight in the near-by Temple of Heaven's blue-tiled, triple roofs. Dark sapphire beneath an azure sky, they hang above vermilion walls and the muted green of cypress and spruce, like three convolvulus blooms, petrified, one over another. Then back we went to the hotel for the breakfast omelette, gratitude and good-byes, and a scramble in the foyer for airmail stamps for the last postings from Peking. We all tried to put as many as possible on each letter, especially the beautiful flower series, or the only less beautiful animal one, both an aesthetic philatelist's dream. Putting on stamps was a protracted business for hygiene demands that stamps be not licked. They had no adhesive, so the postal authorities provided a lumpy, gloylike mixture in sticky bottles, along with a stumpy, still stickier, brush; one's liberally-coated fingers daubed the stuff over envelope, clothes and handbag alike – it really was a confounded nuisance, the whole operation.*

No worry about luggage coming down; the staff were reliable to the last. We climbed into a roomy, oldish Humber. (Why had we never ridden in the new Chinese car – the Red Flag – so proudly shown in 1958?) Through the great arch of the Front Gate we went, myriads of bicycle bells twanging around us; a modern trolley bus paused for a loaded ancient handcart; a woman was pushing it and she grinned at the driver; how could she, possibly, when sweating under the appalling burden? I noted one of the city's most amusing sights – a kindergarten pedicab laden with half a dozen plump four-year-olds *en route* to school.

The Square of the Gate of Heavenly Peace was quieter than before National Day, but here once more were children, this time in lines, trunk-to-tail, elephant-like, each child clinging to the hem of the one-in-front's cotton tunic or seat of baggy pants. The festivities were over, but the scarlet lanterns still blew on the Gate's pavilion and the golden characters caught the sun-

---

* Recently the Chinese have begun to put adhesive on the back of some stamps but not all: I was quite foxed and found myself licking the 'dry-backs' and gumming up the 'sticky-backs'!

light: 'Long Live the People's Republic of China – Long Live the Unity of the Nations of the World.' Peihai Park loomed in the near distance, its white Buddhist dagoba standing out clearly, not beautiful but unique. (It is jokingly, but aptly, referred to as the peppermint bottle.)

We bowled along the wide Changan Boulevard, lined with trees, bordered with grass and flower-beds. The clusters of lamps on top of the light standards had a vaguely Edwardian flavour though the guide books explained they are based on the magnolia blossom. The great rose-pink walls and towers and the golden roofs of the Forbidden City gave way to the five-star Peking Hotel and this, in turn, to new buildings, many finished, many going up behind their criss-cross of bamboo scaffolding. And so to the city's newest architectural pride, the main railway station. The scramble was over; before the train left we had two hours to see the station's glories.

Not quite so monumentally, marmoreally grand as Moscow's underground, Peking's Central Station is still very much a show-piece and is on every visiting-list. It has a long cream façade, a Chinese-style roof and rather fairy-tale ornamental turrets and trimmings. 'Peking Station' is written up, not in characters, but romanized letters, 'Beijing Zhan'. These are still not common but must necessarily increase when China sets to in earnest to develop tourism. Inside the station we found ourselves in a vast foyer, its highly-polished marble floor stretching away on all sides like a flawless ice-rink; a cleaning-woman, hygienic gauze mask over mouth, leaving dustless perfection in her wake, was just disappearing behind the bank of pot-plants found in most Chinese stations. (I think the only stations I saw without them had a real garden.) We went up the wide moving staircase, and Shi-hwa, giving her wise little grin, commented that she knew such things were old hat to us but to the Pekingese they were still a source of wonder and amaze; many people came to the station just to see them – the very first in the city.

At the top we were met by one of the stationmasters himself, led to an attractive private room, furnished *à la chinoise* entirely, and there we sat comfortably sipping tea as Peking's last sets of statistics were given us:

> The station occupies an area of 12,000 square metres and has seventeen waiting-rooms in which fourteen thousand passengers can be accommodated, two being kept especially for mothers and children. There are also a small cinema and post office as well as two hundred booking offices used by 40,000 passengers a day. The station took only seven and three-quarter months to complete, thanks to the voluntary labour of citizens from twenty-one provinces in addition to the two thousand permanent labourers working clock-round in three daily shifts.

We followed him then to a good sample of all of these facilities and found them surprisingly uncrowded considering the great number of passengers.

Our reserved coach looked familiar with its comfortable four-seater carriages, the tea-mugs and packets already on the window table and the falsetto tones of Peking Opera issuing faintly from the loudspeaker. I tried to look forward to the journey instead of backward to the lost wonders of Peking, but the city has a powerful magic and I felt as much under her spell as Marco Polo and thousands of other travellers to whom she will beckon insistently and insidiously to the end of their life.

The music gave way to, presumably, final instructions, for there was sudden excitement; Ling dashed down the corridor on a last-minute check, friends leapt off on to the platform, everybody waved and smiled as we pulled out of the Northern Capital, on our way to the Southern Capital, Nanking. Once away from the city we passed through the patchwork of the Great Plain of China, fertile, intensively-cultivated, for centuries rice-bowl and granary and vegetable-garden for millions.

I woke from a doze when the train drew into a station where the usual panorama of the Chinese travelling public revealed itself through the window. There were soldiers in khaki cotton uniforms going on leave or to new postings, students off on their compulsory work-stint on a distant farm or irrigation project, workers, like Mei-lang and Chung-yi, making the longed-for return visit to their home village, others moving off to the north-east or north-west, where their skill and strength are demanded by the great industrial developments there. Everyone seemed to be carrying some bulky object – perhaps sleeping gear, includ-ing the ubiquitous padded cotton quilt, or a great string bag distended by a saucepan, tin mug or one of the gaudy, flower-covered, enamel washbowls so dear to Asian workers.

I noticed that railway workers included pigtailed women with red piping on their blue uniforms and I recalled that China had several trains manned wholly by women – drivers included. (The best-known is the Peking–Tientsin express.) Music and statistics start with the train, the sweeper appears, though the tea-girl lingers; the performance is on again. I decide train travel in China is unendingly diverting but shall be glad, even so, to get to Nanking after another day and a half of it.

After lunch in the dining-car, we walked back to our 'soft' accommodation through the 'hard', where less pampered pas-sengers sit on wooden benches with high backs in very crowded, very noisy coaches cluttered with bundles and children. In spite of the pandemonium I was not surprised to see many travellers reading the newspapers or instructive comics or telling patriotic stories of one kind and another. Two young men were even deep in a game of what looked like a variation of chess or draughts board across knee. I arrived back in our compartment with the sweeping-girl, who had turned up – just to make sure! By now we were behaving well and there was not a crumb or a scrap of paper to justify her vigilance; she seemed almost disappointed as she went away.

In China headlines can suddenly come alive. 'Devastating Floods in China.' I had read this headline often enough. Now I woke from another doze to find the train had slowed to walking pace and that outside the window an expanse of water reflected the sunlight. Not a lake, I realized, sitting up with a jerk. Here was one of the much talked of 'natural calamities' which, we were repeatedly told, had, along with the 'Soviet defection', caused the shortages and sufferings of 1960–62, halted the

Great Leap Forward, and forced China, hungry if not starving, to begin her controversial wheat negotiations with Australia and Canada. Many Western newspapers stated that China had had no serious 'natural calamities', only man-made ones, and that the tales of flood and drought were face-saving inventions. They weren't in Southern Hopei in autumn 1963. For two hours we crawled along a track shored by sandbags, logs or gravel barely a foot above the water. Sometimes, above the submerged fields, low, muddy banks appeared with a few barefooted peasants in spiky, palm-leaf cloaks and dripping hats splashing their way along, ankle-deep, going one could not guess where in the watery waste. For miles all that we saw of habitations were mud or stone cottages, the roofs often missing, the walls often listing. At other times nothing broke the level waste, the rounding grey, but dripping telegraph posts, wires trailing forlornly around them. Once I saw a cormorant watching the waves for his prey with concentrated glance. Ling joined me, his face troubled.

'Every crop is ruined, of course,' he said. 'And some light industries as well. But probably nobody has been drowned this year. Before Liberation there were hardly any rescue operations; thousands died in the floods and many who lived starved to death because there was no way of getting food to them. Now the army has organized emergency squads which are rushed to the low-lying regions whenever storms are forecast, so that intelligent preparations can be made. The communes, too, make their plans to deal with this situation. But it is not so bad this year, fortunately, either here or anywhere. In 1960 we estimated that sixty-five per cent of agricultural land right through China was covered like this. But we still didn't starve; that is a miracle only we older Chinese can appreciate. Soon, even this amount of flooding will not occur, for we are planning great irrigation works and flood control projects farther up the river.'

The floods thinned out, houses appeared *in toto*, paths became distinguishable and the railway line was cleared; the train picked up speed and I my spirits as we left the disaster area behind us.

13 · SOUTHERN CAPITAL
A Remarkable Woman

I shall always remember Nanking as a city of green, red and gold, for, even more than most towns, it has heeded the exhortation, 'Keep your country green'. Grass, trees and flowers appeared along the sides of the roads, down the middle of roads, in circles at the junctions of roads and around private and public buildings; the Nanking Hotel, much the most attractive I stayed in, spread its bedrooms and public rooms in small blocks throughout its gardens. The National Day decorations threaded the greenery with scarlet and gold and Mao's portrait often peeped out from leafy garlands.

Nanking (Southern Capital), is almost two and a half thousand years old and has been, periodically, throughout that time the focus of warring emperors or nobility. The last century has been especially eventful, for Nanking was the capital of the Taiping Revolutionaries from 1851–64 and here they anticipated some of the reforms of the present régime. Chiang Kai-shek made it the seat of Kuomintang power and the capital of the country, changing the name Peking, meaning Northern Capital, to Peiping, meaning Northern Peace, so that there should be no doubt about Nanking's pre-eminence. It was in Nanking, in 1946–7, that the momentous discussions on the establishment of a joint KMT and Communist anti-Japanese front took place.

The country's most elaborate and extensive national monument, the Sun Yat-sen Memorial Park, built by the Kuomintang, covers many hilly acres on the outskirts of the city. Climbing three hundred steps up the wooded side of Purple Mountain, we paused, *en route*, at flagged squares to draw breath and found that at each stop the view grew grander until we reached the pillared hall at the topmost peak with a tremendous panorama of fields, woods, river and villages. Looking out over this, several times larger than life-size, is the statue of the founder of the first Chinese Republic; the calm, sensitive face, the slightly anxious, remote, benevolently-brooding expression, the simple traditional tunic, have none of the sentimentality of the stereotype figures of many revolutionary posters and statues, both Russian and Chinese. As I stood in front of the figure I was vividly reminded of another national leader, similarly brooding, similarly seated in his stone chair, looking out over his country's capital and I meditated on the irony of a situation in which a country that knew Lincoln's reforming fervour (and George Washington's revolutionary zeal) should now be regarded by the heirs of Sun Yat-sen as the bitterest and most reactionary enemy of their revolution.

My main interest in visiting Nanking was to meet once again its most distinguished woman. Now in late middle age, Dr Wu Y-feng has had an eventful life, reflecting in its many changes, physical and philosophical alike, the experience of thousands of scholars, writers and artists (and, incidentally, as I was to discover in Shanghai, many capitalists too).

I had met and talked at length with Wu Y-feng on my first visit and been moved by her story, which I was all the more prepared to accept because the meeting was arranged at my request. We had not been scheduled to visit Nanking, but, having an introduction to Wu Y-feng and knowing she had been Principal of the Women's College at the University, I asked especially to see her. The Women's Federation had taken a good deal of trouble to reorganize my travelling arrangements and tee up my interview with her.

Born the daughter of a Manchu official, she went to school after the Boxer Rebellion, graduated from Shanghai University, took her Ph.D. in biology at the University of Michigan and returned to become Principal of the University of Nanking's Christian College for Women in 1927. She worked hard with Madame Chiang Kai-shek to found the Women's Comforts Association and in 1938 she became one of the ten women on the KMT's People's Consultative Council. She deplored her students' interest in the Communist Party until she had to realize that Nanking and the whole of China was slipping fast into chaos because of corruption and disorganization. Desperate measures were needed. The Canadian missionary, Mrs Endicott, in her sincere and well-documented book, *Five Stars Over China*, writes that Dr Wu told her she had come to realize that her students' interest in reform was right and should not be checked.

'We have run the College too long like a New England Finishing School for Girls,' said Dr Wu. Finally, she threw in her lot with the new Government, becoming, after a few years, Deputy Minister of Education and Vice-President of the National Assembly of the Province.

This time Wu Y-feng greeted us in the comfortable reception-room of the provincial 'House of Parliament'. She wore a long, black Chinese-style dress, woollen cardigan, low-heeled useful shoes; her grey hair was drawn tightly back and she wore rimless spectacles. Her easy greeting, her firm handclasp, her welcoming laugh and the liveliness of her whole expression attracted us to her at once. She spoke English with the perfection not only of syntax but of intonation and inflexion that only long residence in an English-speaking country can give. Shi-hwa sat back with a smile of relief – an hour off for her.

Unlike our Wuhan professor, Wy Y-feng agreed to go on tape without qualm, so I asked her to tell us, quite simply, something of her early life, her career and, finally, her position as a Christian and an academic in an atheistic régime. Wu Y-feng is a biologist, but she has the makings of a playwright, for she told her story with force and style and a fine sense of the dramatic.

Her family's love of learning did not extend to providing education for 'little sister', she began, so she had to pick up the crumbs of learning that fell from her brother's table, borrowing his books, picking his brains and, finally, after months of pleading, sharing his tutor. Getting parental permission to go to Shanghai University was a miracle she could not to this day explain (she described, *en passant*, what getting to Shanghai had meant in terms of travel in those days; farm-carts, boats, foot-slogging – all were needed to get her from her country town to Nanking and then to Shanghai; robbers and war-lords did not make matters more comfortable, she added). When the Communists came in 1949 she was urged to flee; as a former protégée of the Chiangs, a Christian and a woman, she feared she 135 would have little chance of a position of influence and might be lucky to get away with her life. But she stayed after long agonizing doubt, partly because she believed little could be worse for her country than the state to which the KMT's corruption and inefficiency had reduced it. Much of what the Communist Government stood for, her whole training and belief rejected, and still must, in part, reject; but what it immediately began to do for her country she had accepted with a gratitude that had increased with the years, in spite of her Christian faith, her admiration for democratic ideals, and her affection and regard for old friends in the USA.

As she began to describe the changes of the past fourteen years she really swung into her stride. The light of enthusiasm shone in her eye, but the humorous turn of phrase, the occasional joke against herself, the obvious awareness of Western points of view, the anticipation of our doubts, the answers to our unasked questions all revealed a mind unwarped by fanaticism.

It was immediately apparent that one of the main reasons for her support of the régime was its release of woman from positions of subordination as 'the second sex'. Wu Y-feng explained this to me in detail:

Woman has stood up in the New China; she can say to any man, 'I am a human being like you.' Before Liberation only a few could honestly feel that. Look at my struggle, even in a Christian family, to get the same education as my brother. There is a story about this. A woman was left alone in her house for almost the first time in her life. When someone knocked at the door she was too shy to answer at first, so the visitor knocked again and asked, 'Is anyone at home?' 'Nobody is at home,' came the whispered reply. She just didn't count herself as anybody!

So, as a woman, I had to support a Government that gave us real equality and a chance to fill any position in the land. And also as an educationist. Under the KMT and in the civil war, there were appalling shortages of everything – labs, equipment, books, desks and teachers. Now everyone can go to a school of some kind, for education is a main concern of the Government. Nanking, as you will have heard, is a large educational centre, with many schools and colleges and especially good medical and technical institutions.

And, also, as a patriot, I must do all I can for a régime which has ended corruption, inflation and starvation and already brought us, for the first time in a century, a generation of peace. Only those as old as I, who remember the suffering of pre-liberation times, can know what all this means. Just to have food enough to keep alive is still a marvel to the poor of Nanking. Once when I was a girl I asked a peasant near my home how many children she had – I'll never forget the implications of her reply.

'I have,' she said, 'eight mouths to feed.' In KMT days there was a rhyme about Nanking:

> The electric light is dim;
> The road is not smooth;
> The telephone never works.

You know that isn't true any more.

Finally, and you may find this hard to swallow, I support the régime as a Christian. I believe that I have religious freedom – so do my friends. Bishop Ting and his wife, whom you are to meet at the Theological Seminary this afternoon. And I believe, too, that there is much of Christian teaching in our socialist way of life; we do not live for ourselves but for our country.

At this stage Wu Y-feng must have read my mind, for she paused long enough for me to get out the question that I had been longing to ask – the obvious one:

'What about freedom? Intellectual, artistic, political? Will you please' – I was almost painfully earnest by now – 'please, tell me, honestly, how much of that must you sacrifice in your new China?'

Wu Y-feng put the tips of her fingers together in a 137

characteristic gesture, and replied, almost fiercely, 'Miss Roper, surely you can see that freedom must mean different things in different settings. During a revolution – and long after it – how can the same freedom be expected as in a settled, prosperous country like Australia? You have never known war on your own soil, foreign occupation and mass-starvation. And, please note, even so, we don't do too badly. We have our open criticism-and-self-criticism sessions; the draft of our constitution was debated all over China for months before being accepted. In our Nanking Assembly we have a few "Rightists" who have some freedom to air their views and, as long as they don't advocate violent overthrow of the Government, they fare well enough.'

Taking a deep breath I came at her again. 'Surely, Madame Wu, when you have lived in the United States and know and like many Americans, you cannot accept all this anti-United States agitation – this almost obsessive dislike of "imperialists"?'

The smile was gone from her eyes, the generous mouth hardened, the voice had an edge. 'I used to believe the Americans honestly wanted peace – most of them still do, I hope – but their leaders, their national policy, are aggressive. A peaceful country would not send its biggest fleet to our home waters and keep it off our coast for years; would not put armed forces in bases all round our borders and send planes and missiles over our southern provinces. They would not support a discredited puppet like Chiang Kai-shek and let him keep saying he is going to attack the mainland with American help. The American people are badly led. How can you expect me to believe that the United States Congress is peaceful?'

Well, I asked for it and got it!

I told Wu Y-feng that I had met a former acquaintance of hers in America after I had given a lecture on China. The woman had come up to me and asked if I had heard what had happened to the Principal of the Women's College in Nanking after the Communists had put her in a Concentration Camp. 138 When I said that I had met Dr Wu Y-feng the woman remarked gloomily that she supposed 'they had turned her out of her college'.

'Yes,' I said, enjoying the joke, 'they have; she has just become Vice-President of the Provincial Assembly and before that was Vice-President of the University.'

Wu Y-feng laughed and told me that the story of her suicide had reached many overseas friends and been widely current in Hong Kong.

Nobody could doubt Wu Y-feng's integrity, and what she said made sense, hung together. Here is their strength, I thought; the passionate concern with China's renaissance, the certainty of her 'correct line', her future world-power status. Wu Y-feng is a dynamo of great generating power which can be multiplied by thousands. At the same time it is very easy to see how such force might be turned in more than one direction – internal or external – for better or for worse. Corruption must be dealt with at home, and Soviet 'splittism' and 'revisionism' abroad; Stalin is to be admired, and Krushchev reviled. Every Government forms and guides public opinion; the Chinese Government does it more thoroughly and with more conviction than most.

As I rose, full of respect for Wu Y-feng, I found myself once again quite painfully anxious that driving-power like hers should be directed towards and not against the West; together in peace we could alter the face of the world. The unwisdom of China's exclusion from the comity of nations and the bitterness of China's anti-American attitudes seemed alike more depressing than usual as we stood exchanging farewells and good wishes with this fine woman.

She accompanied us to the Nanking Theological Seminary, whose Principal, K. H. Ting, was also Bishop of Nanking and an elected member of the National People's Congress. Educated in the West and for some years a worker with the World Student Christian Federation in Canada, the United States and Switzerland, he returned to China in the early 'fifties. Ting has a quiet smile, quiet voice and quiet wit. (His wife, Sui May, is, I believe, a graduate of an American women's college.)

My chief recollection of the Seminary – a pre-revolutionary 139 missionary building – is the library. Theological treatises in Chinese and English filled the shelves. (The Bishop told us he bought the Monday edition of the *New York Times* to keep up with Church news.) Students, working at tables, paused to speak with us in moderately good English.

Since all were preparing for the ministry I was surprised to see a girl there and discover that equal opportunity for women had reached the pulpit and parish. I looked at her with almost pitying interest, meditating on the courage and single-mindedness that had brought her from a remote mountain village – holding what her compatriots must regard, inevitably, as a foreign belief – to battle with the Early Fathers and biblical exegesis.

Bishop Ting explained at length the position of his church; what he said was repeated by both Protestant and Roman Catholic colleagues in Shanghai and is reported in later chapters.

The day concluded with a visit to a small theatre for a performance of a local-style opera by the Drama Institute students. The audience, mostly students from one of the many educational institutions in the city, had been told of our arrival and rose to its feet to clap its welcome to the foreign visitors as we marched, rather self-consciously, down the aisle to the front seats reserved for us.

Whenever we went to a theatre the interpreters gave us the outline of the story beforehand and arranged themselves strategically among us during the performance, so that at key-moments they could lean across or over the seat and translate, hand in front of mouth, in a whisper, the main events or conversations on stage. At the more exciting moments their voices would be raised unconsciously and I waited for our disturbed neighbours to make at least the mildest of protests at the extraneous noise – nobody ever did. A very patient people, the Chinese!

14 · THE SHANGHAI STORY
And Some Shopping

More than any city Shanghai has epitomized for the cinema-going, thriller-reading public not only the colour and glamour but also the evil and violence of the East. The verb tells the story: 'to shanghai' – to carry off by force to a nameless and hideous fate on a Chinese junk, in a dope den or a house of ill-fame. Most old China-hands will admit that the word was well coined; that behind all the wealth and glitter of the few was the misery of the many – hideous, almost unbelievable in its sub-humanity.

So many visitors to the city in the 'thirties and 'forties have written up their accounts that there is no need to turn to Communist sources to illustrate the prodigious 'before-and-after' story.

George Adams, an American relief worker, wrote that 28,000 children were found dead on the streets in 1936 and American Olga Lang's *Chinese Family and Society*, a Mather Foundation Study, gives facts more horrifying than any writer of fiction dare invent. Edgar Snow quotes her at some length: 'Many children are virtual slaves to their employers . . . many receive no pay at all and sleep . . . under their work-tables.'

An Australian Member of Parliament, Leslie Haylen, visited Shanghai in 1946 to investigate the fate of Australian UNRRA contributions. In his book, *Chinese Journey*, he tells the horrifying tale of his experiences.

Costs were astronomical – or seemed so because of runaway inflation; he paid one million yuan for a bottle of wine; thousands of refugees poured into the city, sleeping and dying on the streets almost unheeded. Leaving his hotel in one of the shiny limousines reserved, to his embarrassment, for visitors or local VIPs, the car was held up in a traffic-jam; a girl came to the window. 'She was begging – a baby in her arms. The little plump baby seemed fast asleep, and was held up, eyes closed as a suppliant. I touched its face; it was so pretty – it was also dead.'

'It's an old trick; it isn't her baby; she's picked it up to help her cadging!' his diplomat companion remarked.

On the fate of UNRRA supplies he writes: 'There was an

astonishing and frightening story. None – but none – of the food and clothing ever got down to the workers but found its way on to the black market or shops in the Nanking Road. Mankind seemed at the end of the line.'

To patriotic Chinese the city was not only the most febrile, the most squalid, but also the most Western-dominated of their country; here came the Western gunboats (with treaty-agreements for the Western missionaries to follow in their wake, the Communists point out), and here the great industrialists and financiers set up their Western empire in the foreign concessions which operated in territorial isolation beyond the laws of China.

When Chen Yi's armies took over he established, with a speed that amazed the citizens, an efficient temporary Government and his army showed a wholly unexpected lack of the brutality and licence that the KMT forces had prophesied. In line with military policy from the earliest days, Communist soldiers were highly disciplined. They had to observe rules of behaviour; these were set to music and often sung while marching: (1) speak politely; (2) observe fair-dealing in all transactions; (3) return everything you have borrowed; (4) pay for anything you have damaged; (5) don't beat or scold the people; (6) don't damage crops; (7) don't take liberties with women; (8) don't ill-treat prisoners of war.

From the opera-star daughter of a wealthy banker I had a graphic, first-hand account of the arrival of the Red Armies in the city:

> We knew they must take us sooner or later and, naturally, my family and I were especially terrified of what would happen to wealthy 'capitalists' like ourselves. The KMT had filled us with horror stories of Communist reprisals in other cities, so we expected – well [she shrugged], you can guess what I expected. We watched the soldiers arrive from our window. They looked terribly tired and not at all fierce. Many of them were walking wearily along the streets in straw sandals and for some reason those sandals made me very sad. I wasn't a bit afraid; I was just terribly sorry

for them. Some of them later asked if they could camp in our garden and use any spare rooms; we could hardly believe it, because, of course we had expected to be turned out. After even a few days we realized that Marshal Chen Yi had begun the 'clean-up', though nothing very dramatic happened at first.

The spring-cleaning of streets, houses and public buildings, the removal of stinking rubbish and accumulated filth of years of neglect began at once. Apart from a few immediate reforms to ensure the smooth running of food-supplies and city-services Chen Yi made no spectacular effort to eliminate human pests for the first three months. But his officers were quietly, with devastating thoroughness, collecting their evidence and when they started the great clean-up they were equally thorough – drug pedlars, brothel keepers, owners of gambling-dens, and similar types living on wickednesses in the underworld, were easy to round up; much harder, of course, were the big racketeers behind the scenes, the fabulously wealthy merchants bribing and corrupting from offices or mansions. Public trials were common, execution was common but it was not indiscriminate, nobody ran amok and if tycoons were prepared to co-operate with the new Government they were given a chance to do so.

On his visits to Shanghai today Chen Yi must look upon his 'cleaning-up' and see that it is good. We drove along the Bund, famous river-front drive, from which the great European financiers have gone, leaving their office blocks, banks and clubs for Chinese activities in the same field; gone, too, are the beggars, the maimed and the blind, the near-starving street-hawkers, the skinny rickshaw boys with their short life expectancy, as well as the millionaire's Cadillac or Rolls, and his exquisite and expensive women. We turned off the Bund and unloaded at the famous Cathay Hotel, now called Peace Hotel. Owned, like much more of Shanghai, by multi-millionaire Sir Philip Sassoon, it was formerly one of the most expensive hotels in the East. Now there are neither floorshows nor bars, Sir Philip's penthouse suite is available for a mere £7 a day. The 143 food is plentiful but not elaborate, and the only women around are respectable tourists in unadventurous bunches, interpreters of impeccable behaviour and a few members of the hotel staff. We arrived to find it sober as a Sunday-school.

For once our energetic guides hadn't laid on an immediate tour so I asked Shi-hwa if we could do some shopping. Nanking Road is the most crowded thoroughfare in China and we had to elbow our way through thousands of shoppers, sightseers and workers. The window-displays of its European-style shops are a decade ahead of Peking's – and a decade behind Oxford Street's or Fifth Avenue's. Instead of the imported goods of 'concession' days the shops now stock a very wide range of Chinese goods; many of them are advertised on street hoardings, which are commoner in Shanghai than other cities, I thought. Like most other things in print or paint, they are informative, listing the virtues of the wares in some detail and picturing them clearly, none of the 'impressionist', sparsely-worded or 'gimmicky' advertising to which we are accustomed. Patent medicines, wines, radios were pictured and, rather to my puzzlement, tyres; with so few cars available this seemed a work of supererogation! Walking along, staring about me, I suddenly stopped in my tracks to look at two young women, though for a second I couldn't tell what had attracted my attention, for they were dressed pretty much as the others; then I realized that they were wearing lipstick, the first I had seen for a week or two. I was to discover many Shanghai women are better-dressed and fractionally more sophisticated than their Peking sisters, but just as earnest, hardworking and moral.

Shi-hwa took me to the State Department Store where I wanted to buy a pair of slippers. Like hospitals and schools, the stores of China are functional buildings with few 'frills'. I found here the same stone floors and stairs as in Wuhan and Peking stores but the 'display' stands and lighting effects were more elaborate. There was a surprisingly large range of near-luxury goods – wines, cigarettes, candies and cosmetics.* The shoes were on the third floor, so we had to tramp up through crowds

* I found even more in 1965.

so thick that I could believe the reported 100,000 customers per day were all there together with me!

'What size do you want?' asked Shi-hwa when we reached the shoe department. I told her and she translated to the sales-girl, who smiled and pointed to another section. Shi-hwa, try-ing to hide her amusement, explained to me that they had no women's shoes as large as that and I would have to try the men's department! Feeling like Gargantua I moved off to look for my monster size six and a half, pausing, *en route*, horrified, at a case containing a few pairs of Lilliputian six-inch silk slippers made for the poor, bound, twisted, shuffling feet of the elderly women sacrificed in childhood to that dreadful fashion, the 'lily foot', symbol for too long of feminine 'daintiness' and helplessness.

The origin of footbinding – most cruel of all men's sexual fetishes – is not clear, but legend has it that a certain war-lord delighted to think that his mistresses could have feet dainty enough for them to stand within the palm of his hand or, ac-cording to another story, small enough for them to dance on the petals of a lotus. The long pain of the binding process was agonizing.

For generations it was regarded as essential for any young woman who wished to get a good husband. Footbinding was forbidden by a decree of Sun Yat-sen's which the KMT fully endorsed, but it is only in the last few decades that the habit has been finally broken. Today the Chinese are reluctant to talk about the custom; even though it belongs to the unregenerate dynastic days they feel it reflects on their whole nation. (Yet another example of the influence of national rather than Com-munist pride on contemporary attitudes.)

I bought my rope-soled, cotton-topped, comfortable men's slippers for about four yuan* and then spent half an hour shopping around. The store had probably about the same kind of goods as ours but the range of choice in each kind was smaller. Except for embroidered articles such as underwear, blouses and tablecloths, which are beautifully done in traditional designs and fairly cheap, most goods were simpler than our equivalents.

* About 11s. 3d. See p. 30.

But, none the less, the goods were there, in quantity and wholly Chinese – made by Chinese for the Chinese; the floral washbowls, the bright bedspreads and curtains, the bicycles, lamps and numerous radios represented achievement for manufacturer and buyer alike. I watched a stooping, fragile old man selecting an alarm clock, with immense concentration. Fifteen years ago such a possession would have been beyond his dreams. He saw me watching him, lifted up the clock of his choice with a delighted smile which I returned, miming, in nods and becks and handclaps, my approval. I looked at the store with rather different eyes after that.

If any remnants of emporial superiority remained they were quickly dispersed half an hour later when Shi-hwa took me to a tucked-away, shabby little shop which sold second-hand opera costumes and properties. Paintless outside, dark and dusty within, it was like a genie's cave. There were great racks of garments in serried ranks with narrow paths between; ceiling-high rows of shelves and hooks on every spare inch of wall all carried some item of the unique splendour that is Chinese classical opera. On the racks were the lissom heroine's ankle-length silken gowns thick with embroidered flowers – rising-suns or abstract, intricate designs in rainbow hues; the characteristic long overfall of their sleeves trailed on the floor. Alongside, the great, padded-out robes of warriors, stiff with gold embroideries, projected into the aisles, dazzling even in the crepuscular light. On the shelves, higgledy-piggledy, lay the six-feet-long, undulating pheasant's feathers which often decorate the performers' headgear, eunuch's round or hexagonal hats and double or triple royal crowns with fantastic appendages. Swords, daggers, quarterstaffs were there and the tasselled whips conventionally waved to represent the victorious general, the fleeing princess, the pursuing villain leaping to horse and riding away. On the floor lay pairs of the thick-soled boots with which, and his padded robes, hero or villain could loom larger than life.

All was for sale and cheap. I forgot to ask why. I wanted to buy great quantities but common sense prevailed – though with difficulty in such an exotic place. I satisfied myself by buying a black satin mandarin coat with dull gold thread, plate-sized medallions, and a rose-pink, kimono-style garment with elaborately embroidered peacocks sprawling their blue-green iridescent feathers across the back and down the sleeves, tiny lotus and magnolia blooms scattered between; rather surprisingly on the white silk lining of this delicately-coloured garment embroidered tigers, in crudest orange and black stripes, fiercely rampant, claws extended, wound their way from one side to the other. As I was trying this on the lights went out and I stood, swathed, in the darkness until candles were found and lit; the flickering, yellow light, the grey, leaping shadows, completed my sense of unreality and once again, as in the Buddhist temple and the little courtyard of the Imperial Palace, I moved into another dimension of time and space, where emperors and concubines, eunuchs and magicians bodied forth these empty garments in the quiet shadows of the little shop, and I, in my opera-robe, long sleeves drooping to the ground, seemed part of their strange world.

Though she must have been half-dead with fatigue Shi-hwa, knowing I wanted to visit another studio, insisted on taking me to a well-known one nearer to the centre of the city. Intent on gift-buying, I wandered, dazed with indecision, past shelves and cases of porcelain bowls, spoons and vases; past carved jade figurines, translucent green or pink; carved ivory, parchment-yellow or winter-white; scrolls with landscapes and ladies, mandarins and mountains. I bought a few easily portable objects and a necklace of knobbly pieces of turquoise, far more blue than green, as the best stones should be, I was told. 'That's that,' I said, looking at my thinning notecase; but it wasn't!

There, on a teak table, in truly splendid isolation, a foot-high Tang Dynasty funerary horse, of warm apricot-coloured clay, stood with noble head bent over a leg raised to paw the ground in impatient demand to be off. His back legs, stout and sinewy, were solidly planted on the plinth; a warrior's horse, he needed stout legs and broad buttocks. With a beautiful line a cerulean saddle was modelled and painted along his sides, 147 flowing back over his haunches and, in front, rising high above the arched neck and flowing mane. The world-famous terra-cotta horses used to be put into the grave with their lord or emperor; dug up, any one of them bears the discoloration, the patina, of a thousand years entombment in yellow clay; in Oriental museums the world over they are the pride of curators. This one was a modern reproduction only, but so faithful to the original with its slight discoloration, its patches of adhesive clay, its general air of the fragility produced by aeons of subterranean living, that it was indistinguishable from a Tang craftsman's own masterpiece. The horse was, literally, one of the most beautiful things I had seen and at forty-five yuan or so I could just afford to buy him. I realized that the problems of getting him back unbroken was probably insoluble and the nuisance of lugging him around considerable; but I was not deterred. He arrived in Australia cracked in four places but he was repaired and gives pleasure to all who see him.

To keep him company I bought – caution gone with the wind by this time – two smaller horses, six inches high, and two dancing-girls, one of the same terra-cotta, one with a simulated, cracked cream glaze, and both with the same perfection of line and the same air of authenticity as the horse.

15 · THE 'OTHER SIDE' AND THE MODEL VILLAGE

We were determined to get shots of back streets and poorer houses and had been nagging quietly at Feng for some days. We explained, once again, how necessary it was for our record to have balance. On our second morning in Shanghai we were allowed to film older sections of the city.

It was about 6.30 a.m., by which time citizens of the New China seemed to be well into the day's work. Some of the first workers we saw were just limbering up by going through their Tai Chi-chuan – a sort of Chinese Yoga – exercises, favoured for hundreds of years. Oblivious of the passers-by, little groups, varying from ten to three in number, performed the slow graceful body movement with an expression of almost trancelike concentration, indicating mental as well as physical exercise. One man had apparently just paused on his way to the office for,· there on the Bund, he was exercising entirely by himself, his coat and papers in a neat pile on the grass verge.

It was impossible to imagine these solitary, rhythmic exercises amid the city din in any Western country; but they stopped no traffic in Peking or Shanghai, though an occasional pedestrian might pause to admire. Our cameras impeded their progress not at all. The Communist Party was quick to stress the national importance of physical fitness and most factories, offices and schools have an exercise-break at least once a day. Their exercises are much brisker than the old Tai Chi-chuan.

A little farther along the pavement, a venerable old man was energetically teaching youngsters the foot and arm movements of age-old Chinese shadow-boxing. He kept the boys on their toes, effortlessly dodging their blows with a split-second timing, thoroughly enjoying his own dexterity. When he saw the cameras he was delighted and put on a specially active bout, grinning with mischievous pleasure as he teased his pupils. This three-minute sequence turned out to be one of the most popular in our film.

We assured Feng that we had no intention of isolating the slum-scenes and would most certainly make it clear that they were leftovers from pre-revolution days, and inevitable after all the long war and occupation that the city had experienced.

Feng, relaxed, even agreed to let us go off by ourselves to shoot our choice. We failed lamentably to do so!

In the dark alleys away from the tourists of the Bund and the Nanking Road the dwellers in the tiny, crowded hovels rarely see a European, so when one appears, and with a camera to boot, the effect is shattering. Everyone within sight, and beyond, flocked around until, as Harold said, we were shooting the children's eyelashes! Nobody was objectionable but nobody went on with his work; he paused and posed; it was infuriating though understandable and it showed the impossibility of doing much on our own. Even when we rejoined cameraman Cheng his efforts produced nearly similar results. Though a senior person, Feng did not have authority to order people about, and anyway the very nature of the shots we wanted – relaxed, unself-conscious – precluded stage direction. Finally, by a cunning stratagem, we took our camera to one end of the road and created a diversion by pretending to shoot whilst Cheng did his best at the other end. The houses were near-hovels, tumbledown, ill-lit; but they were clean and in moderate condition. Little open-fronted, one-room shops were busy and there were no flies. We were told the houses were due for demolition once new flats went up, but this would be some time ahead. After half an hour Cheng himself was roundly told off by an indignant inhabitant who was not going to have his home taken by or for anybody. 'Go round to the next street,' he shouted at Cheng, 'there are some new places there.' Then, after another half-hour, the police arrived and made mild but firm objections to the congestion we were causing. Feng explained that permission had been given, that the Association for Cultural Affairs approved of us, but in the end we thought it better to stop arguing and move off! It was nobody's fault, really, but we felt frustrated at our failure to show more of what the Chinese workers and the Government still have to cope with.

We had more luck at the model village, where there was no crowding.

It seems to us odd that a housing settlement, with up to

The Tang Horse

Two newly graduated students in an opera presentation of Flooding the Seven Armies

Primary School children doing public work duties in the streets

A scene from the film of the life of Mei Lan-fang, most famous of modern Peking opera stars

Middle School pupils perform their tasks as street sweepers

Temple of the Happy Year in the Temple of Heaven, Peking

Boarders at the part-work part-study technical school in Shanghai doing their washing (cold water!)

Peasants' children at a Primary School in the commune

Residents of the home of Respect for the Aged
come to greet us at a commune near Peking

Above: Students at a part-work part-study school, all of whom are at least Grade IV workers

Left: A Middle School student studies algebra in the park — in the rain

'Spring Morning in Soochow' – *a modern painting in traditional style*

'Red Crag' – a modern variation on the traditional style

Rush-hour at the one commune shop in the village street

Wallboard in a commune near Peking. It celebrates a bigger harvest and new scientific development and reads: 'Production for the sake of the Revolution'.

'*Spring Mizzle in South China*' — *a modern treatment of traditional Chinese painting*

*Exercises for workers at the State Cotton Mill No. 2. In the background
are workers' flats.*

The wallboard reads: 'Proletariat of the World Unite'

The new Primary School at Mei Ja Wu village, built between the author's 1963 and 1965 visits

Workers do their traditional exercises 'Tai-Chi chuan' – in the early morning sun

Right: Little girl standing by a Canton pottery rubbish bin

Top: The author with children, in a Canton street

Below: Brigade leader Liu examines ears of rice grown on the brigade's experimental plot

Overleaf: 'Uncle policeman' conducts children across a road, Peking

60,000 people, in the midst of a city of nine and a half million souls, should be called a village; but everyone refers to Tsao Tang as one of sixty new 'villages' in and near Shanghai.

Finished in 1951, it was the first of its kind, and built to house workers in the large complex of textile factories near by. Our car convoy was met by the Women's Federation representatives and members of the Street Committee – which is another misnomer, for the village has thousands of 'villagers', and the 'Street Committee' represents every one of them! It is affiliated to the Women's Federation.

The title indicates the designer's efforts to give at least a rural appearance, for there were many trees, lawns, and flowering shrubs and, since there were no through-roads, there was even some hint of rural quiet.

Sitting on the grass by the roadside, we scribbled down the statistics given to us by the chief Committee member, Mrs Kuo Ah-mei; families – 12,800; flats – allocated according to family size; one nursery, eight kindergartens, four middle schools, one cultural hall, one big department store, eight smaller shopping centres, eight vegetable and meat markets; one hospital, one clinic, one bank, one post office, one large cinema, one large bath-house for winter use (baths in factories for workers). The family average wage was seventy-five yuan a month and rent was only five per cent of wages, plus sixty yen for light and water;* the average cost of food was twelve yuan a month. Social amenities were cheap, health services free for workers and half price for dependants, so that modest savings were possible. Many families had furniture for the first time.

'This is Hsu Yung-fu,' Mrs Kuo said. She had eight children and for twenty-six years they lived on a boat on the river; six children died of fever or hunger or in an epidemic of some kind. They had so few clothes that they had to share coats and trousers and could never go out together. Now she has a home of her own and her two remaining children are well-fed and are being educated.'

Mrs Hsu nervously twisted her hands as she became the centre

* About 2s. See p. 30.

of attention, but her face, wrinkled as a dried-pea, was wreathed with smiles as she invited us to see her home.

And her lot was the lot of millions. I thought, shudderingly, of the Lang and Adams reports. The dry bones of the statistics lived as I looked at her and my admiration for the small group of committee-women with her welled up as I thought of the tremendous task they were helping to accomplish.

Picturesquely, Madame Kuo was adding, 'One woman like her once wrote on the wallboard, "Before Liberation we lived in Hell; now we have moved into Paradise".' We moved off to inspect their paradise.

First to the kindergarten, where the children were washing their hands before a meal with an amusing little routine. Lined up in straggly fashion, one by one they walked past the teacher giving their hands a desultory rub on the large cake of coarse soap she held outstretched for them; then off to the stone-trough along the wall, where they held hands under a thin trickle from a couple of taps and rubbed vigorously. I smiled wryly as I thought that probably each child not only washed its own hands before meals but made sure that Mum and Dad did so too; for the fervour of the education-drive has urged every student, from kindergarten to university, to pass on all they can to parents and neighbours: 'Each one teach one.' In Peking I had been told of schoolchildren with megaphones on street duty asking young and old to cross the road carefully and not throw litter around; being Chinese they would ask most politely, but I suspected there must be a few little prigs in the New China, though I never met one.

The flats we visited, in courtyards with saplings everywhere, were facsimiles of Mei-lang's at the Cotton Mill in Peking. Two flats had been taken over for a 'Women's Co-operative'. Equipped as a simple workroom with benches, tables and ironing-boards, it housed a couple of dozen women putting together the backs, fronts and sleeves of woollen jumpers knitted in the near-by factory. An old man in a faded, patched, cotton suit, black cap on his thin hair, moved among them, inspecting and advising.

152

'He is a veteran worker,' we were told. 'He got bored without a job.' There is no doubt that the typical Chinese concern about old people's well-being is as lively as ever. 'Houses of Respect for the Aged' are provided for those who have no family to care for them. (Originally they were 'Happy Homes for the Aged'. I think the slight change of name is significantly Chinese.)

The women paused over their work as we entered, smiled, stared a moment or two, then bent over their stitching again. They seemed cheerful, but very silent, hardly exchanging a word. I commented to Madame Kuo on this unexpected feminine taciturnity.

'They like to concentrate on their work and do it as well as possible,' she replied. 'They can't do this if they talk too much!'

The posters on the wall urged everyone to 'Work for the solidarity of all Nationalities' and 'Strive to Strengthen the Worker-peasant Alliance and the People's Democratic Unity'!

I was anxious to get some information about the Street Committee's day-to-day functioning. On the face of it they seemed bodies of formidable Mrs Grundys keeping an eye on what goes on in every corner of their bailiwick. Mrs Fong Chung-tung, chief paid Officer of the Committee, to whom I was introduced as we left the co-operative, looked too young and amiable to be a regular Mrs Grundy and she answered my questions without any of the signs of officiousness and nosiness that a super-snooper might be expected to exhibit.

The Street Committee is undoubtedly one of the major instruments by which the Communist Party not only disseminates its recommendations and prohibitions and its doctrinal developments, but also receives back reports of the actions, reactions, criticisms and counter-criticisms of the populace as a whole. The Committee works with, and is, indeed, part of the Federation of Women, which has its Officers, paid and voluntary, in every city and commune – a vital component of the apparatus of persuasion. I was prepared to find many of the Committee's activities pretty objectionable and distasteful but, as so often I 'had reckoned without the reasonableness of the 153

Chinese, their capacity for compromise, for keeping things amiable and acceptable wherever possible, and above all, for preserving a surprising amount of the 'human touch' in a bureaucratic complex.

Madame Fong was in her early forties, with a tweed instead of a cotton jacket, and a friendly air; her young assistant was very pretty indeed. Throughout, they talked of their work in wholly local, human, apolitical terms. Whether this was accident or policy I could not discover. The village had one Street Committee served by twenty-one paid Secretaries of which Madame Fong was the chief; she had been a factory worker when young, gone to school after the Revolution and been selected for this job from several applicants. The Committee itself consisted of women elected by popular vote and serving voluntarily. Each one represented a section of the living-quarters; there were twenty of these, each with a Lane Committee, which, in turn had representatives from every block of flats – the pyramid again. The main Committee appointed sub-committees to deal with specialist aspects of village life. Every member kept in touch with her 'constituents', reporting grievances and suggestions which reached the main Committee in due course. If considered sufficiently important, they were passed on, in turn, to the Shanghai City Council itself.

Of course, in super-health-conscious China, the Sanitary Sub-Committee was of prime importance, keeping an eye on litter, flies, drains, cleanliness of staircases and courtyards as well as a host of health measures promulgated by the Council of the Hospitals. This would be the sort of Committee that, in Wuhan, worked closely with Professor Lu's teams and they certainly were powerful helpers of Marshal Chen Yi in the early days.

A second sub-committee dealt with education and culture, pressing, like such committees the world over, for more books, teachers and playing-fields for the schools; they were also active in arranging visits of theatrical and musical groups and in 154 organizing discussions and lectures. Discussions on purely political studies were dealt with by the special Political Science Committee. 'Discussion', I was told, covered a wide range of local, national and international topics and outspoken criticism of party policies was encouraged. By now I knew what this freedom of discussion meant – criticism within the circle, fault-finding within the faith. Professor Fitzgerald compares the Party policy with that of a medieval Pope who would encourage schoolmen to contend freely on points of doctrine; but nobody in his senses expected the Holy Father to encourage a basic criticism of Christianity itself – that would be heresy. I doubt if the workers in this model village considered their 'freedom' seriously impinged upon (though some may have grown more than a little weary of meetings).

In 1963 hours were being spent analysing the Sino–Soviet split, as explained exhaustively in the news columns and editorials of the *People's Daily*. The groups had been encouraged to study just how the 'split' affected their day-to-day life; did the break with the Soviet increase or diminish their fervour for hard work, their belief in their country's future; was it, in short, better or worse for them that this situation had come into the open?

Mao has stressed, through the years, the necessity for getting down to 'grass-roots' level, and here I saw how it happened. The 'villagers' could discuss national policy, get things off their chests and feel they were being consulted and kept in touch. The Party hopes by such means to avoid a basic weakness of the planned state, the division into 'we' and 'they' – the people on one side and the bureaucrats on the other.

The Mediation Committee carried out at a purely personal level the national principles of persuasion. One of its tasks was to deal with the innumerable disputes that arose within, and between, families, in the hope that they could be settled without recourse to protracted legal suits or even personal violence. Husband-and-wife situations, parent–child quarrels, neigh-bourly disputes, petty tyranny by local officials or factory supervisors; such situations were usually referred to the Dis-putes and Mediation Committee either by the people 155 involved or by friends and families anxious to cope with the problem before time and anger aggravated it. Madame Fong explained:

> Very often we can help just by listening to people; often they don't even need our advice, they just want 'to get it off their chest'. Sometimes we get the opponents together for the first time and when they are face to face they find they're not so mad at each other after all. Sometimes we investigate their complaints for them and they come back several times to discuss the matter with us. Usually this works and many law cases are avoided [she concluded cheerfully].

Madame Fong expanded considerably on the Committee's work for women. Any woman in need of advice or practical help of any kind would turn to the Street Committee. A sick husband or child might threaten to keep her away from work – the Committee would find a paid or voluntary home-help to take over the household chores. A parent with a backward child needed extra teaching for it or a young wife wanted advice on cooking – just let them ask the Committee and something would be done to help. Joint projects to improve school facilities or the communal gardens in the courtyards were arranged by the Committee; everybody was treated as part of the village 'family'. Clearly immensely significant institutions with an immeasurable effect on national life, the Street Committees of China!

Great goodwill, neighbourliness and real Christian charity were manifestly present; but for us, as Westerners, a couple of disconcerting features emerged. First, it was clear, personal privacy in the village must be non-existent. We would want to be able to escape from neighbours, however helpful, decide for ourselves the way we wished to conduct our private lives; with a Street Committee this would be very difficult. I gathered that the Committee kept an eye on personal comings and goings; boy-girl friendships would be especially noted (where are they not?) and pretty certainly relaxation of the high moral code of

156

sexual behaviour would be commented on and action taken if need be.

An Australian friend living in Peking told me that a girl in her office had become very friendly with, and fond of, a foreigner; the girl talked about him at work for several months; then she ceased to do so and when questioned merely said she didn't see him any more. My friend suspected that the Street Committee, at some level, had demonstrated the unwisdom of the relationship, in their opinion.

Second, in spite of certain permissible variations of opinion, considerable political uniformity must be expected and the possibility of political supervision is always present. Some of the bitterer critics of the régime claim to offer proof that the Committees act as police-agents or at least liaison officers, even *agents-provocateurs*. This may or may not be true, but no casual inquirer like myself could hope to discover the extent of such liaison work. Certainly, the relations between Madame Fong, her assistant and the several housewives she met gave no indication of this; they all seemed relaxed enough. I went with her to a few houses where she seemed to function as a combination of district nurse, parish visitor, Dorothy Dix and chatty dropper-in.

Once again I realized that the situation could only be put into focus in its historical and philosophical context. Chinese life, at its highest as well as its lowest levels, has never seen any need to provide for the privacy of the individual. The gentry and scholar class, the landlords and rich peasants regarded the family, the clan, as the vital, the beloved, unit of existence with the generations living and working together under the one roof in theoretical amity.

So, in today's model villages, housing, education, bread and occasional circuses are still enough for most people; privacy, unknown in the past, is not missed in the present; past neglect is gladly exchanged for present supervision, so the undoubted good intentions and good works of the Committee's Ladies Bountiful are more than welcome to most people at this stage. The small minority who want to think, write, behave – or misbehave – differently from the others, who want to live outside the crowd – how do they view the Street Committee? I didn't ask. If I had done so, I should, I am sure, have been told, sincerely, that such a minority could speak its mind at the Disputes Committee meetings or in criticism-self-criticism sessions, where the rightness or wrongness of their ideas could be sympathetically considered and re-education undertaken if necessary – for everybody's good.

16 · 'CLICK GO THE SHEARS' AT THE WORKERS' PALACE

Fatigued by our energetic researches into model villages and Street Committees, I heard with some sinking of heart that that evening we were to visit a Workers' Cultural Palace. The name suggested a certain solemnity – propagandist art, reading-rooms, political debates. I sighed for a night at one of the popular 'song and dance' shows, with folk dances, singers, sketches, jugglers and acrobats. Ling, whom I had come to like and respect more each day, was quite sure it was just my cup of China tea, and should not be missed. We took the camera, but I could not summon up enough interest to take my tape-recorder. (In Shanghai there are twenty-two of these palaces or clubs, most of them with membership open to workers of all kinds. There are eleven children's palaces.)

The multi-storeyed 'concession-style' building, formerly the Grand Hotel, presented anything but a palatial appearance to the narrow street, and the milling crowd of blue-clad workers in the foyer, a wall-full of not very· attractive exhortatory posters and the usual chipped paint, did not add up to any promise of gayer things to come. The Assistant Director was soon telling us details of membership, numbers of students and courses. He was very earnest and, sure enough, began our con-ducted tour by taking us to a reading-room on the first floor and discoursing on the number of books taken out or read on the spot.

'Ling has let us down for the first time; this really is too much of a good thing for one day,' I said, half angrily, to Harold. But I began looking at the shelves. The books included Chinese classical and modern novels, the works of all the Communist writers, and innumerable treatises on current sociological issues. There were hundreds of foreign books, mostly in translation, but some in the original language. As I expected, after my previous visit, I discovered one of the most popular English authors was Dickens and I smiled wryly as I recalled my efforts to assure a group of Peking university students that *The Old Curiosity Shop* and *Oliver Twist* did not exactly reflect the condi-tions of the masses in England today! Other popular authors are Galsworthy, Shaw and Ibsen – all writers with a social purpose.

Some readers were queueing at the librarian's desk to sign for books to take home; a few dozen others were reading absorbedly at tables. Looking over their shoulders, I found many slowly turning pages of Chinese-style 'comics'. In these every picture told a story by means of simple line drawings, short captions and 'balloons' from mouths, just as in the Western variants. But there was no Mandrake, Superman, Jane or Popeye; instead, historical tales of dynastic days with wicked war-lords and noble peasants; or of the Long March, the establishment of the communes, China v. Western Imperialists and, for lighter fare, idyllic tales of boy meeting girl in factory, farm or evening-class. Sex there was none – not a leg, not an embrace and the only violence was in past wars.

As usual, people seemed pleased at my interest and the readers held up their books or moved over for me to sit beside them, listening, fascinated, to the interpreter's translation. The books meant much to them all, and as much to the thousands of other readers scattered in libraries large and small throughout the whole country – libraries such as I had seen myself in commune villages, primary-school classrooms, factory recreation centres and young Pioneers' Clubs; the newly-literate millions are so excited about their reading ability that almost anything in print is grist to their mill.

Already my fatigue was fading; it disappeared briskly when we climbed the stone stairs to the next floor to see a folk-dancing class. A dozen girls were rehearsing for a performance of provincial dances. In long, bright skirts with gaily decorated aprons, beribboned plaits and stage make-up, they were in the midst of a Parasol Dance. Moving with a rather formal grace, they were opening and shutting, twisting and twirling their gay umbrellas in a complicated series of figure-eights up and down the long room. I discovered, when they had finished, that, among the troupe were a textile worker, a nurse, two school-teachers and a railway porter.

From every room on this floor came sounds of activity which mingled in the long passage in a weird cacophany of gongs and flutes, male-voice choirs, falsetto-voiced soloists, floor-thump-ings, huffings and puffings and, amazingly, a distant hint of a

Tchaikovsky symphony! One by one we traced the sounds to their source.

An amateur Chinese-style orchestra was having a special rehearsal and its tympani, flutes and cymbals were ear-piercingly at it, full pelt; the men's choir was singing, with a beautifully-controlled *forte*, one of the rousing, tuneful national songs such as 'The East is Red' or 'Socialism is Good'. Next door energetic would-be acrobats were throwing one another about under the guidance of a well-known Shanghai performer. After a hurried consultation with Ling, they apparently decided to put on their star turn for us – mass-cycling. Perhaps as many as twenty of them climbed with infinite caution and agility, one by one, on to the same machine, pyramiding to the ceiling, riding round and round faster and faster and then in ever-diminishing circles until the laws of physics seemed outrageously defied. They just *had* to fall down, I thought; but they didn't until they were good and ready! Then they dropped down as gracefully and lightly as petals off a flower.

Delighted by our applause and laughter, they seemed likely to do it all over again. For me, enough stunt cycling is enough, so I slipped away to trace the Tchaikovsky to a Western-style orchestra of about forty players. Their conductor, I learned later, was a noted surgeon; he was not in any way distinguishable by his dress from the orchestra members, who were mostly labourers or tradesmen. Western music is much admired and the Shanghai Conservatorium is well on its way to becoming one of the world's best. Recently one of its pianists was placed second to American Van Cliburn in the Moscow Tchaikovsky Festival Competition.

But the highlight of the visit, the trick up the sleeve, the end that crowns the work, came as we straggled in to hear the folk-song choir, where the boy and girl performers stopped singing on our entrance and clapped enthusiastically. Speeches were made, translated, answers given, translated. Then they asked would we please sing an Australian folk song. 'No, we aren't good enough' (with a bit of luck we'd all be spared 'Waltzing Matilda'). 'Please ask the choir to go on singing for us.'

They continued singing very well indeed, tunefully and with zest. In the end we had to sing 'Matilda' in an appalling, struggling effort to keep in tune and remember at least some of the words. They clapped as if we were the London Philharmonic Choir. Then, whispering and grinning, ten girls stepped forward, eye on their young conductor; deep breaths, silence – and off they went. 'Click Go the Shears!' Australia's best-known folk song sung in Chinese, presto, vivace! Eyes popping, we listened and wondered. They told us they had sung it for years along with English, Scottish and many European ones. Auld Lang Syne and John Brown's Body are in their repertoire, too.

When they finished, the laughter, handshaking and applause continued for many minutes and then Chinese and Australians got together in small groups to talk about the songs and the club's activities in general. It was one of the most delightful occasions of the trip, but my pleasure in it was almost ruined by the absence of my tape-recorder. 'Click Go the Shears' sung in Chinese by Shanghai workers. What a record not to be taking home! I asked if I could come back next night to record it, but other activities would take place there tomorrow; so many cultural groups want to use the clubrooms that none can meet two days running.

Fatigue forgotten, I smiled broadly across the mob at a beaming Ling who called out something like, 'I told you so.' Light-hearted, almost light-headed with all the culture and bonhomie, we moved off to an exhibition-room.

My spirits plummeted with the sickening speed of the Empire State elevator, for here was hatred in double quantity, White v. Black, East v. West. The Ministry of Propaganda had selected, with damaging skill, America's own pictures of Negro persecution. From the newspapers of many states they had culled the hideous record of Ku-Klux-Klan marches, mob-lynchings, Negro shanty-towns and two of the more infamous Little Rock incidents, with white women screaming abuse at Negro children. Many were clearly decades old but who was to 162 distinguish that – or care? The indictment was there. 'This is

USA,' said the pictures. 'This is American imperialism – this is the capitalist West.' One more proof of iniquity in contrast to China's friendship for Afro–Asian people, as shown in these pictures of Chairman Mao welcoming men and women of every colour to the Great Hall of the People and Chou En-lai shaking hands with a self-exiled American-Negro visitor to Peking.

The record was factual, but there was no mention of Civil Rights, of White Americans giving their lives for desegregation, of movie-stars as freedom marchers, of Negroes in high office or the President's stand for the Civil Rights Bill. The indictment was complete. Doubtless, upstairs, the amateur conjurers were producing more 'Smash the Imperialist' flags out of their hats, the gardeners planting 'Go Home, Yank' in their flower-beds; while American newspaper cartoonists back home were producing their time-honoured fanged, menacing Mao, their slave-driven hordes in communes, and the columnists were pouring vitriol into their ink as they wrote of the imagined miseries of a country scarcely one of their compatriots had visited and with which they had no first-hand communications. The situation is at once absurd and tragic.

We had the usual rousing send-off at the door, and we drove back to the 'Peace' through the quiet, near-deserted streets, past the neon-lit Great World – China's most inclusive entertainment centre. (It has some fourteen or fifteen shows each night – Opera, Burlesque, Puppets, Films, Folk Songs and Dancing, Jugglers – and the entrance fee is about twenty fen.*) Then along the sober Bund to the cabaret-less, bar-less, *fille-de-joie*-less Peace Hotel.

My tape-recorder lay on my bed; I picked it up and banged it down on the table in simulated pique! I was less concerned with United States–China mutual suspicion as I fell asleep, than with the absence of a Chinese 'Click Go the Shears'!

* See p. 30.

17 · A CAPITALIST REVISITED

Next morning I realized that, with only two more days to go, there was a great deal I wanted to fit in – opera school, university, talks with the clergy and another meeting with a 1958 acquaintance, Mr Liu. Over the breakfast omelette a visit to a chemical fertilizer factory was announced. This time I was determined to contract out, but I didn't, because Ling assured me so earnestly that it was the largest in China and of great economic significance.

After about an hour's drive we reached the sprawling, half-finished fertilizer works with their great, hangar-like sheds and towering machinery. They were dusty and noisy but I tried to take an interest in them because I appreciated the significance of the policy-change which they represented, the Government's increased stress on agriculture. 'Agriculture is the Foundation. Industry the Leading Factor' ran a newish policy-slogan. I knew that the lean years had made clear the paramount importance of the full development of all agricultural resources, that the steel-drive, the priorities of Anshan, Wuhan, Paoutou and of textile factories, had, for years, relegated the mechanics of agricultural development to second place. So the very considerable amount of time, capital and technical skill now being expended on this plant showed that the Party was taking a closer look at the needs of the country people from which it sprang and from which its first support had come. China is not going to make the mistake of neglecting agriculture as it is said that the USSR has done.

The plant was an illustration of the way the planned, centralized economy could shift industrial – or other – emphases, with an unquestioned ease foreign to the less powerful, would-be planners in a free-enterprise, democratic economy.

It was two o'clock before we got back for lunch and I found a message that the Mr Liu whom I had asked to meet again had been traced for me and would see me at his home at three o'clock.

In the early 'thirties Mr Liu was at King's College, Cambridge, reading for the Economics Tripos and living in the style to which the son of a multi-millionaire was accustomed.

Barely a mile away, reading English at Newnham College, and living in the style suited to any hard-up middle-class young woman in the Depression years, was the present writer; our social paths, not unexpectedly, never crossed.

I had discovered this minor coincidence when I met Mr Liu in 1958. I had asked the Women's Federation if I could meet a representative of the former wealthy class and had been told, in the rather quaint terminology that one often encounters in China, 'We will arrange a visit to a capitalist's house' as one might say to an exhibit in the zoo.

I didn't, and don't, doubt that Mr Liu is a prize exponent of Party policy towards his class, so I met him with appropriate reservation, realizing at the same time that the chance to hear official policy at first hand was, in itself, valuable. With Mr Liu I had to admit that there was something very interesting to expound: something that made sense for the most part and certainly represented an aspect of revolution characteristic of China and comparatively rare in the USSR. Mr Liu was a sample of the highly-valued, co-operative financier carefully preserved by a Party anxious to benefit from his experience and skill. I had met Mr Liu in 1958 in his modest villa tucked away in a poky cul-de-sac in the former French 'Concession'. I learned later that it had been one of the houses on the family property and that in the old mansion, near by, Mr Liu's mother still lived.

A servant admitted me and my host rose from his chair to greet me. He spoke perfect English in the soft tones which many Chinese use, and which matched his quiet courtesy and grace of manner; he had an immediately attractive personality and welcomed me warmly but not effusively. His wife, with oval face and wide, doe-like velvet eyes, wore a Chinese-style silk dress (the first I had seen for some time) simply cut and free of adornment. Mr Liu wore an unusually good European-style suit and a very Western looking tie – not quite 'old school' but very nearly.

The sitting-room, where the servant brought us tea in exquisite porcelain cups, was not large and exhibited that 165 mixture of attractive national, and less attractive foreign furnishings that characterizes the homes of many Asians who have lived in the West. (I have met the same phenomenon in Malaya and Ceylon.) The tea-cups rested on a museum-piece teak table whilst I sat in an unattractive, plush-covered armchair, part of a three-piece suite, and the superb Chinese carpet was marred by a hearthrug in autumn tonings. Mr Liu and I exchanged Cambridge reminiscences and discussed developments in England, whilst Mrs Liu, who spoke no English, sat in silent beauty, smiling occasionally to show, presumably, that she was pleased to see me.

When Mr Liu asked me what he could tell me I said, simply, 'Your life story'. He threw back his head and laughed, for him, quite loudly, and promised not to take too long over it.

One of the twelve children of the 'match-king of China', he had grown up in a home where the accumulation of wealth was seen as the only really absorbing subject of study; money was an end in itself rather than merely a means of acquiring more possessions, of which they had already immense quantities, including textile mills and real estate as well as the match factories.

As a Christian – a Presbyterian – he had almost automatically gone to a mission school and then to England; a purely Chinese education was not even considered in a family modelling itself, at least commercially and socially, on the Western pattern. After working hard in Cambridge and at the same time making valuable 'contacts' and doing the grand tour of Europe, he returned to take part in the family's vast business complex.

He continued his story thus:

I was especially interested in the Stock Exchange, and, if I may say so, I had a flair for investment. I was a pretty successful speculator. But Shanghai, as you know, was a very unsettled city, what with the Japanese occupation, the Communist agitation and, finally, civil war. Even when the KMT were in control there was no security; corrup-

tion was taken for granted. We ourselves corrupted officials as a matter of course when we could; but corruption led to inflation and market instability so that any business negotiations were tricky, and Stock Exchange gains were wiped out by currency devaluations. We sent as much as we could abroad. Naturally, my family were supporters of the KMT against the Communists and we knew both Chiang Kai-shek and the Soongs; but in the end we could not doubt that the KMT was responsible for the appalling mess that the country was in. We were in a dilemma because we abominated Communism but, as Chinese, we resented the KMT's failure to fight the Japanese and its use of American arms against our compatriots. Of course, there was unrest among the workers, too. Altogether, a capitalist's lot was not a happy one!

Just before the fall of Shanghai, in January 1949, we had a family conclave. One of my brothers decided to clear out of the country but the rest of us hoped to stay. If we escaped with our lives it was hard to believe that anything the Party offered could be worse than the uncertainties we were encountering at the time.

He went on to describe their surprise at the lack of unnecessary violence in the Communist capture of the city, and at the speed and efficiency with which a temporary government was established. Later, their father was summoned to Peking to meet Chairman Mao, who asked for the co-operation of himself and all his sons. Father returned, called another family conclave and they all thrashed out the pros and cons for a couple of days. They decided to co-operate by supporting Chen Yi, then Mayor of the city, in his 'cleaning-up' operations.

To everyone's surprise the Party kept its promise to pay five per cent interest on the capital value of the factories, which was assessed, very fairly, by the Party's economists. This was the beginning of the State–Private control of all industries and was expected to last for eight years, after which the State would take over completely, although the dual control has, in fact, lasted 167 longer.* The Government put a trusted Party member in charge of all industries and businesses, appointing their former owners or managers, if co-operative, as Number Two, thus ensuring the best of both worlds – Party guidance for all the factory staff, plus the long-acquired skill of the managers to keep the place running smoothly. Mr Liu became the second-in-command of the family woollen mills.

I immediately asked if this theory worked out in practice. Mr Liu admitted he found things difficult at first, felt down-graded and subordinate, but the good sense and devotion to duty of his Communist 'boss' were soon apparent and a good working relationship set up. In addition, the attitude of the workers improved fast and the whole tone of the factory altered for the better. In the old days it had never entered Mr Liu's head to consult with his workers in order to avoid labour troubles, which he had regarded as a necessary evil. He was paid a good salary in addition to his share of the interest – the Party-member received a smaller salary, as part of the Party discipline, apparently.

'I still work terribly hard but I don't worry now,' Mr Liu smiled. 'And I must say I am delighted to escape cocktail parties for the right people. How they used to bore me! And I'm relieved, really, not to have a Stock Exchange to play; that will save me an ulcer.'

Since he seemed prepared to discuss his affairs very frankly, I went on to ask what had happened to overseas investments, if, when he died, his daughter could inherit and, rather impertinently, what he did with his money, mostly.

Cultural shock again! Mr Liu said, simply, he had far more money than he knew what to do with. He got his overseas dividends, which were considerable, but did not find much to spend them on. His daughter's education was free. She was a star swimmer and even her special coaching was provided by the school. He had his own house; elaborate entertaining and dressing were frowned on. And then he told me one of the stories

* In 1965 I was told that these interest payments were to continue at least until 1966.

which, as much as any I had heard, illustrated the sort of topsy-turvy character that the pure socialist doctrine, as propagated in China, seems sometimes to have for the Westerner.

My daughter came home from school one day almost in tears. 'When are you going to stop being a capitalist, Daddy? Please can you do it soon? I'm called the capitalist's daughter at school and my friends tease me because they say we have too much money!' The last thing she wants is to inherit my fortune, though she can by our laws of inheritance. You may find this hard to believe.

I admitted I found it hard to believe! This fine disregard for money, this rejection of filthy lucre we expect to find in moral exhortations but not in the realities of everyday life.

When the car dropped me at the Lius' house once again in 1963, five years later, it and they seemed quite unchanged. Mr Liu greeted me with the same shy warmth, his wife wore a similar simple dress, the servant, settee and china were the same. Mr Liu was visibly pleased when I remembered his daughter's prowess as a swimmer and proudly showed me her photograph taken at the National Swimming Carnival. 'She would be in our Olympic Team if we had one,' he said. I also, to his amusement, reminded him that in 1958 his ambition had been to weave a worsted cloth as fine as 'Bradford's best'; he thought he had very nearly done it now.

I asked if the country had made much progress or been hindered by the 'natural calamities and the Soviet defections'. Mr Liu did not deny that things had been very difficult for a couple of years. Many had been hungry, even, but nobody had been anywhere near to starvation, thanks to an excellent rationing system and the absence of black markets. 'Now we are round the corner and nothing can stop us.'

Mr Liu explained that he was now General Manager of the China Wool Manufacturing Company but spent less time in the factory because he had been elected as Vice-Chairman of the Democratic Reconstruction League (one of the nine political parties) and had to make many visits to Peking to attend the People's Congress meetings and joint consultations on industrial policy with fellow 'capitalist' members. So here was another kind of link in the communication between Government and governed, between centre and periphery; another tributary to the great river of discussion flowing wider and stronger than the Yangtse.*

It was not until I was on my way back to the hotel that I realized how typical of modern China the occasion was. Here was an exceptionally busy and distinguished man, a 'tycoon' by any Western standards, and a politician too, prepared at short notice to down tools, go home across the city to answer searching personal questions by a comparative stranger from a country which did not even 'recognize' the existence of the Government he served! It was indicative of the importance which the New China attaches to its voice in the outside world. She may deny her isolation, assert her self-sufficiency, underline her doctrinal self-confidence, yet she asks to be noticed, even admired, by the West; and she asks the West to take heed. 'This country can be insulted no longer; China has stood up.' But she asks by implication not by direct demand and, unless all my main impressions were off the beam, she asks to be noticed and respected not as a rival, a threatening power, an old imperialist writ large in new terms, but as an amicable, peaceable equal.

Talking to Mr Liu underlined another paradox; so many of China's statements reaching the West – in *Peking Review*, in quotations from the New China News Agency and many Foreign Language Press booklets – is raucous, inflated, even menacing. Yet the voice of the Chinese at home is more often like his – quiet, reasoned, even relaxed.

My conversation with Mr Liu was interrupted by the driver, reminding me that I was already due at the opera school.

* Mr Liu is also a delegate to the National Political Consultative Conference.

18 · TWO HOURS AT THE OPERA SCHOOL

The school is housed in yet another old 'concession' building off a narrow street. The Vice-Director, a most attractive woman, had, in spite of her businesslike suit, a decided touch of feminine glamour (though the word seems out of context in China today – and, certainly, I'd never dream of writing 'sex-appeal', though she had it). I was not surprised to hear she had been a leading opera star herself.

Students were rushing around the corridors, rehearsing informally in odd corners and even out in the garden; they looked very young, so I asked at once the age and conditions of entry, and received this reply:

> We like them to start at thirteen or fourteen, when they are still supple. As you know, our opera includes acrobatics and fighting as well as song and dance and mime. The course lasts six years. We have so many applicants that we have to set a high admission standard. A student must have good general intelligence and he or she must, of course, show operatic promise and must also have a very high moral standard. We all know that actors and actresses have special temptations to meet as they become very popular and have much public admiration. They must know that their gifts must serve the people; that they must not feel superior and must behave with modesty.

'No prima donnas,' I intervened. 'No tantrums.' Shi-hwa tried nobly to translate!

With the usual thoroughness we were shown round the school. We watched young teenagers making themselves up as old men and women for character-part studies. Some were absorbed in elaborate sword-play routines depending for their appeal and the performer's safety on split-second timing; in another class girls were doing the beginners' course in that Chinese opera speciality 'sleeve-waving'; this is my inelegant name for a specially elegant stage convention. The tie-on sleeves, made of cotton, with the long 'over-fall', were fastened with tapes around the students' shoulders and they were making the sleeves undulate in great arcs over their heads and around their feet, then manipulating them in tiny, shuddering-like motions by their sides and over their faces. They stopped to smile at us and be introduced, but went back eagerly to their practice as soon as they could. A class of young boys was vigorously rehearsing tumbling exercises.

As a finale, a group of students staged two scenes from an opera currently in rehearsal. One was a scene from a popular classic, *The Woman General*. The hero-heroine strode on in her great stiff, gold-embroidered robes. Small flags and pennants were stuck into a padded contraption across her shoulders and these, with the high curling feathers, the big coloured pom-poms on her headdress, gave an impression of great height. The weight of the costume must have been considerable, but the doughty lady also carried a sizeable sword in one hand and in the other the tasselled whip representing her charger. As she entered with the swift, sliding gait peculiar to stage-warriors, the small orchestra in the wings created a pandemonium of excited sound to underline the martial alarums and excursions of the army which entered swiftly in her wake with a series of Nijinski-like elevations, followed by complicated arabesques. Dramatic declamations by the general competed with the orchestra and won by a short head before 'he' burst into an aria in that ear-piercing falsetto which the Western ear at first violently rejects, but, I found, gradually accepts and enjoys.

The shrieks, clashes and reverberations; the scramble, tumbling, leaping; the matching riot of colour and costumes and properties afford me a sense of theatrical excitement that few Western shows can arouse. After the climax the curtain, after the curtain the performers returning to match our clapping with theirs in mutual appreciation.

We went up on the stage and found the young stars dripping with perspiration after their exertions, and full of pleasure at our approval. The air was thick with the dust their acrobatics had raised. Shi-hwa had evidently told the Vice-Director that I was interested in the theatre, giving an exaggerated impression of my experience as an amateur producer, for the Vice-Director 172 came up to me and said, 'We shall be glad to have your comments on our performance and especially your suggestions for our improvement.' The thought of my amateur efforts with school and student plays qualifying me to comment on this remote and exotic art-form reduced me to helpless laughter, and I had to get Shi-hwa to try to explain just how ludicrous the idea really was. The Chinese today always ask for criticism in this way – I suspect sometimes it is a matter of form and politeness; though the national anxiety to learn, to improve, is so strong there may often be an honest wish to pick the visitor's brains. Certainly, visiting scientists, artists, businessmen and scholars get a most attentive hearing.

Alan Marshall, Australian novelist, tells a wonderful story of his visit to the steppes of Inner Mongolia, where he watched the world-famous horsemen performing incredible feats of skill and daring alone or in great hordes; man and horse seemed one as they rode. At the end of the elaborate convolutions the leading horseman leaped from his steed, approached Marshall and asked what suggestions he could make to improve their performance!

The cameras had been busy at practice classes and rehearsal, as both were outstandingly photogenic. Harold and I had the tape-recorder going, mostly at the back of the room as the cymbals and tympani were very fierce. The whole sequence turned out to be so fascinating that it seemed a pity to have to edit out any of it.

19 · NO WOMEN ON THE STREETS

Memories of 'the old days' will always be only too vivid for thousands of women in Shanghai – the pre-revolution prostitutes. One of my most moving experiences in China was hearing their story from a member of the Women's Federation who was made the senior Social Worker when Marshal Chen Yi took over the City Council in 1949.

Mrs Chen (as we will call her) was, at first sight, a rather formidable woman who gave an impression of humourlessness; a missionary light gleamed in her eye and she was rather long-winded. As it happened the interpreter that day was unusually slow and the session so protracted that it lessened the drama, if not the magnitude, of the achievement. I was soon to understand how any woman would find it hard to hang on to her sense of humour after she had worked for years amid the miseries of waterfront brothels and venereal clinics and seen the depths of degradation to which her sex could be reduced. There were in 1949, she told us, eight hundred licensed brothels with about 4,500 prostitutes and an estimated 30,000 unlicensed ones. The 'Big World' was the largest centre for traffic in drugs and women, but only one of many.

Mrs Chen did not exaggerate, for when the University of Princeton and the YMCA made a report on prostitution in pre-revolutionary Peking their findings were horrifying. Peking, along with Shanghai, had the highest number of recognized prostitutes of any country in the world *pro rata*. Advertisements in old Peking newspapers lauded the amorous qualifications of the 'Mist and Flower Maidens' as they were euphoniously and euphemistically styled. 'Her face is like a flower, her body like the moon.' In Shanghai the trade was regulated by the police, who demanded that brothel-keepers be registered and pay fees and taxes according to the quality of their houses, which were rated in grades one to four. Dope pedlars, pimps and prostitutes catered for every sort of appetite, no matter how perverted. Yet many Western writers who have visited post-revolution Shanghai record, with varying degrees of approval, the absence of soliciting in the streets; businessmen, ignorant or daring enough to ask about the existence of brothels, meet with a shocked disclaimer of the possibility of their existence today.

How were the Augean stables cleansed?

Chen Yi ordered the closing of all brothels, though some lingered on until the Shanghai People's Consultative Conference in 1951 demanded that the last ones be shut and any remaining street-walkers taken and re-educated. But closing the brothels was only the beginning of an immense social task. Thousands of women were now out of work, untrained, outlawed by society and too often diseased. The problem was tackled on all fronts with typical Party thoroughness and expedition. First, hospitals were set up and doctors summoned from all over China.

'They could hardly be spared from their own towns but the Government gave this task great priority and spent 200,000 yuan on its medical aspects,' said Mrs Chen. 'For those who were fit the immediate need above all was a job, so training-schools were established for light industrial work – hosiery-, shoe- and glove-making. The more intelligent ones learned to become electricians or clerks. All of them attended literacy classes and learned to read and write.'

Simultaneously, the women were 're-educated'. They had to see that their previous life had not only been bad for them but for their country. They had to join criticism-and-self-criticism sessions, reveal every detail of their past behaviour in order to get the evil of it out of their system and, by doing so, realize that in their new, purer life they would come 'to believe in the motherland and see the damage that their former way of life had done to the health and moral welfare of the citizens'.

In translation, at least, this sounded sent, entious and 'holier than thou'; I bridled a little. Surely, it was obvious that many of them had taken to their prostitution only to save themselves from starvation. But I bridled too soon, because by this time Mrs Chen had begun to change her manner as statistics gave way to personal stories, and she spoke, now, with a depth of feeling that revealed a humanity and compassion which her dry manner had at first belied.

During the various civil wars and the Japanese occupation,

when peasants and workers were starving, a daughter was an extra mouth to feed and many parents sold them to the agents of brothel-keepers who toured streets and villages looking for girls. Sometimes these men represented themselves as factory-owners wanting textile workers and got the unfortunate girls to make their mark on what they thought a contract for a job as a weaver, only to find the truth of their situation when they reached the house of ill-fame itself. A few such houses specialized in providing bed-mates of very tender years for the Humbert Humberts of Shanghai.

Dymphna Cusack, with whom I have discussed this account at length, assures me Mrs Chen exaggerated not a whit, as she herself spent weeks talking with the prostitutes themselves about their experiences. With her permission I quote from her book, *Chinese Women Speak*.

'My value,' one of them told her, 'when my father sold me, was a picul of rice for each year of my age.' (A picul is about fifty kilogrammes.) 'Once there I had to receive customers no matter how I felt. Once I was pregnant so the brothel-keeper gave me medicine to bring on an abortion; after a week I was forced back to work, where, sometimes, I had to receive twenty men a night and often was given drugs to keep me going.'

Utterly absorbed in re-living her experiences, Mrs Chen continued, 'For those who had been cheated into prostitution the most important thing, once they were well, was to restore their self-respect. They would tell me over and over again that they were outcasts; that it was foolish to talk of them as of value to the motherland. Many of them were sullen at first because they believed that we, too, were going to cheat them in some way. When they went into the VD hospitals they screamed as the doctor approached, believing his hypodermic syringe or medicines were to be used to drug or even kill them. I cannot tell you,' she said simply, 'the misery I saw in those first terrible months.'

She then went on to describe how they had recruited women of experience and understanding to go back to the girls' villages and find the parents. Often the girls themselves refused to return because they knew their parents would be too ashamed to let them live in their old home. It was the job of the older women to re-educate (the word again) the parents and make them see that the girls had suffered, often through no fault of their own, but they were now to be good children to their parents and good citizens of the New China; they must not be despised and rejected. The humanity, the imaginative grasp of this particular aspect of the whole rehabilitation plan especially impressed me. I had seen enough of those primitive villages to envisage the earnest, dedicated Communist women in the rice-paddies or outside the shabby huts, patiently, hour after hour, persuading the sorrowing but outraged peasant father or mother that in the New China everyone, even prostitutes, could live again; their daughter must come home.

After the inescapable emotionalism of stories such as these, it was something of a relief when Mrs Chen commented in a sensible matter-of-fact way that, of course, quite a lot of the prostitutes did not want to give up their old life, especially the expensive and successful ones or those with their own flats as kept women of wealthy businessmen. They were reminded briskly that their sort of success was short-lived; once in their thirties they would be less prosperous. Again, it was persuasion rather than force that was used. When these girls were prised loose from their 'profession' and sent off to the training centres they were helped to accept the move when they found that some of their ornaments and possessions had been brought to their new quarters: another imaginative touch.

Even so, Mrs Chen frankly admitted, many girls slipped back to the old trade and had to be brought back to the centre and, though the last brothel closed in 1951, casual prostitution continued for a good long time after that. Besides getting the reformed women steady jobs, the Welfare Committee tried also to get them a husband, by arranging social gatherings and putting them to work in factories with men workers alongside. I was grateful for the complete lack of sentimentality she had shown; any note of false pathos would have been more than dissonant.

Mrs Chen finished on a factual note (as she had started). The average period of readjustment was two years. After this they went off parole if they were (a) in good health, (b) ideologically sound, (c) self supporting.

She added a postscript: 'Of course, there were many children also to deal with and we did this in three ways. First, we established a school at the training centre for children over six years old; next, we sent children under this age to nurseries or kindergartens in the area; finally, we arranged for any young baby with a healthy mother to stay with her and special arrangements were made to help her rear the child well.'

Not at all to our surprise, Mrs Chen in conclusion informed us that the training centres had their own committee, known as the Governing Committee for Democratic Liberty, with several sub-committees for sanitation (inevitably), production and living conditions.

Though it was on this matter-of-fact note that the long story ended, I felt emotionally wrung-out by all that had preceded it, and as we rose to leave I could not easily produce the usual smile and thank you. I was thinking of the young women I had met in Shanghai – the twenty-year-old beautifully executing her morning exercises on the Bund; the pigtailed tea-girl in the train, the sales-girls laughing gently at my too-large feet, the excited students at the Opera School; all these might in the old days have had to experience the horrors of enforced prostitution; one of them may even have done so; after all, thousands of prostitutes had been absorbed in the community since 1950. Now they were free of the shadow.

The breadth of the whole scheme, the tenacity of its organizers amazed me, but the imagination moved me even more. China is an authoritarian state, a land of slogans, a country where the individual must fit carefully into his place in the complex national pattern of living, but, even so, what had, in the last instance, carried through one of the world's greatest social reforms was, quite simply, human goodness.

Mrs Chen, her businesslike manner resumed, saw us off with
178 her limited smile; I felt I had met a great woman.

20 · CHURCH-GOING
The First Congregation

High above the surrounding trees and houses two tall, graceful, unmistakably ecclesiastical towers came into sight as we approached the Roman Catholic Cathedral, early – too early for me – on the Sunday morning of our stay in Shanghai.

We hoped, even in the one day, to record on film and tape as honest an impression as we could of the situation of Christians – clergy and laity – under an atheist government.

At 7.30 the Mass had been in progress for two hours as I slipped into the back pew, recorder quietly turning. The Ziccawei Cathedral, as it is called, is a very large, pseudo-gothic building so European that it seemed odd to find only Chinese worshippers there. These were moving in and out, genuflecting and crossing themselves; children wandered, unaccompanied, up and down the aisles. Most of the congregation were well over middle age, but a few were in their twenties and thirties. It was hard to assess the number of people attending Mass that morning for the service lasted from 5.30 a.m. to 10.30 or 11 a.m., we understood.

A priest, almost invisible, intoned in the shadows of the distant altar, the congregation responding firmly – whether in Latin or Chinese I could not at first tell. Shi-hwa, sitting beside me experiencing her first contact with Christianity, was listening and watching, with eyes wide with surprise, just as I would have watched a tribal rite – which is pretty well what the service was to her! I discovered, when we were outside again, that she knew very little about the life or teaching of Christ. At first, I was taken aback that an intelligent, highly-educated girl like her was so ignorant of comparative religion, but I had, after the usual self-examination, to withdraw my censure when I recalled that there were in China only some three and a half million Christians, a fraction of one per cent of the population, that there had been no missionaries in China for fifteen years and that a young English graduate may have known no more about Buddha or Mahomet. On the way out we paused at the Confessional.

'What is that big box?' asked Shi-hwa, by now really curious. I tried, as an Anglican, to explain the significance of the Confessional in the Roman Church. A sudden thought struck me.

'It's a sort of criticism-and-self-criticism session,' I said seriously, finding the comparison strangely apt, 'and the Priest helps you to do better in the future'.

'How can he help you?'

I didn't feel equipped to answer that one. As when I discussed democratic Western government with her and Mei-lang at the Mill, I experienced the extraordinary difficulty of explaining Western beliefs, briefly, to people wholly without our democratic or religious traditions.

As I dodged the second question I devoutly hoped that Shi-hwa's curiosity was not sufficiently aroused to ask me the difference between the beliefs of this congregation and the Anglican one which we were to visit next.

After the service we talked at the great entrance door with two or three clergy, and a plump and prosperous layman, who spoke excellent English. Then two Priests, the Bishop's Secretary, middle-aged Chen Fui-ming, and a younger one, Shen Pai-chin, led us through a walled garden into a sunny room in the Presbytery, where, over cups of tea, they answered my searching questions with a fluency and conviction which showed they had dealt with them before. The Crucifix on one wall faced a large portrait of Mao on the opposite one.

The Party is very well aware that, small as the Christian Church is, it is none the less significant in the eyes of the Christian West, attracting an attention wholly disproportionate to its numbers. Here again the complexity, even ambivalence, of Chinese attitudes is illustrated. Visitors are assured that China regards herself as self-reliant almost self-supporting, yet she seems to want Western visitors to think well of her treatment of Christians and to have the Christians express their own belief in their welfare in the new society; so that all the clergy we spoke with that morning – as well as Bishop Ting of Nanking and others I had met previously in Peking – were prepared to give us much time, attention and reassurance.

It is impossible for a Westerner to understand how, in mind

and heart, the little band of Chinese pilgrims really regard their lot today. One can only record that the clergy are seemingly cheerful, certainly active, moving around freely, represented even on the Provincial and National Congresses. They staunchly declare their freedom to worship and teach at least in their churches, though they cannot evangelize outside those. Article 88 of the Constitution guarantees complete religious freedom, and all the clergy give loyalty to a government they consider to be restoring the country's national glory and international standing. (Bishop Ting, however, had assured me that no Christian could become a member of the Party; the creeds were mutually exclusive though not at enmity.)

Chen was a thin, intense man with fever-bright eyes, who nervously entwined thin hands as he spoke; he had an air of tension but never of hesitation. His companion, Shen Pai-chin, was plumper, more relaxed, with the famous 'inscrutable' smile so beloved of popular novelists writing pseudo-Chinese tales.

I had learned something of the Protestant attitude from Bishop Ting but was ignorant as to how the Roman Catholics could reconcile allegiance to the Pope and to Mao; to the Vatican and to the Party. So my first question was, simply, what is the relation between Church and State? Chen began on an almost vehement note.

'The freedom which our Church enjoys must be stressed. This at first, surprised us, for we had heard that when the Communists took Shanghai the churches would be burnt and the priests killed. You see, I and Shen Pai-chin have lived safely! The constitution guarantees religious freedom.'

'But surely many missionaries and priests fared worse than you?'

'In the early days there was some trouble for priests thought to have taken part in counter-revolutionary activities. These were the ones who were controlled by the foreign imperialists, who had supported the Church as an instrument of Western influence, and who, when the new Government came, expected all the clergy to plot against it. Clearly, the new Government 181 could not permit subversion; but even during this period many of us continued to hold Mass and offer religious rites to our people. The counter-revolutionaries were arrested and expelled or some of them fled with the traitor, Chiang Kai-shek. Now there is no suspicion of us Catholics, for we admit that the Government has won the support of the broad mass of the people of all faiths.'

When I asked how he could be sure that some of his fellows had been 'controlled by imperialists' he took a deep breath and, for more than ten minutes, produced what he insisted was irrefutable evidence of the subversive activities of some Western Catholics. He assured us that the American Bishop Walsh had been engaged in sending reports on China via the Central Bureau of the Roman Catholic Church. 'A secret news agency,' he said, 'was established to collect any detail of information likely to be of use to Western intelligence services; these were especially active during the Korean war.' He paused and concluded, rather fiercely, 'Catholics were asked to fight against the Communist Government, the People's Liberation Army and the Motherland.'*

In an undisturbed tone, smoothly, Shen Pai-chin added, 'We could not work in patriotic associations and had to oppose the policy of land-reform – for the church itself owned many properties. We could not easily fight the Japanese, even, without seeming to support the Communists and run the risk of excommunication.'

'You now work with the Government, can you also work with the Vatican?'

Either through a certain bafflement in Shi-hwa's untheological mind or from confusion as she translated I was unable to get a wholly clear note on Shen's answer. According to Edgar Snow, and one or two Australian visitors, the church can accept doctrinal rulings from Rome, but no others. To this

---

* In *The Other Side of the River* Edgar Snow writes of a conversation he had with Father Chen Fu-ming about Bishop Walsh, and in an Appendix he gives a report from the US State Department on American prisoners in China which includes Bishop Walsh.

extent the Church is not, strictly speaking, excommunicate; but Shen seemed to say that it was impossible to distinguish between doctrinal and political instruction, and, in any case, even had they wanted doctrinal guidance the Pope would not have sent it. I gathered he considered himself excommunicate.

'The Vatican has slandered our Church,' he said. 'It said we are a people living in darkness, a "voiceless church". It has sent three encyclicals expressly forbidding any co-operation with our Government. How can we live like this? How can we live? Our people need their Mass – they need the sacraments of their church. We are God's priests, we must minister to our flock. But no Government can have a church that plots against it; that plans counter-revolution! Pope John called us a "heretical church". We are not; we are faithful to the true Catholic doctrine.'

I was moved by Chen's passionate exposition of the dilemma of his faith; thousands of devout Catholics must suffer as he does, torn between God and country; rejected by their spiritual father on earth; tolerated, perhaps as an anachronism, by a Government frankly atheist in all its thinking.

'Ye cannot serve God and Mammon,' says Rome.

'I must render unto Caesar,' replies the Roman Catholic in China.

The conflict is irreconcilable; it will be Shen's and Chen's for life.

We walked around the garden, cooling off by talking of flowers, but I was not very cheerful; man's misunderstanding of man saddened me. I recalled an interesting remark of Chou En-lai.

'We Communists are atheists, but we respect all those who have religious beliefs. We hope those with religious beliefs will also respect those without.'

We reached the Anglican Cathedral – a smaller but still substantial building, set among trees with a solid four-square, English parish-church tower; this, I was told, had been repaired by a grant from the Government, which regarded the 183

Cathedral, like the Wuhan Buddhist Temple, as a national monument worthy of preservation.

The church was nearly full and as I peeped in an English-speaking deaconess spotted me and pressed me to sit down, but we had an appointment at the Community Church so, churlishly, I had to rush away.

21 · CHURCH-GOING
The Second Congregation

The Community Church is a less pretentious building than the other two, but its red brick and grey stone, creeper-covered, are very pleasing. The adjoining residential unit, which houses some clergy and all social activities, stands in a walled garden looking disconcertingly like Ridley College, Cambridge.

I entered the church, where the organ was giving a lusty introit to the hymn 'Thou Art the Way' and, as the congregation rose to sing, equally lustily, I slipped into a back pew and found myself joining in, the words coming unbidden though I had not uttered them for years:

> '. . . by Thee alone
> From sin and death we flee
> And he who would the Father seek
> Must seek Him, Lord, by Thee.'

Everyone was singing in Chinese and the volume of sound swamped my alien accents. Looking around I saw the church was crowded and that I had been tucked into a pew already holding its quota; down the aisles and at the back extra chairs had been placed to accommodate worshippers; young and old, poorly-dressed or well-dressed – never richly-dressed – they were singing in full voice. The altar, pulpit, pews, the matting down the aisles, the board with hymn-numbers all looked familiar to me; the two officiating clergy in their white surplices, black cassocks and academic hoods were, at a distance, indistinguishable from Western clergy.

As so often in China, the whole scene seemed not quite real to me. Here I was, joining these Chinese Christians in the same religious rituals as in my Parish Church on the Yorkshire moors or in the vaulted glories of King's College Chapel; yet this time we sang, a little band of pilgrims, among millions of Communist unbelievers.

After the sermon came the organ voluntary whilst the offering was taken; then, most familiar, 'Oh God, our Help in Ages Past' before we slowly left the building. The clergy stood at the door, shaking hands, exchanging greetings and news with their flock in an atmosphere of great cordiality.

The Community Church was an American Protestant foundation which today serves the major nonconformist sects and works closely with the Anglican Church.

After the congregation had dispersed we were joined by the two clergy, both youngish: the preacher, Mr C. W. Lee and his colleague, Mr Y. F. Shen, as well as a second Mr Lee, who is secretary-general of the Shanghai YMCA. All had lived and worked overseas and spoke perfect English, so we needed no interpreters. All had returned to China to serve their religion since the Revolution. Seeming wholly at their ease and pleased to see us, the clergy and Mr Lee led us through the garden to the residence, where, for more than an hour, the sequence was – our question, their answer, joint discussion.

The story they told us that sunny Sunday morning in Shanghai was the same as that of Bishop Ting and the clergy I had met in Peking in 1958. Mr C. W. Lee started:

> The Christian Church has always seemed to have an unfortunate association with Western wars and big business. The Opium War treaty had included clauses not only ceding territory and trading rights, but also specifically granting the entry of missionaries and the rights of church teaching; this showed that political power and religion were bracketed in the Western attitude to China. Therefore the missionaries could not be disinterested. They could not help identifying themselves with Western attitudes and interests. For example, the famous Peking Union Medical College provided many of the leaders of old China; these came back from education in Europe or the United States ready to work according to their interests. The president of that college wrote, 'If you invest two million dollars in the army of the KMT you may lose it; you will not if you invest it in potential leaders now in the colleges.' In this very church, in 1946, the President of the Union Seminary in New York declared, at a time when the KMT were ready to start a civil war against the Communists, 'The issue in China must be settled by force. The frontier of the

United States of America is in Northern China, where the KMT is fighting.' The churches were inextricably bound up with US foreign policy. Overseas, some Missionary Boards met to decide how best to fight Communist aggression in China; this was interference in our national affairs, but even the best missionaries could not see why they should not do this.

I wanted to point out that most missionaries had opposed Communism for religious, not political, reasons and that many had given selfless service.

If I had, I think I would have been told that whatever the motive the results were the same; even the best of the missionaries were the unconscious agents of Western interests trying to maintain a hopelessly outworn and inequitable social system. Instead I asked, 'What happened to foreign missionaries?'

'They knew they could not find a place in the New China and some left of their own accord. Others were recalled; the only ones imprisoned or punished were those who were suspected of counter-revolution or espionage. Many of the Roman Catholic clergy suffered because they resisted land reforms when their properties were threatened.'

'What would happen if a missionary wanted to return today?'

'We welcome them as visitors – an Australian group came in 1957, you remember; if one applied to return permanently the Church would discuss the idea with the Government; but he would probably be refused as he might be a spy.'

At least here no words were being minced!

Then they explained the Three-Self Movement, which aimed at making the Christian Church a wholly Chinese institution by insisting on self-government, self-financing, self-propagation. No more money or guidance of any kind must come from overseas and teaching must be done by Chinese churchmen and only in the church and home. They stressed that this independence had revivified their Church – brought strength and confidence. (I recalled that Marshal Chen Yi and Mr Liu had made the same 187 point, in the economic context – strength through independence.)

Gesticulating and speaking fast and with feeling, Mr YMCA Lee again took over. 'Don't you see, before, people were often Christians for what they got out of the Westerners, "rice-Christians"; in return they had to conform to their ideas, adapt themselves to non-Chinese ways, sometimes; they often went to church because, in some way, it paid them to do so. Now people come to this church because they want to – they have no axe to grind, no "right people" to meet any more. They come for fellowship and Christian counsel. Once we were called in Chinese "eaters of the foreign religion", now we are called "Believers in Jesus Christ" and that is what we want.'

We moved slowly out into the sunshine, still talking, and the session ended, as it had begun, at Ziccawei, with the general problem of religious sects in a Communist country – except that none of these men admitted that there was a problem; indeed, they insisted that there could not be, by the nature of Communist belief and Government policy – in China, at least.

'It is because the Party is atheist that they do not object to any believers practising their faith; they do not wish to exterminate us as another religious body might wish to do, as, for example, Christians and Moslems, Roman Catholics and Protestants, did in the past.'

The other Mr Lee took up the narrative. 'They are realists and materialists, but they believe that religion cannot be eradicated overnight, so the simplest thing is to allow religious freedom. The Party is frank with us – it does not care about us as long as what we preach is not subversive. When you think about it, this makes things easier for us than for an "established" Church, where the state is more closely bound up with it. Then the Church can be exploited and dominated by the establishment. [Mr Lee didn't use that word but it expresses what he meant, I am sure.] An indifferent government is no bad thing for a church.'

'One thing that saddens me very much,' added Mr Shen, 188 the gentlest and least vocal of the three, 'is the attitude of our fellow-Christians overseas, even those who were once our friends and colleagues. They repudiate us, even malign us and, as you may know, we are not members of the World Council of Churches at whose last conference we had no voice at all. Yet we do Christ's work as before; we minister to His servants here. We need their prayers and friendship; tell them about us when you return.'*

Whatever I had thought about some of the other statements during our interview, I felt that here was a cry from the heart, an honest man's distress at a *trahison des clercs* and, as so often before, I felt myself sharing the distress of those travelled or Western-educated Chinese, Christian or non-Christian, who cried out for a greater effort of understanding by those former friends 'on the other side of the river'.

The two Mr Lees and Mr Shen bade us good-bye with cheerful smiles and good wishes for our journey home and greetings to any Australian churchmen whom they had met. I looked back at them waving from the gateway and, as I moved off into the great, unbelieving world of Shanghai, I was impressed by the courage of so tiny a band of the faithful. I could not wholly understand them nor could I then check the details of their carefully worked out case, but I could and did admire them in their isolation.†

* I find that the Chinese Church resigned from the World Council in protest against some members' support for the Korean war. There has been no official move since then but a member of the Australian Council of Churches tells me he believes Chinese initiative would be welcomed by many Churches.

† I have since checked on 'missionary-policy' in China; there is some evidence to support the general contentions of the Protestant clergy. For a brief survey of some of the primary sources I refer readers to Chapter I of Felix Greene's *Curtain of Ignorance* (Doubleday, 1964); C. P. Fitzgerald's *Flood Tide in China* is a valuable reference; and two good books by missionaries are *Through the Chinese Revolution* by Dr and Mrs Ralph Lapwood and *Five Stars Over China* by Mrs M. A. Endicott. In *The Crippled Tree* (Cape, 1965) Han Suyin gives a first-hand account of the attitudes of missionaries in her native province.

It is very convenient for China International Travel Service that Hangchow, one of the most beautiful holiday resorts in China, in the world even, is obligingly *en route* from Shanghai to Canton, so that after the crowded programmes of the great cities visitors can draw breath in this most lovely spot.

We travelled from Shanghai by train and drove from Hangchow railway station along the road skirting the West Lake, mountains rising on every horizon, cypress-covered, pagoda-crowned, the blue lake dotted with wooded islets. Nature has here been prodigal, and for centuries man has striven with taste and skill to improve on her gifts, providing pavilions and parks on the islands, carved and painted bridges between them and, on the coppices and clefts of the hillsides, he has fashioned fishpools, fountains and grottoes. Then, everywhere, in and around the city, the Buddhist faithful have, dynasty by dynasty, erected temples, splendid in design and colour, lavish in ornamentation, filled with paintings, carvings, holy effigies and the occasional grotesqueries of artists' imagination at play.

Built with superb views of mountain and lake, the hotel is modern and very large indeed, with corridors as long as sprinting tracks and a vast dining-room; its food is very good. On arrival there we were given an excellent guide book and told we were to have a day's sightseeing before setting off to survey the commune where we were to film 'Commune Day'.

Looking at the book, we found it extremely hard to choose where to go, for every name seemed to demand a visit. The Mountain of the Snakelike Evening Clouds, the Ravine of Nine Creeks and Eighteen Brooks, the Park of Orioles Singing in the Willows, the Temple of the Autumn Moon in the Calm Lake, the Hill of Precious Stone, the Cave that Leads to the Sky and, perhaps most alluring of all, the Peak that Flew from Afar. 'The Pearl Fountain,' we read, 'is so called because the water bubbles up in pearl-like drops when the visitor stamps upon the ground near it.' And the Tiger Spring was discovered when 'two thirsty tigers, in very ancient times, dug and dug until water bubbled out of the ground'. The writer pleasingly adds, 'Visitors like to take Lung Chin tea made from the spring water.' The

Pagoda of Six Harmonies was planned as a distinctly multi-purpose shrine, for it was not only to hold the Shih Li, the bones of Buddha, but to carry a lamp as a guide for boats and to hold back flood-tides by its magic influence.

We finally settled on a visit to the largest and most spectacular shrine, the Lin Yin Temple. Built in the fourth century, alternately neglected and restored through the years, it has received its latest and most thorough restoration since the Revolution. Climbing up steep, twisting, well-kept paths among the trees and streams, we came to it.

The temple stands at the top of a broad, shallow, flight of steps; divided by a central slab of elaborately-carved marble, they lead to a flagged terrace with great brass incense-burners and flowering shrubs in brass pots. The triple-tiered façade is painted carmine red and has high doors of fretted wood; the sloping roofs are of shining amber tiles. The hall is thirty-six yards long and dominated by a superb sixty-foot image of Buddha made of camphor wood covered with red-gold iridescent lacquer. A dozen larger-than-life images of disciples are ranged on either side; this is impressive enough in all conscience, but our breath was really taken away when we moved to the other side of the screen behind the giant figure; here is 'Fairy Island' with three-dimensional tableaux in fantastic confusion; animals, real and mythical; a fat, grinning Buddha rides on a huge dolphin; other strange creatures appear with whips and snakes, flutes and drums. All these, along with flowers, rocks and trees, completely fill the huge screen. It is not, frankly, in strictly ecclesiastical good taste, but the whole crowded area inescapably reflects the gusto, the immense zest for life its creator must have possessed.

The Lin Yin Temple is only one of many hidden away in these amazing wooded hills; we could have passed days wandering among them, but instead we rushed back to lunch in order to fit in an afternoon's outing on the lake, where similar enchantment awaited us.

There are several new and attractive motor-boats for larger parties, but our boat was a curious vessel propelled from the rear 191

with a punt-like action by a hefty, cheerful wench in patched
trousers and tartan shirt – clan not identifiable – whose muscular arms seemed to make light work of shifting the clumsy boat
and its four passengers. In warm sunshine, fanned by a cool
breeze, we slipped quietly across the lake to one of the several
islands laid out as a park. Completely relaxed, we wandered,
speaking little, through well-laid-out gardens with trim beds of
many shapes. Crossing little bridges, passing grottocs with tink-
ling water, we came to a series of painted wooden platforms
jutting out into the lake; they had rustic-style fencing around
them and a tiny blue- and red-roofed pavilion at the end of each.
This, the deepest part of the lake, has always been known as the
Three Pools Reflecting the Moon. Three bottle-shaped towers,
carefully spaced, rise from the water; the exact date of their
original appearance there is not known but they were refur-
bished by a late Ming Emperor (sixteenth century) and again by
the Communists. Each tower has five round holes and during the
mid-August Festival these are covered with parchment; inside
each tower's hollow top is placed a long-burning candle whose
light shines gently out and is reflected, shimmering golden
in the water. Many boats row out also with lamps and lanterns,
so that the scene is aglimmer with real and reflected light.

It was good to be free for a time, I thought, from Party and
political statistics and social problems, and I was glad that Mr
Yi, our local guide, did not dwell inordinately on the Government's contribution to Hangchow's charms.

After the three towers he led us across the grass, saying with
childlike pleasure, 'Now I will show you something really worth
seeing.' The rectangular pool to which he took us was surrounded by rockeries and rose-bushes; in the depth of the
water faint red-gold patches appeared. Yi, with the air of a
magician, clapped his hands and threw some scraps of food into
the water and immediately the patches shattered into a myriad
splinters as the thousands of goldfish lurking in the depths shot
out; they ranged in colour from deepest red through umber and
orange to amber and primrose; Yi's pride was such that he
might well have caught the creatures himself.

As I watched the fishy mob fiercely fighting for the titbits, I remarked, not unwittily, as I thought, 'They're not good Communists; all that selfish grabbing!' Translated, as a joke it obviously fell flat! It met blank looks from my Chinese companions. With a merry laugh I repeated my comment, adding, feebly, 'The fish have no public spirit.' Still the puzzled look and a request to repeat. Feeling by this time that the remark was one of the silliest I had ever made, I tried again! 'These fish are not good citizens; they are shocking individualists.' Seriously came the answer, 'Ah, but fish are not human beings.'

The Chinese were not affronted; I did not feel I had committed *lèse-majesté*; it was simply that few jokes survive translation; maybe a sense of humour is the last stronghold of national differences.

We were not alone in this rural splendour, for small groups of holiday-makers sat around on the grass or fished from the bridges or banks; children ran races on the grass; families picnicked by the grottoes – but, this being the New China, not one left a scrap of litter in his wake. I was amused to see a young couple holding hands and gazing, lost, into each other's eyes. I had already grown so used to the extreme decorousness of lovers' behaviour that even this show of affection seemed mildly improper. Yi told me, perhaps indulgently, that Hangchow is a favourite honeymoon spot.

On our way back to the boat we entered yet another round pavilion; it had nothing noticeable about it except the stone birds and flowers in the window embrasures. These were exquisitely-carved cranes and plum blossoms silhouetting their shape against the blue of lake and sky in the background. They photographed perfectly and provided some of the loveliest shots in the film. The birds and flowers were chosen to commemorate the poet, Lin Pu, who lived at the foot of Solitary Hill after retiring from the court. Unmarried, he lavished his care on plum trees and pet cranes and so the story was told that he had plum blossom for a wife and a crane for his son! With such uncomplicated relationships ensuring a peaceful life, he wrote by the lakeside until his death in 1028. Characteristically, 193 the guide book tells us that he was dissatisfied with feudal rule; had he supported it I doubt if his memory would be quite so much cherished in Hangchow today, however good his poetry.

'In winter,' adds the book poetically, 'the plum flowers are in full bloom; red as fire, white as snow, they fill the cold air with their sweet scent.' I recalled and approved the famous proverb: 'There's heaven above and Hangchow and Soochow below.' It is a pity that such an idyllic afternoon should have ended in the most acrimonious argument I had during my visit – and with the seemingly gentle Yi, the goldfish lover.

In China politics are always breaking in, as they did on the return trip through some chance remark of mine. I have forgotten what it was but it sparked off a speech from Yi which revealed him as a doctrinaire Party line man some of whose ideas on the West were as rigid as they were inaccurate. I came back at him and a ding-dong verbal skirmish followed in which he produced ready-made opinions with an air of gentle, tolerant infallibility which thoroughly needled me.

This is, more or less, how it went:

Yi. Force will be needed to free many neo-colonialist countries from the continuing grip of Western capitalists.

Me. Well, India, for example, is certainly not in Britain's grip and we are now getting out of the last of our African possessions.

Yi. The workers are everywhere exploited by the bourgeois capitalists and are ready for revolution.

Me. The Australian working man would open his eyes at that! He's doing pretty well for himself! Most of them have their own house and car. ('Even if not quite paid for, I know I should have added!')

Yi. Lenin said that no exploiting government ever gave up power peaceably.

Me. The English monarchy has been forced to give up power peaceably. There has been no revolt in England

since Wat Tyler. Since then the only person who lost
his head, for political reasons, was King Charles I.
(Except Guy Fawkes, I reminded myself, and that was
really the gunpowder! But what of the Irish martyrs?
I uneasily wondered.) And, remember, Charles wasn't
killed by the peasants or workers in revolt but by the
landed gentry; Britain has won democracy by 'the
parliamentary road', whatever Marxism–Leninism
has to say.

I leaned over to Yi, finger wagging like the traditional scold;
only the skilful poling of the boatwoman saved us from a
ducking.

At this stage, I cannot recall how, the argument shifted to
Japan, which Yi promptly identified in its pre-war form with
Western democracies, both being militaristic. I heatedly denied
any Samurai tradition in England, where the army rarely
attracted the best brains, the most ambitious youth; soldiers
were often laughed at; Colonel Blimp, for example, was a
figure of fun.

'Why do you go on like this? Shut up, for heaven's sake,' I
told myself. But I went on, even though Yi remained unshaken,
which actually made me more vehement, and I did not stop my
propaganda until we reached the shore. Yi courteously helped
me out and I felt ashamed of myself. I had forgotten again the
Asian context, the so-different historical and economic background, unless it is allowed for, makes all comparisons of East
and West invalid. I had forgotten, too, that Yi was only a little
more ignorant of our background than we of his before we came
to China.

I felt suddenly very tired. I had been working hard for weeks
planning the expedition at home, then tramping around after
cameras, asking questions, taking notes, making observations,
joining discussions, and, always, expending nervous energy on
the tight-rope act, balancing along the trembling wire across the
abyss of East–West misunderstanding. But this time I wasn't
trying to see anyone else's point of view – Yi put his stock case, 195

I put mine, regardless. It was not very satisfactory and I don't look back on my behaviour with any pleasure at all.

Yi, I saw, once my anger had cooled, represented some of the lower echelons of the Party with the doctrinaire, bureaucratic approach which, in fairness, it is necessary to point out, is deplored by the Party's leaders and criticized by Mao himself.

The *'cheng feng'* movement (literally translated it means 'evaluate, rectify work-style') was directed against bureaucracy and 'getting into a rut'. Mao's widely-discussed 1957 directive, 'On the Handling of Contradictions among the People', laid emphasis on tendencies to sectarianism and meaningless Party jargon and drew attention to wrong relations between bureaucrats and workers: 'Down with dogmatism, sectarianism and bureaucracy, the three evils.' Elsewhere Mao has written, 'Dogma is more useless than cow-dung.'

Before dinner we managed to fit in a visit to one of the silk factories. On the looms we saw the exquisite elaborately-patterned brocade for which Hangchow is world famous. We moved from design studios to spinning, to weaving, to parasol and fan-making, to workers' amenities; one thing impinged very clearly on my tired mind. One of the minor products of the mill are woven silk pictures; landscapes, temples and portraits of the Communist hierarchy. They rolled off the loom, hundreds of them, one after another in a long piece. At a table girls were separating them – click-click went the shears and I watched, fascinated, as head after head of Joseph Stalin dropped into the waiting basket on the floor; it was a macabre sight, none the less so because the Soviet leader was smiling against a floral background!

23 · THE VILLAGE IN THE VALLEY

Although we were delighted to shoot Ming and Manchu architecture and the Buddhist extravaganzas of Hangchow, none the
less the main concern of our film were 'Peking Day' and
'Commune Day', objectively reflecting the life of the average
city and country dweller – what Australians would call the
'ordinary blokes' in ordinary places. So it was with rather mixed
feelings that we viewed the idyllic beauty of our commune
location in the pale sunshine of the next morning. The village
of Mei Ja Wu, one of eight or nine in the West Lake Commune,
nestled in a valley in the hills near Hangchow and it reminded
me so much of Shangri-La that I almost expected Ronald
Colman to turn up for a retake of the romantic nonsense of *Lost
Horizon*.

Its buildings clustered together at the far end of a wedge-
shaped valley with steep hills, tree-crowned, rising on three
sides. We drove along a bumpy dirt road into a blue-green
world; a large fish-pond reflected both the azure of the sky and
the verdure of the woods; the sharp yellow-green of rice-paddies
glowed beneath the dark green of tea-bushes growing, squat and
stiff, in meticulously-planted rows on terraced hillsides; an
occasional peasant passed by in the perennial blue cotton suit,
faded, patched, but never ragged.

As we moved down the narrowing valley we began to distinguish other colours: grey-brown stone or mud houses, a
red-brick shed; girl tea-pickers wearing multi-coloured blouses,
cartwheel plaited straw hats slung over shoulders, black hair
in a long bob or beribboned pigtails.

Rounding a slight bend we found ourselves in the heart of the
village at the narrow end of the little valley, which was blocked
by a dramatic, sharply-pointed peak; wreathed in wisps of
morning mist and capped by slivers of cloud, it represented a
living replica of Chinese classical landscape painting.

The village itself could have changed little in appearance
over several centuries though it had been tidied up, and, here
and there, extended. The small cottages and the few larger
houses (these presented blind walls to the street and opened on
to courtyards at the back) all had grey-tiled, moss-covered roofs.

One of the larger dwellings had been turned into a clinic, another into an open-fronted shop and a third, the largest, judging by the voices issuing forth, had become a primary school or kindergarten. Though shabby and unpainted, all these were clean and in good repair.

A swift-flowing little stream, cutting its way through the rocks, had worn a steep ravine which split the village into two; it was crossed by a surprisingly elegant bridge with carved stone panels in the sides and six praiseworthy miniatures of the Imperial Palace lions on top. This led, we were told, to the former landlord's property; so it was, presumably, the creation of one of his artistic forebears.

Beneath the bridge the stream had been partly dammed and given a concrete bed to form a large pool for the dozens of fat geese, cackling away like the sentinels on Capitol Hill; their ceaseless din formed a background to all our activities in the village itself; occasionally, they competed with the loudspeaker fixed in the branches of a tree, which blared forth the usual songs, alternating, presumably, with the usual news items and exhortations. It was a noisy intrusion on the quiet of the village but we were told that when it was on it had to be very loud, as the houses at the far side of the village wanted to hear it, too! Fortunately, it was less continuous than the geese.

A few villagers were going about their business (the work-teams were already in the fields). As we crossed the bridge lively chatter broke out by the stream-bed below, punctuated by a series of dull thuds and vigorous splashings; we looked over to find four middle-aged women had just arrived at the stream with the day's laundry and there, in cold water without benefit of soap, they were washing pants and blouses, banging away at them with great wooden sticks on rocks made smooth and hollow through centuries of washerwomen's labours. A little higher up an elderly woman was washing the fish for lunch. A few children paddled alongside, and an aged man drifted past us, smiling, with the vacancy of the very old, at the great-grandchild cradled in his still strong arms.

198   We were met and officially welcomed at this stage by the

brigade leader, who led us at once to the brigade's committee-
and meeting-rooms. We gathered that all the villagers formed
the one brigade. Liu Chen-hau was, by any standards, an impressive person; the more so because he was quite unaware of it.

Shortish, stocky, sun-tanned, he gave an impression of sinewy
physical and moral strength. Still in his early thirties, he had a
boyish air and an open countenance, with a pleasing expression,
combining firmness and friendliness, and a quick smile, at once
mischievous and self-confident. His clothes, faded and shabby
like the peasants' we had seen in the fields, detracted in no way
from his air of gentle authority. Three other members of the
Brigade Council joined us and we walked, chatting about this
and that, to the hall where we were to get down to the facts and
figures of commune life.

The meeting-hall was the main room of what had been the
home of the wealthiest landlord in the district (we were to hear
his story later). It had a stone-flagged floor, painted wooden
ceiling and wide casements opening on to a courtyard gay with
pot-plants and flowering shrubs. It was furnished in wholly
traditional style, with many scrolls, porcelain vases and heavy,
elaborately-carved teak furniture. We sat at a magnificent long
table in arm-chairs so solid they were an effort to move even the
few inches required to sit down and stand up. Tea was immediately served in cups as light as the chairs were heavy. Liu
explained proudly that we were drinking the best tea in China,
for this was the region from which tea had long been sent to the
Imperial household in Peking, the first choice of Emperors of
all dynasties.

Liu gave a gracious little formal welcome 'to friends coming
from afar' – from 'Adaliya', as the Chinese call Australia. He
then began to tell us about the commune in general and his
brigade in particular, speaking fluently and with scant reference
to the notes in his hand. It soon became clear that his fluency
was the result of the complete identification of himself and his
own interests with those of the brigade he led; here was his life
and it was the easiest thing in the world to remember everything
about it.

He told us that the greater part of the commune was given over to tea plantations, with rice and vegetables as subsidiary crops. Fish farming was being developed. This village had a population of 1,102, scattered through 228 households; its 603 able-bodied workers (as Liu described them) were divided into five teams working together under his leadership, just as he worked with the other brigade leaders under the Commune Chief.

'This,' he said disarmingly, in conclusion, 'is not one of the best communes but it is not one of the worst.'

After the statistics Liu began to talk about his own experiences, through them illustrating the lives of millions of his kind and putting into personal terms the growth and character of this, China's greatest social experiment.

He had lived, he began, all his life in this village, as had all his forebears for generations. They had always been desperately poor, ill-fed, ill-clothed and, of course, wholly illiterate. Eighty-five per cent of the land had been owned by five per cent of the population (percentages seem inescapable in China today). He had gone tea-picking with his mother almost as soon as he could walk in order to eke out their scanty income with a few extra yen; his father was an invalid and he and his three brothers usually went hungry to bed. He remembered only three people from the village going to Middle School in Hangchow, all the children of rich peasants; now forty-five attended this school and eight had even gone on to the university – peasants' children these, imagine that!

As so often before, I noticed that one of the measures of the régime's success was its provision of education facilities and I recalled how often in undeveloped countries – including New Guinea – I had found the demand for education second only to the demand for food. Liu said that he himself had been illiterate until the Liberation – when he would have been about sixteen years old – since then by means of part-time classes he had reached senior Middle School standard and was continuing his studies still.

The Kuomintang, he explained, had promised land reform,

but nothing had been effectively achieved, so that when the Communists promised land redistribution, and actually carried it out in the provinces they took over, they naturally won great support. Sure enough, as soon as the Party leaders entered the village in 1949 each family received the land it had worked for the landlord; debts owed to him were cancelled and, as Shi-hwa translated quaintly, 'there was everywhere great rejoicing that, at last, all were free'. But it was soon seen that the plots were too small to be worked profitably, that each family needed to work with the others, so the village organized the mutual-help groups, which soon developed logically into co-operatives; there were twelve in all in this district. 'Date please, Shi-hwa,' I whispered. 'Ask him the year.'

'That was in 1953,' came the answer, 'and these lasted until 1956, when they merged into higher co-operatives and then in 1958 came finally the organization of the commune.'

We gathered that the commune had had growing pains but that these were over and the pattern firmly established. Under the 'General Line of the Communist Party' West Lake Commune managed most of its own business, administration, education, amenities, militia-service and, above all, agricultural planning. Liu then recited, unhesitatingly, comparative figures of the yield per acre of the tea, rice and vegetable acreage since Liberation, showing a steady increase year by year. Tea crops had increased by thirty-five per cent since the commune was formed; rice by forty-six per cent – and both by four hundred per cent since 1949.

They were still very short of mechanical aids; but by this year the commune had acquired one hundred and fifty simple tea-processing machines and ten water pumps each of twelve horse-power; his eyes glowed with pleasure as he told us the amount of labour they saved. In addition every house in the village now had electric light and had been put into a state of good repair. Nobody was hungry or homeless any more and old people were specially looked after.

Ordinary Chinese still love poetry and are encouraged to write poems for wallboards or to be recited at concerts. One old 201 peasant woman in her House of Respect for the Aged had written these lines:

> Although I am old I am ambitious;
> Although I am old I am young in heart;
> If I wish to conquer the sea it will be moved by me;
> If I wish to remove a mountain it will fall down.
> We are so energetic and enthusiastic,
> Because our leadership is correct!

Incomes were below those in the cities but were slowly increasing – again an unfaltering series of figures, of which the most important was that today's income was six times that of 1948; an average household earned sixty-eight yuan a month.* In addition all had a home of some kind, schooling and medical care. They all had holidays, too. This was undreamed of once.

I noticed with interest that Liu often referred to the household rather than the individual. In the main Chinese tradition, though in a very different context, the family is still the unit at the base of the social pyramid.

From the households are created the teams, five or six of these making a brigade, which is often, as in Mei Ja Wu, coterminous with the village. The teams elect representatives to the Brigade Council, which considers all aspects of local affairs, and in turn the Brigade Council sends members to the Commune Council, which is represented on a regional body. At every level contact is kept with the Communist Party and through this comes the link with Peking, the apex of the pyramid of authority. Directives are sent down but recommendations are also sent up, so that the traffic is always two-way; the vast interlocking system of communication is maintained throughout the country and the leaders in Peking keep contact with the people.

To prevent rigid stratification any production-team member could take a complaint direct to the commune leader himself, but Liu made it clear that this rarely happened, because brigade members lived and worked so closely together that suggestions or complaints could be aired and dealt with after full

   * See p. 30.

discussion – more or less on the spot. It made me quite dizzy to contemplate the volume of talk, the gargantuan volume, that such a system envisaged; but nobody was gagged, so long, presumably, as he did not attack the whole system and the Party on which it was based.

'You see,' said Liu earnestly, 'the brigade can tell the commune it is wrong in its directives. Last year the Commune Council, on the recommendation of its Agricultural Committee, told us we must raise one hundred and twenty more pigs and five per cent more tea. We did not think this as sensible as raising one hundred and thirty more pigs and two per cent more tea because we knew our special needs and abilities in our own brigade, so the commune agreed.'

We asked at this juncture, inevitably, if they could refuse to accept the commune ruling.

'No,' said Liu firmly, 'the Commune Council has the final say.'

As he paused for breath someone popped in a question, 'Do you pay income tax?'

Liu explained that the commune paid nine per cent of its income to the State, then allocated twenty per cent for the management and administration of the commune and eleven per cent for reconstruction and development plans. Wages were paid from the remainder. Side-occupations were not taxed. We asked him to expand on this statement and discovered that each peasant had a garden-plot whose produce he could eat or sell; pigs were a side-line for some, and women could keep monies earned from any co-operative efforts they cared to start. (I recalled the women making fireworks in the Canton Commune.) He himself had quite a large garden with especially good fruit trees. (We photographed them later.) Wages, as such, were not fixed but money earned was based on work points. A quota of tea would be worth ten points and payment made accordingly; tea picked above the quota would receive *pro rata* payment. Bonuses and honour awards were given by the commune to star-workers; last year one hundred and twenty-five had been so rewarded in his brigade. He was proud of this record. 203

Someone asked Shi-hwa to try to translate, 'All work and no play makes Jack a dull boy.' She grinned widely and said she'd have a go.

Liu laughed and told us they had pictures three times a month, and that amateur and professional groups provided plays and concerts on holidays and festivals.

'How many holidays?'

'Four days a month for men; six for women.'

His next-door neighbour at the table, a woman, broke in cheerfully asking him not to forget that they had two basket-ball courts and that last year their A team had won the commune tournament. We could watch them practising in the lunch hour that day, she said. China adores basket-ball and has reached, in its usual thorough way, a very high standard indeed among its topline national teams.

Liu explained that everyone had to work hard to advance the economy of the commune, but that they all tried to help anyone who was falling behind in work points because of illness or family trouble. Old people, too, were looked after by the Brigade unless they had a family, which was expected to look after the ageing relatives.

Everything fitted in, everything was logical, planned, organized. It was, in principle, unacceptable to the individualist from the West but yet it did not seem impersonal for 'cheerfulness kept breaking in' – the concern for the old and ailing; the pride in the basket-ball win; the passion for education and, as ever, the friendliness and warmth of our hosts. I found it difficult to assess the commune's achievements as objectively as I should when the people were so kind, the garden so beautiful and the inquisitive children peering through the window so wide-eyed and appealing. Firm judgements can be more easily made in the study from carefully compiled documents when one is not diverted and confused by human behaviour!

24 · 'COMMUNE DAY'
Morning

When our small filming team arrived at the village about eight o'clock next morning there was an air of subdued excitement. Some villagers were at work but the tea-pickers, young women in teens and twenties mostly, were waiting for us by the goose-pond. They usually left at six o'clock but since the light was not then good enough for filming they had been held up for our benefit.

As soon as we climbed out of the cars and John, Feng and Cheng had consulted on sundry technicalities – the major plan of the film had, of course, been made the previous day and in a long evening conference – the cameras began whirring. The girls had put on clean cotton blouses, probably their holiday attire, to celebrate the occasion but otherwise they were dressed as on the previous day. Some wore their large hats, others slung them over their shoulder; all carried on their hip a willow basket over which they stretched their arm as they swung along with a graceful, if slightly lop-sided, gait. As they passed beneath the National Day celebration arch of pine leaves, tinsel and red paper, the whole scene looked picturesque to the point of musical comedy and I expected the marchers to break into the opening chorus.

Once beyond the street they fanned out over the tea-slopes and got down to the day's work quota. Both cameras followed, with Harold and me scrambling up the twisting paths with recorder and notebooks at the ready. We were glad to find our-selves soon beyond reach of the village loudspeaker.

Liu, in well-pressed shirt, moved about among the pickers, having explained that he did this every so often, as much to let them know he was interested as to keep them up to the mark. We climbed up some 1,200 feet – the hill was about 1,500 feet – and then paused at a group of pickers to take close-ups of their action. The girls were picking with two hands, and we watched, admiring their speed and dexterity; their flying fingers plucked the tiny, tender leaves from the low bushes – not a twig was taken – and then dropped the leaves into the basket; the eco-nomy of their movements would have pleased a time-and-motion-study expert.

When we marvelled at the speed of the two girls Liu laughingly admitted that he had brought us to the women who had won bonuses and medals as the champion pickers of the brigade! The older of them was Vice-Director of the brigade. We paused while the champion made a formal speech of welcome to visitors from 'Adaliya'. Harold busily bent over the recorder to catch the faint, sharp twang of the leaf leaving the twig (he bent too far, it seemed, for when we played the tape back that night the noise was thunderous).

One of the girls in the near-distance was singing softly to herself so I asked if they could all sing for our soundtrack. Liu quickly consulted with the nearest girl, who called together the others. Dropping their baskets they all seated themselves under a tall tree – by now the sun was pretty warm – and for a quarter of an hour entertained us with solos, duets and choruses. Shi-hwa discovered for us that they sang several traditional old tea-picking songs – one described the seasonal changes of work – selections from Shao Sing opera, and modern 'uplift' ditties on political and social themes. With the chorus, the 'musical' was complete, and the show was a remarkably good spontaneous effort at my request.

Everybody seemed very happy and I certainly was more relaxed than I had been on the whole trip. After all, the strain was nearly over; we had taken thousands of feet of film, some of it unique, we had permission to take it out of the country in the next two days and here we were recording folk songs with these friendly people on these beautiful tea-slopes. As an extra cause for rejoicing Liu produced a basket of food and drink for our mid-morning break. As we ate hungrily the girls got together and sang for us again. We left them reluctantly and moved across to the 'animal husbandry', as Shi-hwa translated it, telling us that this was almost a new development as there had been little of it before Liberation.

At the farmyard we were met by the brigade Jack Spratt and wife – he tall, thin and dour, she plump and smiling. We were probably the first Europeans he had seen, but he expressed no more emotion than if we were fellow-villagers and watched rather gloomily, as his wife led us proudly to the sow with her litter hard at work sucking in its midday meal. I did not note down Mrs Spratt's figures on the numbers, weight and value of the pigs; I was prepared to believe they had got fatter and more philo-progenitive every year since Liberation! Then to the goats, where Mr Spratt came alive. Thrusting a handful of feed at each of some half a dozen goats, he smiled at them almost as broadly as his wife at the pigs; and certainly, for a goat-fancier, his animals were most appealing, healthy and kempt. They ate the fodder rather disdainfully as he talked to us about them.

The whole farmyard and pens were as clean as pigs' and goats' dwellings could be and the grunts of the pigs along with the sloshing sounds of their guzzling at the trough reproduced themselves amusingly on the tape. We tore ourselves away with a fine semblance of regret before Mr Spratt could take us off to see more goats in another part of the farm.

We set off down the hill towards our next location – the fish-farm at the lake. Feeling almost irresponsible by now, I started down the last stretch at a trot which quickened to a run, and then, slipping and slithering down the last five hundred yards to the road, I landed almost at the feet of a surprised peasant off to join the men for the fishing sequence at the lake. We walked on together, silent, but with occasional smiles and nods to show we wanted to be in some kind of communication though words were denied us.

Shooting the fish-farm sequence gave us the most amusing two hours of the whole expedition. In a sense it was staged for us because at the time of our visit the fish were not quite ready to be caught, but the men were called together to show us what the routine was at the correct time of the year.

Liu, outwardly his unruffled self, but obviously quite excited, took charge, unobtrusively. The great net was carefully examined, being held by some twenty men whilst the inspection was made. A tiny hole or weakness had to be attended to and Liu's advice was sought. There was a quarter of an hour's delay until it was repaired.

The men then entered the water, pants rolled up to the knee, 207 slowly spreading out along the edge of the pond until they had spaced themselves evenly, net in hand; keeping it taut they moved along the shallows at the sides. Suddenly, I called out in surprise, even though I had, of course, known what I was expecting. The first of the fish began to leap out of the water in a gasping, futile effort to escape the all-embracing menace; their shining silver bodies piled up, writhing helplessly, one upon another in an ever-increasing heap as the net enmeshed them. The water splashing beneath the onward march of the men's feet, the tumbling of the fish, made a steady background to the growing excitement as the team, shouting urgent instructions or commenting on the catch, strode slowly on.

I began to run around the edge of the lake recording water-noises and getting as close as possible to the fish; then plomp – in I went up to my ankles in the mud! Two of the fishermen rushed over to help me, not a smile on their concerned faces, and only when I recovered enough to burst into laughter at my plight did they show any amusement; my laughter struck the note and guffaws spread through the company. It was all tremendously good fun, I thought, wiping my shoes and washing my feet in the water.

The men sorted out the catch, carefully throwing back fish beneath a certain size. With his usual, quiet efficiency Liu told me that the baby fish, some two inches or three inches long, went in during January and were fed chiefly on grass and soya bean husk. After a year they weighed about one and a half to two kilos, after two years three to four kilos. There was another pond and both were looked after by one peasant, who checked for disease and water impurities. The fish were sold at a low price to the villagers and were not regarded as a commercial product.

Leaving the men to collect and dry the nets and return to their day's proper work, we crossed over to a small but especially fertile-looking rice-paddy. On closer inspection, we found that this contained several little boards with numbers on them. This, Liu pointed out, was their experimental plot and the boards recorded yields and quality; both were improving annually.

One of the best of the Commune Day shots was of Liu, cartwheel hat on his head, waist-deep in the rice, holding up a great sheaf to show us its specially fine ears.

Then we went off to lunch, calling briefly, *en route*, at the tea-processing sheds, one of the few new buildings in the village. Men and women sat stirring the leaves (after they had been dried in the sun) in slowly-revolving metal bowls made bright by constant friction. This process, I gathered, removed twigs and impurities. Simple mechanization was now almost complete, we were told by the shed-supervisor.

The morning's work had gone so well that we were all feeling pleased with ourselves and very much part of a team, so it was with real camaraderie that we sat down to lunch in a sort of back courtyard at the Brigade Headquarters. Here we were joined by the commune leader – a former peasant from the next village.

A refectory-style table was set ready for us with bowls and chopsticks. The meal was generously planned and very well cooked and every course came from the brigade's land – the cigarettes being the only exception.

We had fish with a subtly-flavoured, sweet-sour sauce; pork (Mrs Spratt must have been grieved over that pig) with walnuts; beggar's chicken, a speciality of the district; a delicious clear soup and, finally (from one of Liu's own trees), a great platter of red-gold persimmons, dripping with juice as we ate them.

As we shifted our chairs away from the table to sit back in more comfort after the Lucullan banquet, the old woman and young girl waiting on us brought six pots of tea and several cups each. As we looked up in surprise Liu told us that he had asked for their six finest teas to be prepared so that we could taste them all, and decide for ourselves which was the very best tea in China.

The task of selection, difficult enough for connoisseurs, was impossible for us, but we went through all the motions of tasting and rolling on the tongue and passing comment just for fun and to please our beaming hosts. The choicest of all, it turned out, 209 was a large-leafed, green variety which made a pale primrose-coloured brew. Harold took a coloured photograph in close-up just for the record.

Since Liu was to 'star' in the second part of our film, I wanted to fill out a sketch of his life-story which he had given us that morning. In the post-prandial glow he seemed sufficiently to have accepted us as well-meaning people for me to pluck up courage and ask him to tell us about himself.

It was a tale of suffering and triumph typical of millions of his peasant contemporaries. He told it with feeling but without rancour. He was born in 1933 and the Japanese occupied the area in 1936 so that all his early years had been shadowed by war; food was scarce, life was cheap and school out of the question. His father had died when Liu was nine years old, worn out by overwork and under-nourishment. During his last illness the family had borrowed from the landlord sixty silver yuan for which, after a couple of years, he demanded one hundred and twelve yuan. When Liu's mother said she could not pay he demanded, instead, a piece of their land worth far more than this sum. When his mother protested vigorously they had an argument, in the course of which he seized a stone and flung it at her. She died soon after as a result of the injury.

Liu's voice, and Shi-hwa's, were non-committal, undramatic, free of self-pity, but the depth of Liu's emotions was communicated to me very powerfully even through the language barrier. 'After that,' translated Shi-hwa, 'Liu and his brothers and sisters had a very poor life, like beggars.'

For a second, I wondered if the characters were overdrawn, then I recalled that the derelict condition of the Chinese peasantry has often been impartially recorded, and my shadow of a mean doubt was routed.

'When things were at their worst the Communist army arrived,' Shi-hwa continued, 'and immediately began redistributing the land and organizing the village.' As soon as he was eligible Liu joined the Party himself.

After a pause to allow the unspoken tension to be dissipated I asked Liu what had happened to this and other landlords and rich peasants. Liu explained that, when the fighting was over and the Communist armies were in charge, they rounded up the landlords but did not kill them out of hand. Public trials were arranged when the peasants could make their case against any of them. The landlord who had been responsible for his mother's death was shot after his trial as many others had suffered from his greed and wickedness; rich peasants and landlords who had exploited less cruelly had not been shot but allowed to work out their punishment on the co-operative farm. Both received their share of the redistributed land and indeed one was now part of Liu's brigade and working very well. He had been 're-educated and now realized the importance of combining with the masses under the leadership of the Party'.

Liu had used until now, little jargon and, though this seemed a hackneyed note on which to finish such a tragic, yet triumphant, story, I realized that after all that Liu had suffered in his short life, he was sincerely paying tribute to a government which he served with gratitude.

I congratulated him on the flourishing condition of his brigade and then asked what he most wanted for it. He looked at me with his wide smile, and said, 'That's an easy one; I want a truck and a new building for the primary school.' He was confident that within two years or less they would have both. They deserve them.

When I returned in 1965, there across the bridge, bright in the spring sunshine, was the new Primary School of white stucco. A triumphant Liu had all the facts ready. The estimated cost had been 75,000 yuan, but so much voluntary work had been given that the final cost was only 30,000 yuan. There were six classrooms, two laboratories and three activity rooms (for hobbies, art and music), as well as a clinic, offices and staff rooms. There were three classrooms in reserve for the increased numbers of the next few years. At present there were two hundred and forty children. He showed me proudly a Chinese-made harmonium in the music-room.

As for the truck – they were half-way to buying it.

During the afternoon John and I hoped between us to cover the social aspects of the commune, so whilst he went off to shoot Liu's house and the clinic, I was to be allowed to take Cheng and 'do' education and culture.

Cheng had happily agreed to let me direct the schools sequence and promised to let me have a free hand, proffering only technical advice as the man with the camera.

I was quite elated as we set off down the street for the group of dwellings that housed a nursery, kindergarten and primary school. Shi-hwa was with John, as Cheng had enough English to understand my needs and instructions. *En route* we passed the little shop so I paused long enough to make a note of some prices. A man's woven vest cost 4 yuan, canvas shoes 2 yuan, washbowls 3 yuan, cotton curtaining (1 metre wide) 2 yuan per metre.

When we reached the basket-ball court, where two teams – one in blue, one in red jerseys – were just warming up for a game, Cheng's brisk walk slowed to a saunter and his eyes kindled, so I said in slow, basic English, 'We stay-watch; film basket-ball.'

'Yes, yes, basket-ball film well.'

So down the bank we went to the dirt court to join the small crowd of spectators, women, children and a few men. The blue jerseys were the A Team, the inter-brigade winners, and the red jerseys the B Team; both got extra time off during the lunch-break to practise. They played a fast game with the intense concentration and formidable energy that characterizes the youth of the New China.

Cheng was in his element and was taking shots from all angles. I knew we could never use so much film and, though I did not grudge him the footage, I was a little concerned lest there should not be enough film left to do justice to my precious education section. At last the teams paused. I met them, shook hands with captains, mimed congratulations and steered away the fascinated Cheng down the path, over the bridge to the kindergarten.

This was in the smaller of the two courtyard buildings and we passed through the gateway in the whitewashed wall to find ourselves amongst some fifteen or twenty children, rushing about after balls, playing with wooden bricks or busy at a round-game. Each wore long bright pants, sandals and a white cotton pinafore with an embroidered animal.

Teacher, instantly alert, was determined that her pupils would do her justice, so, clapping her hands like teachers the world over, she immediately stopped their play and lined them up in a stiff, straight line.

'Tell children – play – not stand still,' I said to Cheng, who did not quite grasp the point. So I seized a ball, bounced it, ran after it; seized a child and danced a few steps; waved my hands to the others and got them moving with me.

'Play, play,' I cried out to Cheng. My antics were at least informative, for teacher suddenly disappeared and returned with, to my surprise, two large, inflatable rubber animals – they seemed rather expensive and elaborate for that simple little kindergarten. Squealing with delight, the children rushed forward to seize them and the two lucky ones were surrounded by envious would-be blowers-up. Cheng got some attractive studies of a boy and girl puffing away, though it took them some time to get the toys thoroughly distended as they kept breaking off to watch the camera, allowing the deflated beasties to shudder to the ground.

After this I played ball with them for a few minutes and then they all sat on the shallow steps outside the one big room that was their classroom, and sang for us. The first song, gentle and sweet, was obviously a lullaby, for as they sang the children cradled a baby in their arms, shut their eyes, rested head on hands and finally dropped chin on chest to indicate slumber. Then came a more rousing ditty which I guessed was a political 'top-pop'. Later, through Shi-hwa, I got the names – 'I am a Good Baby' and 'I Must Grow like Chairman Mao'; the expected combination. By this time the children were so much at ease with us that they took my hand and tried to drag me off to show me some special toy or their sand-pit, but we had to be off and departed to the adjoining nursery to shouts of 'Good-bye, Uncle and Auntie; come again.'

The nursery, looked after by volunteer mothers, with the help
and advice of the clinic's nurse and medical assistant, was in an
old outhouse, dark and dingy, but weatherproof, clean and
warm. There were four babies, two asleep in wicker baskets made
from local osiers by an old peasant, and two who regarded me,
owl-eyed, from the playpen. One of the babies was in his cradle
wearing a peaked velveteen cap which reminded me of the one
that Jen-bao wore at the Summer Palace, and I wondered how
'our family' was getting along back in Peking, and if they still
talked of our visit.

We went on down the street to where there were four classrooms around a flagged courtyard with an ancient tree in the
centre. Everything except the tree looked shabby and down-at-
heel. A flight of steps leading to a low terrace, worn hollow with
generations of the feet that had trod them, clearly indicated the
age of the place; no wonder Liu put a new school building at the
head of his list of priorities.

A taller, shyer, but equally likeable version of Liu was his
headmaster-brother, who met us at the gateway and gave us the
usual speech of welcome before taking us off on a tour.

The converted classrooms were cramped, with their old-
fashioned desks crowded too close together and allowing too
little room for teacher and blackboard. Fortunately, one of the
rooms had large windows which let in enough light to enable
Cheng to take shots.

The teacher, taking a writing-cum-reading class, put three
characters on the board; they looked complex enough to me but
Cheng said they were simple. The children copied these down
in their exercise books, pencils held almost at a right-angle,
looking carefully from board to paper. They worked at differing
speeds, the four on the front row being noticeably faster than
the average. I walked round admiring the tidy books and,
against all reason, thinking how clever the children were to be
able to write any sort of Chinese characters! They were learning
romanized script, too, I discovered, for the teacher then wrote
up the phonic equivalent of each ideograph: *mao, gou, niu* (cat,
dog, cow). At this stage down went pencil, arms were folded on

desks and three times the class repeated after teacher whatever word she pointed at.

So loud and clear were their voices that the rafters literally rang and Harold had to tune the recorder to its lowest. Each tone was copied faithfully to the last inflexion, the childish voices rising and falling with those subtle variations of sound and rhythm that distinguish an Eastern, multi-tonal language from our own. This would make such unusual, informative and amusing viewing that I asked Cheng to film long shots of teacher and class, mid-shots of the children, mouths agape, as they recited, and close-ups of the two best writers and the decorative pages of their exercise books. Cheng was moving around a good deal during all this, of course, and, though the children were most interested in any unusual goings-on, they still managed to concentrate enough to get through their exercise. The young man who was star-writer of the class went on unflappedly as Cheng shoved the camera right over his shoulder, almost on to his page. At this stage what I had feared befell; Cheng ran out of film! The last five minutes of that confounded basket-ball had done it – if there were no more film in the car my one and only precious sequence would be ruined. I tried to appear as unflappable as the star-writer whilst Cheng tore off to the car, where, mercifully, he found a last roll of film and we started over again.

Then we went to a senior class where an incident both amusing and disconcerting occurred. The class read a sentence in characters on the board; it was written, presumably, to illustrate the verb 'determine'. 'We are determined to liberate Taiwan.' It was at least a fortnight since I had heard this one, it having been driven from the number-one position in the slogan-parade which it had in 1958; I should have expected rather 'We are determined to destroy revisionism'. I have no idea whether the teacher did this to interest or impress the foreign visitors or whether it was simply a stock grammar-book example.

The songs that this class sang for us were 'Unity is Strength', composed during the struggle with Chiang Kai-shek; 'Hold high the Revolutionary Banner' and a folk song about telling 215 stories to the children in the fields. I was glad they finished on this more childlike theme. I never grew used to the Chinese insistence on political songs for children.

As a final shot I wanted to take the children streaming through the gate and the courtyard wall on to the village street with their headmaster among them. This was heaven for the pupils, but, rather unwisely, just for effect, we asked them to make a noise and say something to us as we left – the hullabaloo was indescribable as they laughed and yelled out some farewell message, rousing the somnolent geese to a rival din; it made a very good finale if a rather boisterous one!

There was a typical postscript. As we left I noticed that the children were told to go back into the school, so I asked Shi-hwa later to find out why they had not gone home, since it was past 3.30 when, I understood, the day ended. She reported that, since the children had missed some schooling because of our activities, the teachers thought they should have an extra hour so as not to fall behind in their programme of work. No time must be wasted in the New China.

I also asked Shi-hwa to find out why the children learned two lots of script, as I thought it must make their learning task even harder. I was told that it had proved easier for children to learn their own characters if, alongside, they chanted and memorized the romanized phonetic version and, in addition, it prepared them for the time when this script might be widely used in papers, books and place-names. I was relieved that the youngsters' task was made a little easier for I knew that it takes them at least two years longer to reach the equivalent reading-writing standard of their Western contemporaries – and they have to learn to use chopsticks, too, poor things.

We all sat by the stream and the others told me, briefly, that they had shot the house and children with Liu watering his very own plot, then the clinic with its resident nurse and medical assistant and its visiting doctor, commenting that the health posters on the walls were particularly decorative and numerous – Wash your hands! Swot that fly! Get your polio injections! Get 216 enough sleep! Keep the backyard clean!

We collected our traps ready to go and were greeted with a blast from the public speaker overhead – 'Socialism is good', with its tiresomely catchy tune. Liu smiled with pleasure, not guessing we hated the noise disturbing the rural quiet. It faded into the distance as we drove off along the bumpy road – past the tea factory, leaves drying in the yard; past the fish-lake, now silent, fish invisible; beneath the tea-slopes where the pickers paused to wave and cry out to us; past the experimental rice-paddy through the ever-widening valley, back to the main road, *en route* for the irrigation project that served several communes in the district. Liu was, to our joy, still with us but we all fell silent as we rounded the bend and saw our last glimpse of Mei Ja Wu village and realized we should never again share its busy, purposeful, daily round.

We were able to get a few shots of the great barrage formed by the irrigation project's giant dam before the light failed. As I watched the cameramen I noted an old peasant woman, patched pants, faded jacket, going home pulling a loaded hand-cart; it did not even have the valued rubber tyres and must have been tugged by her weary forebears along the same road time out of mind; old handcart, new dam. Old China, New China – a typical juxtaposition.

We left the cars a little farther on and tramped a mile or so through lush meadows to the headquarters of the whole commune. This was a larger but shabbier house than the Brigade Headquarters, and, to our surprise, it had none of the fine furniture, the scrolls and porcelain of the brigade house, but only the minimal desks, chairs and cupboards required for its administrative officers. The Commune Headquarters had, presumably, occupied a house from which the landlord had managed to escape with his possessions, but it had not commandeered the brigade's possessions, even so. The commune leader was older than Liu but still young for his responsible tasks. He was a little haggard, a little anxious, but obviously intelligent and respected by his colleagues. At our lunch party in Mei Ja Wu, though he was a senior member of the local hierarchy, the commune leader had been happy to let Liu be 217 the host, answer queries and do the honours. Now various clerical staff joined us for the briefing and with these also the leader was on easy terms. Again it seemed that Party instructions against rigid stratification of the ranks, in civilian as well as army personnel, were observed.

There were thirteen members of the headquarters staff in all, in charge of the militia, women's affairs, civil affairs, tea-growing, rice and vegetable production. (Sales were arranged by the local State Sales Commission.) Others dealt with loans to brigades and co-operation with neighbouring communes on joint projects. Like Liu, the leader was a local boy made good. He had been elected to office and was a member of the Party.

There seems little doubt that some of the early Chinese claims for the staggering successes of the communes have to be discounted, as they were by the Chinese themselves. Joan Robinson agrees that part of the early trouble seemed to be that too many Party cadres descended on distant villages knowing little, maybe, of agricultural, and nothing of local, conditions; they met with obstinate lack of co-operation and were finally recalled. They certainly weren't in evidence at the West Lake Commune, which exhibited at every turn a grass-roots democracy, a down-to-earth realization of local conditions and traditions; and leaders were farmers as well as administrators, peasants as well as Party members.

The meeting was short because we were all tired and hungry and were due back for a farewell banquet at the Hangchow Hotel. Cheng arranged to come back to film the headquarters next morning as soon as the light was suitable.

We walked back through the meadows in gathering twilight, cicadas noisy in the long grass, frogs in the sunset-reflecting ponds; the path was narrow, permitting only two abreast and our little group broke up from time to time to let peasants pass with bundle, basket or tools; they looked up in surprise at our European dress and voice, but it was a pleased surprise and our smiles were returned. We reached the cars as a crescent moon appeared, with an excellent sense of timing, to illuminate the 218 lake as we drove along it on to the famous Shu Causeway. The shining waters stretched on both sides and the pagodas, the islands, the pavilions, the Peak that Flew from Afar, the willows where the orioles once sang were all bathed in a soft radiance – it was an almost too-suitable closing curtain for such a remarkable day.

We said good-bye to our commune friends with a warmth and gratitude that would have been effusive had it not been wholly sincere. For two days they had given up their time and energy to helping a group of strangers from the 'imperialist West', members of the officially deplored capitalist society, and given them with every appearance of pleasure and goodwill. We had made, we thought, a rare film and we had reason to be grateful. We also had reason to be exhausted – and we were!

Harold and John went off to the farewell banquet; they felt in need of good doses of *mao-tai*; I went to my room to tidy up notes and impressions. I could do neither; 'Commune Day' was too close and the relief from strain that the end of the filming had brought found me unable to concentrate. From the balcony I looked out over the silver-painted lake, across the shadowy causeway, towards West Lake Commune; all its peasants would be in bed; the shouting fishermen, the singing tea-pickers, the earnest teachers and sloe-eyed kindergarteners. Only Liu and the commune leader would be awake, looking back over the day's events – over there in that almost too-picturesque valley.

They all worked extraordinarily hard for a standard of living well below average in the West; their possessions were scanty. Farm workers in Australia live in fine style by comparison. But I had a curious impression of something very near leisureliness – an unfebrile, almost relaxed atmosphere and, certainly, a sense of buoyancy. They were simple, hopeful, endearing people and in my two days as a welcome guest they had taught me something about communes and something about living.

As I lay on the brink of sleep, recalling the sights and sounds and songs of 'Commune Day', I heard faint strains from the revellers in the dining-hall; 'Socialism is Good', 'Auld Lang Syne'. Before 'Waltzing Matilda' I was, mercifully, asleep!

Next evening began the long train journey, two nights and a day, from Hangchow to Canton. It gave me a chance to draw breath after the strain of filming and find time for long hammer-and-tongs debates with my Chinese companions, protracted but amicable.

After a last day and a half in Canton all three interpreters, Li, Liu and Shi-hwa as well as producer Feng, cameraman Cheng and Ling came to the border with us. A tinge of sadness coloured the journey. Making the film had not been an easy assignment; although we had found it stimulating and, mostly, enjoyable; occasionally doubts had prowled and prowled around, and per-haps because of this very fact, certain links had been forged between the two teams.

Shum Chun looked just as it did on our arrival a month earlier. The Customs Officer, unruffled as ever, passed us through briskly; on the long march down the postered corridor Ling again carried my suitcase, and the soldiers smiled at the straggling children crossing the bridge with bundle-carrying parents going 'in' and 'out'.

The parting came a few feet on the Chinese side, where we paused for good-byes. Ling cracked one of his last jokes, Shi-hwa smiled as cheerfully as she could, wrinkling her nose characteristically; Feng handed over the last batch of film, which he had been carrying for us. Now, I wanted the whole thing over quickly and was relieved when the slightly charged atmosphere was disturbed by an impatient hoot from our wait-ing train, forcing us to seize our cases – Ling could carry mine no longer – and dash for our carriage. Harold clutched the recorder and tapes; we had to make two journeys for the film-cases.

Pausing for a second, we looked back to see our companions waving to us beneath the red and gold of their flag; and we, beneath the red, white and blue, put down one handful of luggage to wave hastily back.

In the scramble we had to abandon my plan for a final shot of the two flags flying symbolically in the frontier wind. Maybe 220 it was a corny idea but, in my heightened state of fatigue and excitement, it seemed bright enough and I abandoned it with regret.

Once in the train, with the film really 'in the can', mingled relief and melancholy flooded over me; I felt like a good cry!

As the train pulled away I expected, for an unintelligent minute, opera music and news; but they didn't come, of course; nor the zealous sweepers, nor the tea-girls with hot-water cans. Instead an attendant moved along the carriage with a little tray of wares, all sorts of packets forgotten in the last month, salted peanuts, Wrigley's chewing gum, mild Craven A cigarettes instead of the stronger Double Happiness, movie magazines for *China Reconstructs*, Coca-Cola instead of Five Goats. One of these would ease the transition. I surveyed them with unusual care, finding that the disproportionate attention given to a triviality helped me settle down.

I bought a packet of Rowntree's pastilles, to me the most English thing in sight because it took me back to my child-hood's threepenn'orth of weekend sweets. Slowly peeling off the tinfoil, I picked out my favourite flavour and stared, still a little dazed, through the window as the train carried us back towards Her Majesty's Crown Colony of Hong Kong: from one of the newest Communist countries to the last, very nearly, of the possessions of an Empire on which once the sun never set; from the simplicities of West Lake Commune to the cosmopolitan pavements of Kowloon; from the vast, unified realm of Mao Tse-tung to the scattered miscellany of the British Common-wealth. A period of adjustment was needed, I decided, as I surveyed the parked cars, the stiletto heels, the sexy cinema-posters which at first seemed strange and not particularly pleas-ing. But their familiarity was asserting itself by the second pas-tille. 'At this rate I'll soon be back in my own world.'

But, of course, I wasn't, because for me there are no longer two worlds, mine and theirs. I would be glad to be home again in Australia, familiar and loved; still recognizably British, still, most of the time, recognizably democratic, still offering the privacy and comfort which my middle-aged bones require; but, as a visitor, I could feel at once at home with cheerful and 221 strenuous patriots like Ling and Madame Huang, and with my fellow academics; I could identify myself, in imagination, with all the Chinese men and women I had met who were steadily striving to create for their country the good life, as they, by their own lights, saw it. Certainly, I could dislike in China the same sort of people and attitudes that I disliked in Australia, England or America. It seemed to me, then, in a moment of deceptive clarity, that if this awareness of our common humanity were everywhere accepted, not as a sentimental concept but as the main cold, hard fact of international relations, the chances for peace would be brighter.

My portentous meditations were interrupted by the noise and bustle of our arrival at Kowloon station. As far as I was concerned, the solution of world problems would have to wait, for personal ones were beginning to press in upon me. How were we going to edit, script and distribute the film lying there in those battered round tins? Who would want to show it in Australia? Would we be able to sell it overseas? Ahead lay the jungle of international TV – of which an awareness of common humanity is not a noticeable denizen!

I pushed the problems aside; I would go on a shopping-spree in duty-free Hong Kong and let them keep until my Australian landfall. One job, I believed, was accomplished; we had made a documentary film, which recorded, as fairly and faithfully as we knew how, the people of the New China as we had seen them.

APPENDIX I
UNITED STATES – CHINA RELATIONS
The Mirror Image

In 1961 I talked about China in the United States and in 1963, in China, I talked about the United States. Sometimes I felt I was moving in a looking-glass world. People, places, seemed real to begin with but when questions started I grew confused by the almost indistinguishable attitudes and apprehensions in both countries. The Common Room at Barnard College faded into the English classroom at the East China Teachers' University; the Shanghai YMCA into the Mid-West Rotary Club; voices with an American accent, English with a Chinese inflexion, merged, emerged and merged again bewilderingly. *Mutatis mutandis*, my auditors were, in the early 'sixties, saying pretty much the same thing: and always the core question was, 'Who is going to attack whom?'

'Why is China so aggressive towards the United States? Look what our missionaries did for her; the Peking Medical College, the schools, the university scholarships. And why can't she leave her neighbours alone? Why must she try to dominate them. She believes Communism will destroy capitalism. We like the Chinese people – we always have – how could they "go red"?'

On the other side of the river the argument runs:

'Why is the United States so aggressive towards China? What harm have we done her? We don't threaten her frontiers or send military advisers to her neighbours, and we have no ships in Western waters. Why can't she leave Asia to the Asians? We don't dislike the American masses and believe they want peace, too; but their leaders are controlled by the capitalists and the Pentagon who hate China, and want to destroy Communism.'

The wish to understand, the bewilderment that 'they' seemed prepared to use force, these were evident in people of goodwill in both countries. There was little people-to-people hatred but much nation-to-nation fear. It was clearly impossible for either side to see itself as an aggressor – that role was unthinkable; 'Surely "*they*" can't think we want war?' The peaceful national image was interchangeable.

With a quite painful anxiety to do so fairly, I put what I thought was the American case to the Chinese something like this:

> Your major fear is American aggression, and you cannot believe that this fear is reciprocated in terms of Communist aggression. That Communism is a 'good thing' is to most of you so acceptable that you simply cannot see it as a devouring monster and your country as the 'Red Terror'. But anti-Communism is an integral part of United States life and only some knowledge of her history can explain why.
>
> The United States is still young enough to be dogmatic and idealistic, noticeably more so than the more sceptical countries of Europe. She regards herself as the main protagonist of individual freedom, often identified with 'private enterprise'. She is proud of her tradition of anti-imperialist struggles begun by the Pilgrim Fathers and enshrined in the superb Declaration of Independence. 'All men are created equal' and the 'pursuit of life and liberty' mean, above all, liberty to be free from government dictation, because; to the Founding Fathers, government had meant tyranny. The familiar hymn still echoes national belief: 'Sweet land of liberty, of thee I sing'.
>
> Early anti-colonialist struggles are part of the national memory and criticism of the British Empire stemmed largely from this. So, for the Chinese to accuse the Americans of being imperialists and neo-colonialists seems particularly inept. Economic or political imperialism is your concept not theirs.
>
> Again, historically, Americans are a church-oriented people, because the Pilgrim Fathers were at least as much concerned about religious as political freedom. In spite of so much materialism, they still see, idealistically at least, the Christian way of life as the best, if not the only, way; so atheistic Communism is anti-Christ.
>
> The Americans' long search for freedom led to the de-

velopment of the two-party system, to preclude tyranny and keep the politicians in their place. To such people Communism seems monolithic – against freedom, against the individual. The millions of Americans who still suspect their own central, federal government must clearly suspect, a thousandfold, a Communist form of centralization and planning.

There is, of course, a paradox here. Proud of their own revolutionary tradition, deifying the founders of it, Americans see nothing odd in their present fear of your revolution. It undoubtedly scared them to hear Chou En-lai say prospects of revolution in Africa were excellent. They want to help the underdog; they are on the side of the angels, but they are parliamentary, not revolutionary ones.

You must realize that Communist doctrines and actions have done everything to increase these traditional beliefs and fears. The gospels of Marx and Lenin are unreservedly anti-capitalist; capitalism is the ENEMY. Until Krushchev began the *détente* with the West, it was never admitted by Communists that mid-twentieth-century capitalism has a different face from its nineteenth-century counterpart. Then the Chinese, it seemed, howled Krushchev down!

The Cominform has long been disbanded but its belligerent aims of international revolution stamped indelibly on Western minds the concept of Communism as the international aggressor. Revolution *can* be exported, it seemed to insist.

Communist leaders' statements recently have hardly been soothing. Krushchev's 'We will bury you', Mao Tse-tung's 'The Bomb is a paper tiger' are remembered because of their vivid imagery.

Even the American liberal who wishes to interpret everything for the best must feel concerned at China's ignorance of many aspects of the American life and spirit. Just as Washington is extremely well-informed about the facts and figures of the People's Republic, so in Peking there is a wealth of factual information about what goes on in the

United States, as even the casual reader of the *Peking Review* will notice. But one cannot escape the fear that the steady denigration of the capitalist system, the continual playing up of the less attractive sides of American life, may be making the Chinese the victims of their own propaganda and leading them to a dangerous underestimation of American quality and of the United States' strength and determination. In a delicately poised balance-of-power situation, wrong assessments of this kind are good for neither side.

In the United States there is a sizeable minority of Americans who have made themselves better informed than the average by studying the material provided by their own State Department and their own and overseas writers. Books like Felix Greene's *The Wall Has Two Sides* and Edgar Snow's *The Other Side of the River* have sold in their tens of thousands. There is a Committee for the Review of United States China Policy. On my visit to the United States I was besieged by groups of many kinds who wanted to quiz me about China as I had seen it, because they felt they knew too little about it.

What parallels are there in China? What groups are addressed on political issues by visitors who know the United States well? What meetings, newspapers or magazines air criticism, right or wrong, of your foreign policy in general and towards the United States in particular? Though you say, and, I believe, with truth, that you do not hate the American people, the masses, you still know very little about them; and maybe you could press for a relaxation of tensions in spite of all the military bases and advisers and in spite of the American pressure to exclude you from the United Nations. Only when the present alarming out-of-touch situation begins to change will two great nations see each other as human beings rather than great agglomerations of humanity labelled 'Communist' or 'capitalist'.

The steady flow of your anti-American cartoons and

slogans contribute their share to American fears. They have similar campaigns against you, of course, and you are provoked, admittedly; but your hitting back, though human, does not relieve tensions. When I tell my American audiences that you express no personal hatred for them they find it hard to believe.

It seems to many Westerners, even friendly ones, that you see the United States not only as the greatest, but the only, villain of the international piece; if only the U.S. ceased its 'imperialist' activities the world's problems would be solved. This disturbs Western liberals, who fear that China is diverting too little attention to other causes of world unrest. A young, self-critical American once said, 'I admit we are sinners but are we the only sinners?' By her very insistence, say these liberals, China is tending to create an atmosphere which exacerbates instead of lessening antagonisms and misunderstandings. The voice of reason on both sides is drowned; and the voice of a China, mature, patient, true to her old philosophical traditions as well as her new inspiration, could be a very persuasive one indeed.

Moreover, your own foreign policy, at least as seen in the West, seems often to show you as expansionist – as Great Power chauvinists, to use your own phrase! People hear India accusing you of attacking her territory; they suspect that you took over Tibet against the wishes of the Tibetans. They believe they see your hand in unrest in your neighbouring countries, and also in Africa.

The Chinese case in all these 'foreign relations' is, virtually, unknown to the ordinary citizen, which means you cannot be judged fairly on the facts. This tragedy of misrepresentation is the result of lack of contact, of public ignorance and, whatever its cause, has to be taken into account. Most important, all Western countries – even those 'recognizing' your régime – have been shaken by what they have heard of China's pronouncements on the recent Atomic Treaty.

The horrors of atomic warfare are very much in all our 227

minds and we have long feared that the strains between the USSR and the United States may lead, perhaps inadvertently, to the holocaust. So, to us, the Tripartite treaty, with all its imperfections, seemed a step to world accord – a notable easing of the cold-war situation. To you this treaty is 'a gigantic fraud'. We heard that China was not afraid of the Bomb. We read in the *People's Daily*, 'The atomic bomb is a paper tiger; in the debris of a dead capitalism the victorious people will create very swiftly a civilization a thousand times higher than the capitalists' system and a truly beautiful future.' (I was more than disconcerted to find two seemingly intelligent Chinese acquaintances comparatively unmoved by this statement. They made no reply when I remarked that their attitude seemed to show a strange refusal to face the facts of the atomic age.) It is perfectly natural and good morale-building for your Government to assure you that you would survive the bomb just as British leaders assured their people during the war that they would survive anything that the Luftwaffe could do to the tight little island. But a too-confident approach to the atomic threat is alarming.

Your continued recriminations against your fellow-Communists for what millions regard as a desirable *détente* seem out of touch with the changing nature of capitalist society and the realities of the Atomic Age, in which, we believe, any drawing closer, any bridge, however tenuous, across the gulf, is welcome. We know, after our interview with Chen Yi and talks with people we meet in this country, that your attitude is not so extreme as we feared, but we had to come here to be sure of this. Most liberals in the West agree with you that total disarmament is the only answer but think it possible only step by step as suspicions gradually lessen; meanwhile they believe the Tripartite Treaty is a move in that direction. Of course, liberals believe that any atomic treaties without China make little sense and that wide-range plans for world disarmament are useless without you.

To my American auditors in 1961 I would put the Chinese case much as follows, oversimplified but, I believe, basically accurate:

China suffered, in civil wars and Japanese occupation, a toll of human life and property beyond anything that Americans can imagine. Because the Chinese have paid this terrible price for peace they value it inestimably and a government that ensures it is supported, whatever shortcomings some of the people may consider it to possess. China needs peace, she wants peace, but not at any price.

The United States and Britain have to face the unpalatable truth that they are, good works notwithstanding, identified with commercial exploitation, military intervention over many years, and racial superiority.

The West, last century, virtually compelled China, then a closed country, to trade with it. From about 1830 Britain thrust opium on to the lucrative Chinese market in spite of imperial decrees against the smoking of it and its deleterious effect on the people. Two humiliating treaties were made after two long wars and, amongst other things, European powers were given extra-territorial rights in certain Chinese cities. In these 'concession areas' Chinese law did not run and the Chinese residents' only municipal right was that of paying rates; in this sense they were aliens in in their own country.

Unfortunately, the Americans cashed in on British and French victories, obtaining special rights for their ships and, later, control of Chinese Customs. This had a most adverse effect on the nation's economy. By the Open Door Policy of 1899, certainly, the United States foreswore any territorial claims but she demanded every other advantage wrested by her allies from the nerveless hands of the moribund Manchu Dynasty. And it is particularly unfortunate that the Treaty of Tienstsin legalized, in the same document, the sale of opium, the entry of gunboats to harbours and the entry of missionaries – the coincidence could not but do damage to the servants of Christ in China!

In recent times the United States' identification with Chiang Kai-shek, whom the Chinese regard as a discredited, defeated leader, amounts, in their eyes, to interference in a purely internal struggle – one thing the United States claims it disapproves of on principle. To many Taiwanese the KMT are not patriots but 'carpet-baggers'.

So now, when China says, 'Yanks, go home', she is repeating a long-standing, anti-Western cry from the heart. Like many Asian countries, she wants the West as a trader, visitor, friend, but never again as arbiter of her destiny.

It must be remembered, too, that the American is seen by South-East Asians mostly in uniform, in jeeps, in reconnaissance planes or in social enclaves cut off from all neighbouring nationals except 'the power élite'. The Americans at home talk peace but in the East, around the place, they look like war. China has seen no American civilian, had no contact with peace-loving men- and women-in-the-street and the vast majority have had little access to American publications for over fifteen years. Pointless now to discuss the reasons for this tragic lack of contact; it has happened and its disastrous effect cannot be minimized for it has precluded those relations between people of goodwill which alone can counteract the mass propaganda stereotypes.

So your image as the peace-keepers is your own; the Chinese do not know it – on the contrary, I believe you are genuinely feared. Don't lay to your souls the flattering unction that Chinese fear of America is all Government propaganda. China sees your most powerful fleet off her coasts, your military and civilian advisers on her frontiers, in Japan, Thailand, the Philippines, Vietnam, and fears you nearly as much as when General McArthur threatened her industrial life-blood by his proposed crossing of the Yalu River.

And she is afraid, too, because American politicians and public servants have made several unequivocal statements which have become, for the Chinese, classic references on

American anti-China policies. Idle, again, to argue whether they are meant to be taken literally; they make very uncomfortable reading in newspapers and Communist Party publications.

John Foster Dulles said, 'We will do all we can to contribute to the passing of the Communist régime in China.'

In 1954 Mr Walter S. Robertson, Assistant Secretary of State for Far Eastern Affairs, declared in the House of Representatives, 'It is the heart of our policy toward China to keep alive a constant threat of military action . . . in the hope that at some point there will be an internal breakdown . . . a cold war waged under the leadership of the United States led by Formosa . . . the United States is undertaking to maintain for an indefinite period an American dominance in the Far East.'

American support of Chiang Kai-shek is, to put it mildly, a running sore. You do not need to turn to Chinese Communist sources to see why this is so. Your own country has honest records, honestly made public. Read the State Department publication *United States–China Relations, 1949* or the *Stilwell Papers*, including 'Vinegar Joe's' bitter comments on the Generalissimo. Or look up the history of Formosa and see what you think of the Chinese claim that the island is part of China proper. In 1950 the Secretary of State said, 'China has administered Formosa for four years. Neither the United States nor any ally has ever questioned that occupation.'

There is an interesting point. While seeking information about the history, diplomacy or policy statements over the last four or five decades in China, I have been struck by the large amount of it available through American sources – the books of scholars, State Department White Papers, reports of diplomats, articles in newspapers and journals – all these indicate that, in the United States, one has a chance to build up, piece by piece, at least on paper, a pretty accurate picture of the People's Republic of China. Nobody in the United States need go ignorant of the facts, 231 and nobody will stop him writing about them. This is very much on the credit side; but it makes the misleading impressions given in mass media the more discouraging.

The busy general reader, without time to ferret around, sees China's foreign policy as aggressive. She has 'raped' Tibet and 'invaded' India, and that is that. Few people have time to find out, for instance, that Tibet has been subject to the hegemony of China for many centuries (Kublai Khan appointed the Grand Lama as early as the thirteenth century and Britain recognized Chinese suzerainty in 1729). Chiang Kai-shek always has, and still does, lay claim to it as part of his China and in 1943 the State Department stated, 'The Chinese constitution lists Tibet among the areas constituting the territory of China. . . . This Government has at no time raised a question regarding (this) claim.' This is not to say that Tibet, ideally, may not wish to be autonomous, but no support was ever given to this by the KMT and its allies. In the meantime, many social reforms are being carried out. An impartial record is given in a recent book, *The Timely Rain*, by an English reporter and his wife, Stewart and Roma Gelder, and in a film which they made during their 1963 visit to Tibet.

As for the Sino–Indian dispute, this is presented as an invasion by an aggressive neighbour. The story of this most unfortunate encounter, and the rights and wrongs of the territorial claims of each country, is long and complicated; But one fact is clear – it *is* a genuine border problem, in a poorly charted area where borders have never been properly delimited; any idea that China is all wrong and India all right is misleading. There were many discussions between the two governments and China made certain offers to solve the problem, as she solved similar boundary disputes with Burma, Afghanistan and Pakistan, for example.*

Looked at carefully and coolly, in actual fact China's

* A well-documented account is to be found in *The China–India Border* by Alastair Lamb. Oxford University Press, 1964.

foreign policy has been just that – careful and cool. She has made no attempt to take over Hong Kong from Britain or Macao from Portugal, though she claims that they are part of China and, in a day when overseas possessions are universally regarded as imperialist hangovers, they may certainly be seen as Chinese. Even Taiwan, given back to China along with other Japanese-occupied areas at the end of the Second World War, has never been seriously threatened by mainland forces. There is an oft-repeated slogan, 'We are determined to liberate Taiwan.' I asked the Chinese repeatedly how they meant to do this, and usually received another slogan in answer, 'We will liberate Taiwan by suitable means at a suitable time.' Nobody ever said or implied that it was to be recaptured by force. A United States Rand Corporation Report says, 'Evidence indicates that China made no early plans to commit the army to combat in Korea.' Elsewhere a Rand comment is: 'The foreign policy of the Chinese Government has been rational, cautious and calculating.' Beneath the threats and outbursts, the drum-beating that any country makes, rightly or wrongly, when it sees itself threatened, the Chinese leaders have been most obviously averse from military adventures. When they claim they have had enough of them to last their lifetime, they may be right. When Chen Yi told me if there was another war he hoped he wouldn't be in it, he probably meant what he said. The Soviet Union has, indeed, chided the Chinese for tolerating imperialist enclaves in their territory.

It is interesting and significant that, in spite of the vehement 'Yanks, go home', one is always told by the Chinese people that they do not see the American people, the masses, as their enemies. The American masses want peace, too, and do not know what is being done in their name to others.

Translate the Chinese position into American terms; put the Chinese fleet to sail between Florida and Maine; put Chinese military and civilian 'advisers' in Cuba, 233

Mexico, even Canada, to 'preserve the integrity of these countries from United States expansionism'. Imagine members of the Chinese People's Congress declaring openly that they will support Communist subversion inside the United States and will try to dominate North and South American affairs in the interest of 'containing capitalism'. Then you will get an idea of the view which the Chinese, rightly or wrongly, hold about their present position *vis-à-vis* the United States.

Church-going Americans who are horrified by China's atheist government do not realize that she has never had a nation-wide religion, certainly never a national church. Taoism is not a mystical religion, nor was it ever institutionalized, and Confucianism is not a spiritual creed demanding a trained priesthood to help interpret God to man. 'Respect the spirits, but keep them at a distance.' Buddhism and Mohammedanism, like Christianity, were foreign imports and never accepted by more than a small proportion of Chinese millions. So the national attitude to 'godless Communism' must be very different from that of countries in which institutional religion is an unquestioned part of the way of life. In a sense China has always been agnostic – even her saints. There are other parallels – indeed one can work out a fascinating if sometimes over-ingenious list of them – proving that, in some ways, the new Communism is but old Confucianism writ large.*

Unlike any land mass of comparable size, China has been unified both territorially and culturally for centuries; in spite of difficult communications and peripheral discontents, unity was the norm – in striking contrast to tribal Africa, fragmented Europe and even princely India.

The Emperor was the sun that shone over all, the *roi soleil*, as long as he kept his effulgence; but if his bright complexion dimmed, the battle was then to the strong and, if imperial weakness provoked a rival successful enough to seize the throne, the mandate of heaven passed to the

* Professors C. P. Fitzgerald and J. Needham have elaborated on this.

usurper and his heirs for so long as they could hold it. In the seventh century a Sui Dynasty official turned out his emperor, establishing the great Tang Dynasty; then the Mongol Dynasty was overthrown by the Ming in 1328, to fall in turn to the invading Manchu in 1644.

The place of Mao Tse-tung and his régime can, then, be seen in some dynastic perspective by any Chinese who knows his history; and today millions do.

Every Chinese schoolboy knows that the Chinese have always absorbed their conquerors; the lesser breeds without the Han law were assimilated by the traditions and ideals of the scholar-gentry class on whom the conquerors most depended to govern their vast domains. Permanent beyond the dynasties they served, these men, the civil servants of their day, established a lasting pattern of sovereign greatness – almost the philosopher-king with a reverence for learning, for teaching, for improving. So Mao, as scholar, writer, philosopher, calligraphist, is as much in the main stream of succession as Mao the strategist and military leader. 'To govern is to rectify,' said Confucius; the latter verb is a favourite of Mao's; one of his famous lectures is 'Rectify the Party's Work Style'; the late 'fifties saw a Rectification Campaign.

Finally, it is more than interesting to note that, alone among great countries, China has made few alliances; avoided balance of power politics; accepted and rejoiced in an isolation originally geographic but long perpetuated as a mark of superior status.

Clearly, there is danger in over-elaborating this recurrence of the pattern, but it supplies, in part, an answer to the puzzled cry of the American one-time Sinophile, 'How could China go red?'

In both countries I saw more of the younger than the older people, and I found myself constantly comparing them. I was struck by many similarities. Both were articulate, inquiring, extremely friendly; both free of personal malice in their attitude 235 to each other; both were much concerned about the state of the world, though the American youngsters were less sanguine, more shot through with doubts and, of course, far more critical of their own and their allies' attitudes. American Youth Corps men and women, dedicated, diligent, trying to be open-minded; our interpreters solicitous for our welfare and their country's good; the opera-school students thrilled by our applause, campus co-eds sacrificing lunch hours to question me about China; all these would quickly learn each other's quality if they could meet. (Even earnest American Church workers would be surprised at their similarity to earnest street committee members.) The essentially outgoing spirit of American youth, and many adults too, would quickly assure at least the beginnings of mutual understanding. Certainly those few travellers like myself who have friends in both countries long for the time when the one can meet and learn to know the other.

In this sort of way I presented my case in '61 and '63. Then, I believed, on balance, that it was from the West that the thaw must begin; the first move be made. After 1965 I was sure of this, for the escalating war, the ever-nearing presence of United States military forces on China's southern borders, had inevitably increased her fears and deepened her suspicions of United States motives. In 1965 the mirror image, though not destroyed, was flawed; the intensity of anti-American sentiment in China had multiplied and calm presentation of the West side story was not exactly easy.

The people were as friendly, the service as good as ever; for the Peking May Day Celebrations the city was *en fête*, but always the shadow of Vietnam loomed large behind and through it all. The militia, the civilian defence force, was frequently seen drilling, girls and boys, men and women alike, often practising with wooden staves for rifles. There were more of the regular forces on the streets than I had seen before; the People's Liberation Army was receiving much publicity. People wrote, painted, acted, sang, talked and demonstrated their 'anti-imperialism'. Posters with figures in fearsome postures
236 appeared in school-playgrounds, university campuses and fac-

tories as well as on the streets and in the parks. In the theatre there was scarcely an opera or play that did not in one way or another bear on the Vietnam situation, on China's revolutionary struggles and victories, or on American interference in the Dominican Republic and elsewhere. The funny men in the May Day playlets were usually terrified GIs or a near-demented President Johnson. In schools one was sickened to hear the children singing songs about the need to drive out the aggressor or see them drawing sketches of American planes shot down in flames and of GIs captured in jungle ambushes. I remember especially our visit to one of the Children's Palaces (Youth Clubs) in Shanghai. After two most enjoyable hours watching folk dancing and singing, model-aeroplane-making and mouth-organ-playing, we were taken to see the drama group perform their latest little play. It was called *Five Letters.* One of the young performers made a speech welcoming visitors from 'Adaliya' and then they were off. An eleven-year-old girl entered and told us she had received letters from five friends (these were standing in the wings). Dressed as a Chinese, a Japanese, a Vietnamese, an Indonesian and an African boy or girl, each appeared in turn.

We needed no translation or explanation. The intensity of the feeling, the depth of emotion would have communicated itself in any language. 'The Americans must go home . . . we must all be free of the Western aggressors.' The little room was vibrant with intensity of the children's emotion.

Thoroughly distressed, I asked our interpreter if it was necessary to draw children into politics in this way.

'Of course we must,' he answered. 'Don't you see our country is threatened. It has already been attacked and our neighbours are occupied by enemy forces. We hate war but even our children must realize that it now threatens us all.'

The young actors returned for applause. My guide, smiling at our strange language, led me back down the stairs. Dozens of children left their activities, dashed excitedly to the front door and lined the drive, shouting, 'Come back Uncles and Aunties, come back.'

The Western imperialists were aggressors, but we, the people, were their friends. It was a cheerful pandemonium – but the young actors' voices, thrilling with fear and indignation, rang still in my ears and I could not smile good-bye. I was wrestling with the problem raised by the answer to my anxious query.

On my last day in China I saw a mass demonstration in Canton against the landings in the Dominican Republic. Large and small groups began gathering early in every corner of the city. By noon the enormous procession was under way, twisting away beyond sight in both directions. Scarlet flags and pennants of every size waved dazzlingly in the tropical sunshine; the great posters and banners with their Chinese characters, gold on red or black on white, were everywhere and needed no translation, for any Western visitor at all familiar with the Chinese scene: 'Yanks go home'; 'Oppose US aggression'; 'We support the just struggle of the Dominican people'.

The crowd seemed vehement, intense, involved but quite unhysterical; in well-behaved fashion they kept to one side of the road to allow traffic to go on its usual way with a minimum of interruption. People on the pavements watched quietly, the few police cleared up occasional congestion with the help of volunteers.

Our interpreter explained that the groups came from factories, trade unions, shops or offices and from every educational institution in the city. The whole performance was clearly highly organized on familiar lines; nobody, we were told, was compelled to join his or her group, but the pressure of public opinion, the power of group-solidarity, the strength of national feeling were such that few failed to march.

Once it was finished, normalcy took over and the dispersing marchers gave us greetings and smiles.

But, apart from posters, plays and the occasional demonstration, we were not personally brought up against the Vietnam situation unless we raised the subject. Ordinary life went on as usual and plans for developments of agriculture, industry, education and even tourism were promulgated and 238 discussed.

Even when we received news of the decision to send Australian troops to Vietnam there was no change of attitude by our hosts. They did not hold it against us as people and their main reaction was one of puzzlement. 'What have you to gain? Don't you want to be our friends? Why don't you let Asia manage its own affairs?'

Where they did crop up, the 'anti-imperialist-aggression' manifestations were unpleasant enough for the ordinary tourist, but for those of us with friends in both countries it was a cruel thing. The shadow of the plays, the banners, the marchers falls today on everything I think and write about China. The whole confrontation is tragic, dangerous and, above all, unnecessary.

In such an atmosphere I could no longer tell the Chinese that the United States sought only to 'contain' her; made no threats against her safety; because the Chinese now fear that Vietnam may not be an end in itself but a stage on the way to China.

They see history repeating itself. 'This,' they said, 'is where we came in.' Once more the gunboats, the armies, the threats; but this time, they say, there will be no unequal treaties, for Western aggression is no longer faced by a tottering dynasty but by an armed and united country. Unless they are asked by their neighbours for help, they told us, they will not move outside their own boundaries, but if the Americans set foot on Chinese soil . . .! 'This animal is dangerous; it defends itself if attacked.'

China is not without evidence for her apprehensions; and they publish it frequently in their foreign-language papers. A Senator from Georgia asked for a 'preventive' atom bomb (this was echoed two months or so later by a colleague from South Carolina).

But, above all, they know that American planes have been identified over Chinese Hainan Island off Vietnam, and that bombs are falling within a few score miles of their border; they see the conflict escalating to their southern provinces and the possibility of the Seventh Fleet entering territorial waters. Our tourist party – at its own request – was taken to see three 239 pilotless planes which the Chinese said had been shot down over their country. They were on show in Peking. The Chinese must, then, show the world that they are strong, well-armed and united; what else can they do and how else can they do it without actual fighting?

The anger and suspicion, the shouting and the drum-beating stop short of the American people, the masses. The foreign troops, the White House and the Pentagon are the targets. I recall no poster or slogan directed against the American people.

Given past history; given world-tensions; given the demands of vocal United States extremists, the noise of war in the near-distance and bombs on the neighbour's back garden, the Chinese reaction is logical and to be expected. The surprising thing is that, though she has said so much, she has done so little. In the circumstances, government techniques would be similar anywhere. Play down the enemy's strength, play up your own; declare national unity and invincibility. 'We shall fight on the beaches, we shall fight in the fields and in the streets; we shall never surrender.' The Chinese leaders are saying just this in encouraging the demonstrations. It is echoed in the riproaring speeches of Marshals Chen Yi and Lin Piao in September 1965, promising annihilation for any attacker. 'Come the four corners of the world in arms and we shall shock them.' The Chinese believe their safety depends upon showing national unity and confidence to the watching world. They too ask, 'What sort of people do you think we are?'

The sad truth is that the Chinese people have not been left alone to show what kind of people they may be in a world where they are accepted as equals and treated as friends.

APPENDIX II
The Arts in China

It is one of the safer generalizations that a significant pointer to any government's character is its treatment of the artist and appreciation of his contribution to national life; and it is a commonplace to observe that China, with the longest continuing civilization in the world, was producing painters, poets, philosophers, mathematicians and craftsmen when most Europeans were semi-literate 'barbarians'.

The present régime is much concerned with its artists and the lively continuance of the ancient traditions to which they are the proud heirs. In the midst of the fiercest revolutionary fighting Mao Tse-tung found time, in the caves of Yenan in 1942, to write his much-quoted treatise, 'The Yenan Forum on Literature and the Arts'. This has now become the definitive statement on the Communist Party's attitudes and policy.

Mao himself is a poet and calligrapher as well as a political philosopher. Many of his oldest and most immediate colleagues such as Chou En-lai, Chen Yi and Kuo Mo-jo are highly literate and cultivated men.

The artist in any medium is encouraged, almost pampered, by the state and the people. Any youngster showing promise as painter, musician, writer or actor can receive both a free general education and a professional training at one of the institutes, studios or conservatoria in the larger cities. Work is guaranteed on graduation. Older, pre-revolutionary artists have found work either as teachers in these institutions or as performers in city orchestras, theatre companies, radio and television stations or publishing houses. Craftsmen are busy in workshops and factories producing *objets d'art* or training apprentices.

All these men and women are paid well above the average wage and a successful actor may receive one of the highest salaries in the country; though none ever reaches, of course, the astronomical figures of Western film stars. Authors collect royalties. A leading lady in opera or films might receive as much as five hundred yuan a month, compared with a factory-worker's sixty-yuan average or an engineer's two hundred yuan. Young graduates from academies start at eighty yuan. There are artists on the Provincial or the National Congress and many receive public acclaim, along with Party cadres, army heroes and model workers.

When the best-known painter, Chi Pai-shih, died in 1958 at the age of ninety-four, he was universally mourned and is remembered with pride and affection. Reproductions of his paintings have sold all over the world, along with those of his much admired younger colleague, Ju Pei-hung, whose superbly vital, black, rearing horses have captured the imagination of thousands in the West. (Art reproductions, along with traditional crafts, are amongst the Republic's best foreign-currency earners.)

Mei Lan-fang, most brilliant and famous of traditional opera stars, well-known also in the West, died in his own country full of years and honours – and wealth. (He was said to be one of the few really rich men left in the New China!) A film of his life and art is always on circuit.

Folk-arts are cultivated and each province and minority group is busy reviving its special skills. The old art of paper-cutting is especially attractive. Paper-cuts have a wide range of style and theme, which vary from province to province; some are bold and simple, with a remarkable economy of line, others are so delicate and complex that it is hard to imagine how the maker could wield his scissors with such hairsbreadth delicacy. I saw how it was done at the Folk Art Institute in Shanghai, where the leading 'paper-cutter' offered to make one of his 'simpler' ones for me. I watched him fold in two a small rectangle of dark-red paper, then, for six or seven minutes, without pause, he manipulated scissors and paper, turning and twisting each in turn, finally handing me a pair of matching birds with sweeping plumes, peering out from leaves and flowers. I have watched ivory-carvers, embroiderers, weavers and potters similarly at work. In the far North ice-carvers are now encouraged, and the festival in Heilungkiang Province has, apparently, produced ice-carved animals, flowers and miniature buildings of great artistic merit.

Painters are commissioned to decorate new buildings with canvases or murals. Poster art is pop art and there are literally

242

tens of thousands of posters all over the country. Illustrated magazines are numerous and 'comics' for children and adults everywhere in demand. Most books are illustrated and lithography is regarded as an art.

In music the scope is probably as wide as in the pictorial arts. The larger cities have both Western and traditional orchestras which give concerts and broadcast on radio and television. In Shanghai I heard a gala concert given in the city's new Town Hall auditorium by the conservatorium students' orchestra. The programme included a violin concerto, 'The Butterfly Lovers'; seven violins and a piano accordion playing a medley of folk songs, 'The Four Seasons'; two Chopin études by a girl pianist, and the first Chinese women's quartet playing two pieces by Handel. One orchestral piece was a joint composition by four students working, the programme note said, in combined inspiration on a theme celebrating the building of the Ming Tombs Reservoir! This was an interesting amalgam of Eastern and Western melodies and rhythms but, for my ear, too lyrical, oddly lacking in the energy which usually characterizes Chinese youth.

Gramophone records are in great demand and, like many things in the country, they are produced by the million. Folk music is 'in' and there is a long list of titles. Choirs and places where they sing are everywhere, for both professional and amateur performers.

The theatre story is similar; the Chinese have become addicted theatre-goers. Not only do the towns have their several theatres, but there are travelling troupes reaching the remotest commune. All performers, even the most distinguished, have to spend some time with these to ensure that the peasants have a chance to see the 'stars'. Travel by mule-train or farm-cart is common and performances often take place in barns or fields. Theatre prices everywhere are very low, ranging from a few cents to half a yuan. This is really the people's theatre.

There are four kinds of theatrical companies. The first presents that extraordinary blend of singing, tumbling, miming, fighting and dancing, along with ear-piercing orchestra and 243 fantastic costumes that constitute Chinese classical opera; a theatrical form wholly *sui generis*. The beginnings of Chinese opera have been traced back to the Sung Dynasty, but Peking opera, as it is known today, is a mere century old. Some of its themes are grist to the Communist mill. *Resisting the Tartars* is a good example of the patriotic theme; *The Fisherman's Revenge* shows the peasants fighting against feudal oppression. The famous *Storming the Heavens* has no message; it tells the story of Monkey's exploits over earth and heaven, and is Chinese fantasy at its most bizarre and diverting. I doubt if any performance can offer a more exhilarating exhibition of sheer theatrical virtuosity than a good performance of this opera. This was borne out by the great popular and critical acclaim which the Peking Opera Company received on its recent visit to Paris.

Next, there are the song-and-dance ensembles offering precisely that – folk songs and dances, modern songs and dances, playlets and mimes based on workers' and peasants' activities or some national or international situation.

I saw on every visit short sketches bitterly portraying, for example, 'American imperialism' in Taiwan, the Congo, Latin America and, in 1965, Vietnam. On the home front there were tales of the new education developments, of new mental health treatment. One of them, for example, told of the development of the Homes of Respect for the Aged. A starving old beggerman limped on to the stage, to him slithered painfully a poor old crone with the pathetic six-inch foot; they mimed acute despair and resignation. Three or four young people danced on and, expressing loving concern for their misery, led them across to a modest little house with welcoming characters and posters on the wall. From inside came others to mime the feeding and clothing of the old folk, who in turn acted out their combined amazement and gratitude; then old and young joined in a song of praise for the army of liberation, the generous Government and the bright future for all old folk throughout the land in the Homes of Respect. Third, and, I suspect, the most popular are 'Acrobatics', which include not only acrobats but jugglers and magicians as well.

Last, there are the straight drama companies which I glimpsed only in passing, since they do not provide very interesting entertainment for non-Chinese-speaking visitors.

Some foreign plays are presented in Chinese or their original language and on my visits to Peking I could have seen, for example, Ibsen's *Doll's House*, Goldini's *Servant of Two Masters* in Chinese or a student performance in English of *Othello*.

China has taken enthusiastically to Russian-style ballet. The Director of the Ballet Classique de France said, on his return from the ballet's 1965 tour, that the Chinese ballet would reach world standard in four or five years.

Children's theatre is everywhere encouraged. One of our most amusing afternoons was spent at the Children's Theatre in Shanghai. The play was about two city youngsters going with grandma back to her childhood village and meeting young cousins for the first time. Of course, the main object of the play was the bad old days before Liberation and the good ones after it. Now the melons are bigger and better, the wheat more golden, the fairies much happier and kinder to mortals; all country children now work gleefully with their parents on co-operative farms and even help to build a desperately-needed hydro-electric station. Once again the moral tale, once again the high standard of acting, staging and presentation – the sets were like the story, a delightful mixture of realism and fantasy. In the harvest scene, for example, huge melons slid noiselessly on to the stage, giant beanstalks dropped from the heavens and shining red tomatoes rose majestically from trapdoors.

For the writer, even the poet, China also has a good deal to offer. Like all newly-literate 'masses', the Chinese are avid for the printed word. In clubs, on trains, in parks, I saw men and women, noses in book, oblivious to passers-by. Bookshops are well stocked and for children the range of choice is almost bewildering. Children's books cost very little. Sometimes they are referred to as 'egg-books' since they are about the same price as that commodity.

Polemicists and pamphleteers are, of course, much in demand. Amateurs in all the arts are equally encouraged.

Festivals for dancers, musicians, poetry-readers and story-tellers take place everywhere. For the great amateur arts festivals held in Peking hundreds of performers come from all parts of the country. Immensely elaborate affairs, they are favoured by the visits and comments of Chairman Mao and Premier Chou. Seats for these performances are sold out a few weeks ahead and the progress of the various competitions is widely reported, even in the Foreign Language Press publications.

The People's Liberation Army has tens of thousands of performers in its drama and song-and-dance groups; its amateur writers are very active.

Story-telling and poetry-reading sessions attract large audiences. Here are a few samples of prize-winning entries in inter-commune and minority peoples' poetry competitions; they include love-poems, described as having a 'new salty tang, very different from the wistful sentimentality of much of the old'.

Don't scowl, you naked mountain!
We shall make you a set of new clothes.
With a green gauze cap, and garlands of red blossom,
You'll have to change your name from 'Bald-Top'
To 'Flower-Fruit Eminence'.

On either end of the springy carrying-pole
The girl balances two full water-buckets.
Lithely she moves ahead, not splashing a drop
While the lad follows close behind.
'Stop for a moment,' he begs her,
'Let me tell you the longing in my heart!'
Without pausing, the girl laughs –
'Look at the beads of sweat on your face!
You can't even keep pace
With a woman carrying two full buckets!
What has your heart got to say about that?'

Brother goes on winged feet, carrying baskets of earth
Close on his heels comes a girl, also with two full loads.
'Even if you fly into the clouds,' she says,
'I'll not let you outdistance me!'

'All this is more than admirable, it is remarkable,' Victor Purcell, Cambridge Sinologist, writes. 'Never before in the history of China has there been such cultural activity.'

But, clearly, there are certain serious disabilities. The professional artist is a public servant, owing everything except his talent and his staying power to the State. When Mao wrote at Yenan, he stressed the value of the artist not for art's but for China's sake:

> Art must serve the masses; art must serve socialism. . . . All literature and art are for the masses of the people. . . . We will have no more literature and art of the ruling class of China's feudal era. . . . Writers should create a variety of characters out of actual life and help the masses to project history onward. . . . Their works are the products of the reflection of the life of the people. . . . For revolutionary writers and artists the targets for exposure are aggressors, exploiters and oppressors.

Theoretically, then, all are to be didactic, exhortatory; they must 'point a moral and adorn a tale'; they must help the people to become better citizens, better socialists and nurture 'the revolutionary spirit'. Esoteric, off-beat or 'abstract' art, as we know it, is out.

At the opening of an Arts Festival, the Vice-Minister of Culture said:

> Literature and Art is political and ideological work. Our duty is to assist the ideological consciousness and morality of the masses, speed up socialist construction and bring about the early achievement of Communism. Workers in the field of art and literature can shoulder this great and 247

glorious task only by becoming revolutionaries and one with the workers.

And an editorial in *Renmin Ribao* stated, 'Art comes directly from the life-struggles of workers'.

In the visual arts the influence of the Moscow realist school is apparent. Peasants and workers, printed or sculptured, are romanticized figures, larger-than-life heroes, tough and muscular, looking onward and upward to an ever brighter revolutionary future. This, of course, is revolutionary romanticism, not revolutionary realism. When an exhibition of British painting went to Peking, many Chinese visitors could not understand, for example, Joseph Herman's Seated Miner; Denis and Anna Mathews, who accompanied the exhibition, write, 'The miner was a seated figure. He was not standing smiling in an awareness of a glorious future. He was unglamorized, self-contained and about to smoke a pipe.'

Because of the need to serve the masses, standards of taste must inevitably fall at times and some of the ceramic figures I saw at Wusih and the pottery at Fushan were, to me, in disappointingly poor taste.

As for the theatre, the Communist Party, like the Greek city-state and the medieval church, regards it as a preaching medium. Especially in the last three years the *People's Daily, The Red Flag* and, for foreign readers, the *Peking Review* have carried their typically prolix, schoolmasterly exhortations to use the stage as a pulpit.

When Peking staged a mighty Festival of Opera on Contemporary Themes in 1964, a national conference of writers and artists met also to debate the issues. The *Peking Review* records their queries. 'How can today's reality best be reflected in the drama, especially in such old, traditional dramatic forms as Peking, *kunqu* and Shaohsing opera? What should be the proper approach to China's cultural heritage? How shall certain old operas be reassessed and adapted to today's needs? What about myths and legends?' The *Peking Review* continues, 'The week-long festival brought together eighteen Peking and provincial operas as well as modern plays and puppet-shows. Fifty thousand people came to see the shows. The aim was, without losing the essential flavour, to make these operas more comprehensible to today's audiences.'

The opener of an East China Theatre Festival went to the heart of the matter when he stated firmly, in characteristic jargon, 'Our plays must foster a socialist theory, they must serve to build the socialist economic base.'

That a fair number of writers and audiences raised their voices against at least the excesses of this trend is clear, for they sparked off a quite vehement defence of the worker-revolutionary-hero concept in the *Literary Gazette*, and two subsequent issues of *Peking Review* in 1965. Thus writes the editorial department of the *Literary Gazette*:

Someone put forward the idea of writing about 'middle character' and down-grading the importance of writing about heroes. His main reasons may be summed up as follows:

1. Positive heroes are a minority among the masses of the people whereas 'middle characters' make up the majority.
2. Literary and artistic works should reflect contradictions and these are often concentrated in middle characters.
3. It is mainly the middle elements that art is called upon to educate.
4. In our literary works too much has been written about heroes and too little about middle characters.

Middle characters will, of course continue to appear . . . but the central and most important task of socialist literature and artistic creation is . . . the creation of heroes . . . writers must not be tainted by the spiritual burden of the individual peasant or a gloomy psychology.

In 1965, as the Vietnam war escalated and drew ever nearer 249

China's southern borders, contemporary themes took over almost every theatrical performance.

The first indigenous ballet, *The Red Detachment of Women*, was a full-length dance-drama based on incidents in Hainan Island during the war against the Japanese. *The Seal*, telling the story of the defeat of commune reactionaries by cadres and team-workers, was first seen as a Peking opera, then as a straight play in the repertory of two hundred companies. It was also made into a film. It is reported to have been treated in forty different styles.

Another widely popular story, that of a revolutionary railway worker and his family, *The Red Signal Lantern*, I saw in its operatic form. The captured revolutionary hero sings:

> As I go to my execution I see
> The red flag of the revolution flying high.
> The day will come when
> The stormy skies will clear
> And a hundred flowers blossom in beauty.
> A new China
> Rising like the sun,
> Sheds its rays over the land.

The Yi minority people adapted an old play to the new times; one of its songs went thus:

> 'How wonderful if I could pluck the stars from the sky
> And hang them in the kitchen as lamps!'

> 'The more you sing, the crazier you get,
> For stars to be turned into lamps
> Is something I have never seen.'

> 'Why, that is nothing unusual.
> Here we have built a power station –
> A string of stars hangs in every home.'

> Unison: 'All praise to the General Line for
> Socialist Construction!

Our gratitude to Chairman Mao has no bounds!'

In literature the same themes are demanded and provided. Guozi Shudian (Foreign Bookshop) lists the following titles: *Keep the Red Flag Flying*, *Harvest*, *An Ordinary Labourer* and *Guerilla Hero*.

In Peking I met the novelist, Chou Erh-fu, who gave me a copy of his *Morning in Shanghai*. It tells the story of the 'transformation of the capitalist concerns and the changing outlook of the businessmen. It is a fast-moving account of the devious ways in which the businessmen set to work to get round the various Government regulations.' Chou Erh-fu also devotes considerable space to the everyday life and struggle of the Chinese workers. Volume I is six hundred and fifty pages long, an enormously detailed, often doctrinaire account of revolutionary versus reactionary characters. The monthly, *Chinese Literature*, carries some well-written short stories, but the repetitiousness of theme becomes monotonous to the Western reader.

One of the most depressing things that I came across in China was a little booklet, *The Debate on the Literary Front*, which made sadly clear official disapproval of any individualistic, non-revolutionary approach to contemporary problems: 'This sort of writing cannot at present serve the masses at all.' By our standards the writer is the most circumscribed of the artists because he cannot find refuge in the apolitical themes of the traditional painter, nor overlay his message with the choreographic or musical diversion of the theatre. He is more naked to the Party and didactic winds from which he has little shelter. Writers' outspoken criticism of the basic concepts of the régime cannot be expected. Hu Feng, a Party member, fell from grace and ceased to find publication after he had written a long article attacking the writers' union and demanding that the arts be taken out of Government hands.

In a key speech on Party policy, the Director of the Propaganda Department declared, 'Letting flowers of many kinds bloom and diverse schools of thought contend means that we stand for freedom of independent thinking, of debate, of creative freedom to maintain one's opinions on questions of art, literature and science' – which seems as liberal as you wish, until it is 251 realized that he markedly omits freedom of expression in the political field, and elsewhere equally clearly says, 'While we hold there must be democratic liberties among the people no freedom can be extended to counter-revolutionaries; for them we have only dictatorship.'

This was in 1956, and a year later the *People's Daily* carried the curious comment that 'it is necessary to be lenient with rightists who take no destructive action for these educate us in negative aspects'. No wonder Professor Fitzgerald comments 'The question of how far freedom to criticize really extends is still entangled in the thickets of Marxist theory.'

Edgar Snow says succinctly, 'No one but a fool would say that writers are free to noncomform.' I agree, and certainly do not say it!

Where then, on balance, does the creative or interpretive artist stand today? The interpretive artist clearly never had it so good. The creative artist, like the Christian, the scholar, the academic, the philosopher, stands within the circle drawn by authority and if he does not wander beyond he can be envied by many of his Western counterparts. It would be foolish to cherish the illusion that all, or even many, Chinese artists are kicking against the pricks. Their creative ability is not, in actual fact, wholly cabined, cribbed and confined. No open-minded, open-hearted visitor could fail to be impressed by the vigour and, Party line notwithstanding, the variety, of the arts in China today.

The most significant aspect is, of course, the general acceptance of the arts as an integral part of everyday living, not just a sort of fringe-benefit for the cultivated few. The artist or crafts-man feels he is deeply involved in the community, making an important contribution. The majority of Chinese creative and executant artists know for what they are working and love what they know – the glory and well-being of the Middle Kingdom. A young painter may be busy on health posters, he may have to make his pictures speak loud and clear about litter-louts, bumper harvests or part-time education, but he believes this is 252 worth doing and feels, too, that, within certain bounds, he can do it in his own way. Many posters, illustrations and wood-cuts are obviously banal, even crude, but many are gay, amusing and most competently designed. Book-illustration, especially for children, is excellent and a visit to the Canton Fair handicraft section reveals a renaissance of the plastic arts. There are faithful copies of classical porcelain, carvings, embroideries. There are, admittedly, elaborately ugly chinoiseries, with that sad *mésalliance* of good craft and poor art, which sell both on the home and overseas markets; but, side by side with these, are beautiful *objets d'art* where artist and craftsman have combined to produce modern things of beauty in the twentieth-century idiom as well as in traditional style.

And it is important always to realize that artists in the People's Republic may be Communist, but they are also Chinese. Sir Herbert Read, leading English art critic and historian, visited China in 1963 and concluded that ninety per cent of the best painters worked wholly in the main Chinese tradition. Chi Pai-shih was revered not for social realism but for his exquisite flower and landscape paintings, which, with their remarkable economy of effect, are the antithesis of the meticulously-detailed offerings of the Moscow school. Like their Sung and Tang predecessors, the modern Chinese masters are known by what they omit, and Western critics have agreed that many of their works might come from the brush of the greatest 'old masters'.

I was interested to note that nine of the twelve reproductions on the 1965 Guozi Shudian calendar were labelled 'Traditional Painting', though every artist is contemporary. Several are simple flower or bird studies, indistinguishable in theme and treatment from nineteenth-century Ching paintings, and even the Long March landscapes and the famous Peking Zoo pandas are variants on classical themes and treatment.

Of abstract art in the Western sense there is none; but China has always had its own style of abstract and symbolic art. Sir Herbert comments, 'I think the Chinese answer to the West's modernism is to go back to their tradition which they feel is rich enough to include our modernism, but far more expressive.' 253

In theatre the story is similar. The theatre perpetuates national traditions; it adapts them to modern needs; it makes its moves into new subjects on official lines, and it also breaks away from them, just like the other arts.

The companies of jugglers, musicians and acrobats, the folk-dancers and singers, are, to some extent, traditional, for they are the lineal descendants of the wandering players who entertained the court and gentry and, occasionally, the peasants of dynastic times with local song and dance. Today the troupes are planned on a wider scale. From the local performers the province selects its first troupe, which tours China and sometimes foreign countries. I saw the Liaoning Company – rather uneven, but its best performers would have topped any bill in the Western variety theatre (provided anti-imperialist banners weren't drawn from the conjurer's hat, or praise to the Party sung by the chorus).

Classical opera is still played; I just missed a performance of 'Monkey' in Canton. Its traditions have been taken over and adapted to the present demand for 'contemporary themes' and this has proved fairly easy to do. The old opera often dealt with social themes and, in addition, it clearly differentiated, like medieval miracle plays and modern Westerns, between hero and villain. Make-up, especially, drew the distinction hard and fast so that the audience knew, literally at first glance, what kind of character had entered; red or black paint on the mask-like make-up meant a loyal 'goodie', white the treachery and guile of the 'baddie'.*

The long modern realist novels also perpetuate tradition, for they are the descendants of, for example, the famous medieval novel, *The Dream of the Red Chamber* and the equally well-known *All Men are Brothers*, besides the early twentieth-century stories of Lu Hsun.

The poet's path is reasonably smooth. The nature poem continues and the short philosophic meditation; even the old

* Though many of the dated operas and their traditions may be abandoned, it is devoutly to be hoped that many examples of this unique theatrical form will be retained. There were far fewer in 1965 than '63.

legendary fairies, gods and goddesses reappear, especially in the work of commune poets. Many of Mao's own poems have no party theme or political overtones, and they always reveal an intense love of the countryside:

Snow (sung to a popular melody)
This is the scene in that northern land;
A hundred leagues are sealed with ice,
A thousand leagues of whirling snow.
On either side of the Great Wall
One vastness is all you see.
From end to end of the great river
The rushing torrent is frozen and lost.
The mountains dance like silver snakes,
The highlands roll like waxen elephants,
As if they sought to vie with heaven in their height;
And on a sunny day
You will see a red dress thrown over the white, Enchantingly
    lovely!

Kunlun (to a well-known melody)
Rising straight in the air above this earth,
Great Kunlun, you have witnessed all that was fairest in the
    world of men.
Your three million white jade dragons in their flight
Freeze the sky with penetrating cold;
In summer days your melting torrents
Fill the streams and rivers over the brim,
Changing men into fish and turtles.
What man can pass judgement
On all the good and evil you have done these thousand
    autumns?

But now today I say to you, Kunlun,
You don't need this height, don't need all this snow!
If I could lean on the sky, I would draw my sword
And with it cut you into three pieces.

One I would send to Europe,
One to America,
One we would keep in China here,
So should a great peace reign in the world,
For all the world would share in your warmth and cold.

So, Party ultimata notwithstanding, there is a great deal of the past in China's present in the arts as much else.

When we talk about the curbing of the creative spirit, which is rightly to be deplored, we have to take note of the different East–West ideas on the workings of the spirit. It has rarely been a Chinese aspiration to be different. For a young artist to be told 'he paints like the master' is a very great compliment. He wishes to be part of a whole, a harmonious whole.*

Nor has the Chinese artist in any field usually been averse to practical goals, to statements on clearly moral problems. He has been happy to leave curious speculations about supernatural powers, fate or salvation of individual souls (the soul-body dichotomy has not exercised Chinese thinkers). 'Respect the spirits,' said Confucius, 'but keep them at a distance.'

But even if the Western visitor to China knows a modest amount about its artistic tradition, he must be often bored or irritated by their modern manifestations. This is, in part, because realism has become so discredited in the West that we are perilously near the assumption that realist art is, *ipso facto*, poor art, and certainly art with a message is deeply suspect. Western critics are prepared to look down on pictures, plays, music that speak simply to ordinary people. Yet there is a more than even chance that the great artist may well do better for believing in some of the things that most of his fellows believe in. Shakespeare, Dickens, Balzac, Molière, Rubens were not odd-bods, outsiders, but creative beings well within the main stream of a world they may have criticized but, even so, much enjoyed; a world whose material rewards they gladly accepted.

When Sir Herbert Read complained about Chinese realist

* Victor Purcell talks of China's 'organicism' as one of its most
admirable concepts.

art, it was not because it was realist but because it was mediocre. There is no reason why plays about revolutionary heroes or commune intrigues should not, intrinsically, be as interesting and as theatrical as the personal problems of adolescent lovers or the psychotic 'misfit', provided the dramatist knows his job. For the Chinese audience there is an immediacy about what is going on on the stage. Much to my surprise, I found myself caught up in the sheer strength, vigour and conviction of the dancers of the *Red Detachment of Women*, in spite of its off-putting title and my strong prejudice against women militia 'on points'. The performers meant every step of what they were dancing and, since Chinese audiences still feel they are living their revolution, incidents on the stage reflected first-hand experience for many of them.

The steady beat of doctrinal drums in the theatre and the recurrence of the same themes were most noticeable on my last visit because of the tensions generated by the Vietnam war. Even making allowance for this, I became, from time to time, exasperated and longed for more of the apolitical acts on the programme.

When we are tempted to make sweeping generalizations about the danger of limitations on the artists' freedom of expression, we do not always concede the existence of certain limitations in 'the Western world'. It has its own curbs and strait-jackets provided by commercial, popular and 'establishment' demands, especially in times of war or national crisis. Commercial artists, radio and television script-writers and popular dramatists must provide, within pretty narrow terms of reference, goods which meet these demands. The sort of artist who most suffers in China by existing terms of reference is the rebel, with or without a cause; the one who wishes, come hell come high water, to create as the spirit moves him, with no reference to tradition or popular demand. Such a one is lost to China today.

But situations change – in China as everywhere else. It is significant that, though Mao said that art must serve the masses, that it must build socialism, he also said, 'Our first task 257 is to popularize art and then raise standards. Only by representing the masses can you educate them. First popularize, then refine.' This would seem to imply that a wholly doctrinaire or popular approach to the arts may be a transitional stage. Provided there is peace and some sense of security, it seems possible that, after a couple of generations, the taste of an increasing number of people will become more sophisticated; didactic and moralistic art will be less acceptable; and conformity less necessary.

It is unlikely that Mao, the poet and calligrapher, will wish to see the lowest common denominator of taste become its highest criterion in a country with an artistic heritage like that of China. Art must serve the masses and the masses must have what they want, but they must be taught to 'raise their standards'. The task of the leader, as Mao sees it, as Confucius saw it, is the task of the teacher. 'To govern is to rectify.'

APPENDIX III
Education in China

Like all so-called 'newly-emerging countries' Chi̵ ̵ ̵
education only slightly less emphasis than she denotes to
industry and agriculture; education is as much an investment
as the others and as much needed to make sure that China
will 'catch up'.

The Chinese have added reason for stressing educational and
cultural development; their country's age-long reverence for
learning placed the scholar at the top of the social hierarchy;
ahead of the merchant, the farmer and, certainly, the soldier,
who came very low on the prestige-scale.

When the Communist Government took over in 1949 it faced
tremendous problems. Not only was the country impoverished
after years of savage war and foreign occupation, but even
before that, it had never had enough facilities or teachers. The
Nationalist Government had done its best job in higher education, but, even here, provision was scanty and primary and
secondary schools were tragically few.

In 1949 the number of potential students at all levels was
almost overwhelming, for it included not only the usual proportion to be expected in a population of more than six hundred
and fifty million, but also tens of thousands who had had no
opportunity of schooling before or during the revolution. Some
eighty-five to ninety per cent were illiterate.

Though the régime was reasonably sure of its position, it
still had 'to consolidate the revolution' and cope with what it
calls, 'bourgeois and reactionary' opposition from within and
the strongest opposition from without by many of the Great
Powers. Excluded from the United Nations, it did not share in
any of its rehabilitation schemes.

Paradoxically enough, the very strength of the scholarly
tradition was a liability, for it had led to the divorce of the
intellectual from the people and perpetuated a *corps d'élite* concerned with the niceties of learning, especially in Chinese
language, literature and philosophy, whilst its interest in science
had been limited. To meet the needs of an industrial, tech-
nological age, therefore, the whole climate of educational
opinion had to be changed without, at the same time, alienating

the intellectuals whom the Government knew it urgently needed. Reading through Party literature on plans for the New China, one is struck by the amount of attention given to the position of this group. All but the most reactionary and anti-Communist of them were fairly well-treated, and a slow, steady effort was made to persuade them that their future was assured if they would co-operate with the Government in building the new educational structure. 'The declared policy of the Communist Party is to win over, unite, educate and reform them,' wrote Mao Tse-tung.

Two of the most outspoken critics at the time of the open-criticism period, known as the 'Hundred Flowers' (1956) were Lo Ching-chi and Chang Po-chun, both leaders of the Democratic League political party. They were subjected to merciless criticism in return and were deprived of their ministerial portfolios, but they were allowed to keep their membership of the People's Political Consultative Conference, on which they still serve. Chou En-lai in his speech 'On the Question of Intellectuals' admitted that 'irrational features and sectarian attitudes had handicapped the Party's policy towards them' and promised to try to remove these.

On the financial front, the Party made equal efforts, spending every yuan it could spare (more than ten per cent of the budget in 1957) and giving provincial governments, trade unions, industrial concerns and, later, the communes, the task of providing certain educational facilities. In addition, if parents could afford it, they paid small fees for some primary and secondary education, and college students were pressed to earn their way by part-time work. Many scholarships are available for needy students.

According to an article in the January 1963 edition of the British quarterly, *The Arts and Sciences in China*, there were, in 1963, thirty-one million children in kindergartens, ninety million in primary, ten million in secondary and about nine hundred thousand in tertiary institutions. Compared with pre-revolutionary 1949 this means that there were two hundred and thirty-seven times as many pupils in kindergartens, three times as many in primary, five and a half times as many in secondary and over three times as many in tertiary institutions, as well as tens of thousands in part-time classes.*

Somehow, funds have been found to convert or erect an extraordinary number of buildings for the education of children, adolescents and adults. Some of the buildings used are old and, by our standards, some of the new ones bare and certainly lacking in frills; but they are there and the basic minimum standards for teaching, residence and recreation in new schools is by no means ungenerous considering the many calls on time and skills. Many university libraries are generously stocked and laboratory equipment has favourably impressed visiting scientists from the West.

Teachers have somehow been found. In the early days some returned from overseas, some were recruited from business and industry, and many were Middle School graduates barely a couple of jumps ahead of their pupils. Now that the Teachers' Colleges are turning out their graduates, the position is improving steadily. There are said to be three million full-time teachers at present. At the East China Teachers' College I found well-planned four- and five-year courses.

The whole country joined in the great 'literacy drive' of the 'fifties. With its huge eighty-five to ninety per cent illiteracy rate, the People's Republic, in 1949, faced its most urgent educational task, and faced it with characteristic determination and almost demonic energy. 'Each one teach one' was the word; primary-school children taught mother at home and uncle in the fields; the army passed on what it learned to the peasants, who, in turn, evolved ingenious devices for teaching one another. Often they wore ideographs on their backs as they ploughed or sowed so that comrades behind them could learn.

Factories, farms, schools, educated families, all set up teaching centres. The task was Herculean, for learning to write

---

* Chinese statistics are sometimes self-contradictory or presented in forms which made annual comparisons difficult, but these figures march well enough with those for 1958 given by Leo Orleans in his *Professional Manpower and Education in Communist China.*

Chinese at any age, let alone in one's forties or fifties, is a tough job. By 1957 Chou En-lai estimated illiteracy at sixty-six per cent in rural areas, twenty-four per cent in the cities.* On present showings illiteracy will be as rare in the under-forties by 1967, as it is now rare among under-twenties.

Because, as Communists, the Government sees the need to remove any lingering traces of reaction and to create a China dedicated to both socialist ideals and national glory, the whole tone of education must be both socialist and Chinese. The prime and final arbiter of the country's educational destiny is the Education Committee of the Party, and they see the schools as their most powerful means of ensuring that China 'will stand up'; that 'the East wind will prevail over the West wind' and that it will be a socialist wind.

'The educated must be developed morally, intellectually and physically to become workers with a socialist conscience and culture.' 'Education must serve the political ends of the proletariat.' 'Professional knowledge must be combined with politics.' 'The broad masses of students and teachers must criticize the individual in pursuit of personal gain and fame who seeks to become vocationally proficient without becoming red; who follows the road of the "white expert".' Such statements recur again and again in Party documents and newspapers. All this is often summed up in the one simple dictum, 'Education in politics'.

One of its clearest practical effects is shown in the National Regulations for the Enrolment of Higher Education Students, one of which reads: 'Candidates are chosen for the best health and scholastic conditions provided that political quality is assured', and a second test for health and political quality is given after enrolment.

One would naturally conclude that this state of affairs would demand a high degree of centralization, and certainly the central planning authorities determine, among other things, which subjects shall be expanded, which cut down and where, when, and to what extent this shall be done in the light of

* Anyone able to read 1,500 simplified characters is classed as literate.

national needs. University admissions and graduate employment are determined by the national planners, who balance the respective demands of industry, agriculture or teaching and research. Transfer from primary to secondary to tertiary institutions is made by a national examination system.

There is no doubt whatever that the bond between education and the Party is a close one. I believe that there is a trusted Party member at the head of all institutions; this was true of all those which I have visited over a seven-year period. Sometimes the man or woman was a former revolutionary with a long and faithful record of service and a single-minded devotion to the Republic, but rather scanty educational qualifications; sometimes I found Party membership and educational distinction combined. Always the second-in-command was 'professionally expert'.

In addition, the curriculum of every institution includes the study of politics. In primary schools the subject is called 'Communist Morality' and is taught for the first fifteen minutes of the school day. Called, usually, political science or political economy, it occupies about two periods a week in secondary schools and one or two longish sessions a week in higher education centres.

There can be no doubt that some must long for freedom to speak up or at least to contract out – just to keep quiet and get on with their own business, avoiding political activities. This, I gather, may not be easy, for there may be an implication that 'he who is not with us is against us' and so overt, even vigorous, support of Government policy is found to be desirable. I have met two young Chinese graduates who, with their families, are now living abroad but who went to school and university in China. Both said they had been very happy in their middle school and joined in its many group activities with enthusiasm and enjoyed their physical labour. But at their universities they had not liked the continuous pressure to take part in so many political activities. After several years of overseas studies, they were both in many ways keen to return to their native land, but not keen to breathe continually the Party air! They 263 believed that, in the past few years, the increasing rather than diminishing concern with student political orthodoxy was caused chiefly by increased external pressures, a belief I share.

Dissident students are dealt with not by violence, which must always be eschewed except in time of war, but by the 'vast apparatus of persuasion'. An Australian student–visitor was told by a university teacher, 'If a student writes up an anti-Party slogan, the writer is not punished but shown it along with other students, and made to see the error of his way.' Public opinion, the steady, sweet reasonableness of one's peers, must exercise a piston-like pressure on the would-be non-conformist. And there are periodic political mass demonstrations in which students are expected to take part.

All this sounds as if it should produce a sense of frustration and rigidity in teachers and taught, and a doctrinaire approach antipathetic to true scholarship.* Fortunately for everyone in China – and outside it – the realities of the situation are less disturbing than China's own pronouncements often suggest.

To begin with the intellectuals: many European Sinologists report that they have found their Chinese colleagues back at work, often very happily; some of them still grumble about this and that, even express considerable reservations; but they are seeing results, and there is peace. No doubt they sometimes tire of the jargon and the slogans, and would prefer to get on with their research and teaching instead of attending meetings or going off for physical labour stints; but when some of them say they have learned a good deal from their time in field or factory, and have profited from some of the criticism-self-criticism sessions with colleagues and students, there is no reason to disbelieve them.

In his famous oration 'On Contradiction Among the People' Mao Tse-tung showed understanding of the demands that had to be made on older scholars: 'Some are reluctant to accept Communism; we should not be too exacting in what we expect of them; as long as they comply with the requirements of the

---

* It certainly presents a hurdle for the Western scholar who wishes to look impartially at the Chinese education scene.

state and engage in legitimate pursuits, we should give them opportunities for suitable work. The feelings of some of these have been hurt; this is not good.' And he has a few words for the Party die-hards: 'Many of our comrades are stiff with intellectuals; they lack respect for their work and interfere in cultural matters in a way that is uncalled for.'

Academics' support is more easily understood when we discover what was their lot before 1949. Professor Fitzgerald, who lived in China in those days, writes, 'The universities were suffering the heavy hand of the special secret police; students were suspect; professors watched; freedom of thought and publication suppressed.' We know that even their lives were not spared; a well-known professor was executed in Kunming. An American writer, Frank Kiernan, states, 'They [the academics] loved China and the Communists gave China an international status greater than anything the KMT had been able to.' Sir Marcus Oliphant says, 'Chinese scientists are used to fitting their interests to national needs and they take part in planning at the highest level. A few scientists who wish are given freedom to work in their own way.'

For today's students the situation is one they have grown up with; the majority accept it either gladly or at least uncomplainingly; certainly those belonging to families that could never, in the old days, have dreamed of any education for their children, probably do not complain about the present climate of opinion. They may not have the final choice of courses or jobs, but they can list their preferences and the regulations are often administered humanely and sensibly enough. Many get pretty much what they ask for; if not, they accept the situation as a national necessity in their developing homeland.

I found that the political studies were not as limiting as might be expected. Communist morality in the primary schools is really citizenship in a socialist setting; it teaches children to be clean, honest, hard-working; to have reverence for parents and old people, to serve the community, look after public property, love Chairman Mao and be ready to defend China against aggressors.

In middle schools and universities there is, of course, a thorough study of Marxism–Leninism and Mao's writings, but there is also discussion of current affairs, international, national and local; though sources of information are limited, university libraries at least take some non-Communist overseas journals for consultation.

Even so, undoubtedly this aspect of Chinese education remains, in theory, a constant challenge to the Westerner's cherished beliefs in academic freedom. It is essential to translate the theory into terms of human behaviour and the greatest happiness of the greatest number. And here one moves on to greener fields. Chinese youth seems cheerful enough.

Individually and in groups young people are well-mannered and well-behaved, and disarmingly friendly with foreign visitors. Youngsters on the move across cities to parks or playing fields walk in groups or in unregimented, rather straggling, 'crocodiles', and classroom discipline is not rigid.

Hero cults are a necessity for the young; in China the highly efficient public communications media pay great attention to these. Men and women, usually, but not always, young, are selected as examples of those virtues which the socialist state most wishes to develop. Once selected, a hero, or, equally often in sex-egalitarian China, a heroine, is featured in posters, stories, newspapers, films, plays and on radio and television. Each has a 'good revolutionary spirit', wishes to become a good Communist and to defend his country against aggressors. But the spirit must show itself in humility and unselfish service for others. Heroes are ready to do hard and unpleasant jobs, 'clearing muck and carting manure'; they are unendingly cheerful, thrifty to a degree, saving the private and the public purse; they are tidy, morally pure; they love old people and they work very, very hard. They study the works of Mao and, in the light of his advice, tackle problems successfully.

Forgetting the revolutionary label, one sees the pattern of the good Scout or Guide, or, foregoing the Christian label, the boy and girl heroine of Victorian moral tales.

266 Most publicized in 1965 was a country boy and soldier, Lei

Feng, who died in a tractor accident at the age of twenty-two. His diary, published after his death, was quoted constantly and was praised by Chairman Mao himself, who said, 'Followers of Comrade Lei Feng are displaying his revolutionary spirit of rendering wholehearted service to the people.' In his diary Lei Feng wrote: 'I feel that I must live in such a way that others may live better. I must devote my limited life to the boundless service of the people. The greatest happiness belongs only to those who work diligently and energetically for the prosperity of the country.' A picture of Lei Feng shows him telling a group of Young Pioneers how to start a 'thrift-box'.

Some of the accounts of Lei Feng and other 'heroes' read, at times, a little comically to us, in our debunking age, and we are tempted to think of a race of revolutionary Pollyannas, but the fault is on the right side. It is all very much in the plain living, high-thinking tradition with which Highlanders, Yorkshiremen and New Englanders are especially familiar!

Lessons on public responsibility seem not wholly wasted, for there is little hooliganism or vandalism. In museums, gardens and palaces there are very few guards or attendants. I saw a large group of youngsters at a display of bonzai trees in Canton; they pushed one another about and made a bit of noise – thank goodness – but never did more than gently touch a leaf or flower. In the same park I saw a group of ten-year-olds, like so many little elves, sweeping up leaves and weeding as part of their public-work chores for the week.

With all the university students I met I felt at ease, and, though their outlook was doctrinaire, this did not prevent their questioning us about our life and opinions and in turn answering questions frankly about their own. Talking with such students one finds the wallboards, the slogans, the jargon, fade out of mind.

One has to ask how far time and energy spent on political studies and physical labour affect academic studies. It is hard to give certain answers unless one has seen a good deal of work over a fair length of time. My only first-hand experience was with English-language students. I was impressed by the spoken 267

English of graduates of the Foreign Languages Institute in Peking and the final-year students at Sun Yat-sen University in Canton, but have no knowledge of their written work or the extent of their reading in English literature.

I have discussed scientific standards with Australian scientists who have visited China. Professor Sir Marcus Oliphant of the Australian National University commented favourably on laboratory equipment in the Institutes of Physics and Atomic Research. Professor W. Christiansen, well-known radio astronomer of Sydney University, writes after his visits to observatories in China in 1965, 'The young people at the Purple Mountain Observatory near Nanking had built a 3cm wave-length radiometer with which they are observing the sun. The construction job had more than a little of the heroic about it because the radio astronomers had not merely built up the complicated equipment from components which they had bought; they had constructed the components themselves, the antennas, the wave-guides, the ferrite devices as well as the electronics.'

Sir Lindon Brown, Vice-President of the Royal Society, said in 1962, 'Chinese scientists seem fantastically well-acquainted with Western scientific literature. There is a lot of good work that anyone in Europe would be glad to have in his laboratory.'

Centralization appears less formidable on closer inspection. There is considerable devolution of authority, for Mao Tse-tung and Party leaders seem aware that bureaucracy is now a greater threat than reaction, and there are frequent warnings against red tape, routine and remote control. 'Dare to think; Dare to do!'

Yung Chi-min, Chinese historian, writes, 'Party members made a thorough analysis of their own thinking and examined Party leadership, special emphasis being laid on tendencies to subjectivism, sectarianism and meaningless Party jargon.' In his 'Contradictions Among the People', Mao writes, 'Contradictions arise from the bureaucratic practice of state functionaries in their relations with the people!' The three evils, 'bureaucracy, dogmatism and sectarianism', are widely recognized. (Their cure is not, it is made clear, a multiple party system. It is 'rectification under democratic centralism'.) The local authorities which run schools are allowed some freedom of adaptation; principals of some schools and colleges are given considerable responsibility for administration and organization.

Finally, we must assess the significance of Chinese development of its vast work-and-study programme. This was enunciated by Lu Tong-yi after a meeting of the Communist Party Education Committee in 1958. The statement, 'Education must be Combined with Productive Labour' will remain for the Chinese a sort of gospel for years to come. 'Pedagogy is a branch of social science and must be guided by politics. The principle of divorcing mental from manual labour has dominated education for thousands of years,' he says, and quotes a formidable array of scholars, including Confucius, Mencius, Hsun Tzu, as well as socialist writers like Fournier and Owen (he might have included William Morris), to show the folly of this dichotomy, which, of course, for the Marxist is one cause of class distinctions.

'We believe that all-round development provides versatile people going over in sequence from one branch of production to another,' he continues, quoting Mao's famous remark that the ideal is a 'cultured, socialist-minded worker – a working intellectual and an intellectual worker'. He urges an increase in the movement for schools to set up their own factories and farms and for factories and agricultural co-operatives to establish their own schools.

Since 1958 the momentum has increased and there were indications on my 1965 visit that further steps were to be taken, perhaps in the direction of more physical labour, but I had an impression that some teachers may prefer to consolidate the present schemes before further adaptations are made.

Theoretically, the work-and-study concept, if applied reasonably, is hard to fault by either educationalists or sociologists, and that it is producing valuable results we must believe, in spite of some mistakes through the over-enthusiasm of Party planners. We have to discount some of the near-miraculous results lyrically reported to us: 'The students throw themselves 269

into the furnace of productive labour to get themselves tem-
pered and refined and work without caring for reward. With
hardened hands they have changed their stand; with skins
tanned their thinking takes on a red glow.' Clearly knocking
off school to be farmer's boy or factory-hand will not please
all the people all the time, any more than compulsory games
or cross-country runs please every English schoolboy. But most
Western observers I have talked to seemed to think that the
work is usually accepted equably, often enjoyed, by the young
at least. The children of a European resident in Peking told
me, 'We get awfully tired sometimes, but we have lots of fun.'

Many projects on and off the campus produce results in the
way of improved techniques, increased crops or cultural
activities and more campus swimming-pools and athletic
grounds for the students themselves.

The social significance of companionship between worker and
intellectual, blue overall and white collar, is considerable, and
an obvious solvent of some labour-relations problems that
plague us. Work-and-study is a most valuable bridge between
city dweller and country cousin. Altogether I should say it is
one of the more interesting pedagogical experiments of our
time, and aspects of it would be of value if adapted to Western
conditions.

For readers interested in figures, I append a few tables.
Some of these are based on Leo Orleans's admirable collation
of statistics in his *Professional Manpower and Education in Communist China*. Though these are already six years out of date,
they are valuable. The 1965 figures were given me in Peking.

But statistics, in education, far more than industry or
agriculture, have meaning only in terms of what human beings
are doing or having done to them, so I expand on my generalizations and other people's figures by briefly describing some of
my visits to education centres over the past seven years.

SOME OF MY VISITS

KINDERGARTENS

The kindergartens which I saw at the Peking Cotton Mill and later at the Hangchow commune* are, with a few minor variations upwards or downwards, duplicated in their tens of thousands; for there are now, according to official statistics, several millions of children in pre-school centres.

PRIMARY SCHOOLS

Similarly, the primary schools, for children aged seven to twelve years, were representative in these two places, allowing for poorer ones in remoter country areas and newer ones in recent housing estates. There are now ninety million children in the primary schools. Exact numbers in 1949 are not known, but only two and a half million children graduated from these schools into secondary schools in that year.

MIDDLE SCHOOLS (HIGH SCHOOLS)

In 1960 there were about ten million children in general or specialized secondary schools.

My longest visit was to a Nanking Middle School† which was typical of the general – i.e. non-technical – high school. Built in 1954, it was a large, grey stone building, with characteristic up-sloping, Chinese-style roof, standing in large grounds generously planted with young trees. ('Plant a tree and watch it grow' the children were told, and they had done both to good effect.) There were, I noticed, at least three courts for the widely-popular basket-ball and for the daily exercises in which the whole school took part. When I arrived I saw three classes performing these, and very nice it looked, this mixture of dancing and physical jerks with overtones of traditional *tai chi-chuan*. We were met at the gate by the Principal – a woman, I was delighted to find. Over tea she told us that the school had some 1,800 students from the age of thirteen to

* In 1963.
† In 1958.

nineteen and one hundred teachers; the day started at 8 a.m. and finished at 4 p.m., with students remaining for two hours of homework or extra-curricular activities. Since the school served a wide rural area, facilities for boarding had to be provided. I visited the dormitories, where four hundred girls and boys lived in Spartan conditions with bunk-beds on a stone floor with mats, tin wash-basins and a cold-water tap in the yard. The pupils themselves kept the place clean and helped to cook the simple but well-balanced meals served in the school canteen. All pupils stayed to sixteen or seventeen, and those who were sitting for the highly competitive university entrance examinations remained a further two years for special studies.

There were thirty-six classes – six grades with six 'streams' in each. All studied Chinese language, literature and history, and there was strong emphasis on the sciences, as well, of course, as on political philosophy, which included not only Marxism–Leninism and Mao Tse-tung's works but also discussion of local, national and international affairs. In each week there were twenty-five periods of forty-five minutes each for younger pupils, and twenty-nine of these periods for older ones. A week consisted of five days' study, one day's holiday and one day's manual labour, which was done partly in one of the two small workshops set up in the school grounds and partly in city factories, on neighbouring communes or in the school's own farm on the outskirts of Nanking. 'Our students must be all-round workers; we must inculcate good morals, good work and good discipline,' said our Principal in her peroration, and a slogan over her head read, 'All should be socialist minded and professionally expert'. I saw children assembling simple radio parts in a special workshop in the grounds. Others made nails.

HIGHER EDUCATION

Peking National University,* on the edge of the city's western suburbs, comprises the old and beautiful buildings of the Yen Ching missionary university founded by American churchmen

* Visited in 1958.

and large numbers of modern buildings erected since 1949 on a campus of some three hundred and twenty acres. It is a comprehensive university, offering all courses except professional ones, for example, in medicine, engineering and agriculture. There are about 10,000 students in all, of which about a third are women. The entrance examination is a stiff one, and the university highly selective, attracting the most promising students from all over China. Most courses are five years long (some are six years), and no degree is given at the end, but there is some statement of standard reached and successful candidates are known as graduates. The campus has good sporting facilities, including a large swimming-pool built in eighteen days of twenty-four-hour shifts by voluntary student labour. Everyone was very proud of this achievement.

The usual wallboards with posters, announcements and news bulletins were common, and large slogans appeared on banners and posters and walls. 'Education must serve the politics of the working class', 'We must have intellectual workers and working intellectuals', 'We must train ourselves to become educated Communist-minded workers.'

Among the new residence-halls we ran into groups of students hurrying along with bundles of clothes and bedding to foregather for their month's work-stint in the country; a few staff members would join them. Where possible they would do manual work somehow connected with their studies. This would obviously be easy to arrange for biologists, botanists or agricultural scientists, but I was interested to learn how arts students fared. Apparently, many of these helped with teaching, especially in literacy classes, and some had written local histories or made dictionaries of local dialects. I found conversation with the students very easy, for the girls of the senior English class accompanied me and made most articulate companions, determined to learn from me as much as they could about the English language when they weren't telling me about their work and their country. They were all most cheerful, and the highly-organized life they led seemed not to make them tense or inhibited.

273

I talked to them about their political science studies. They told me they had one longish session a week with a lecture, followed by discussion, which ranged over Communist doctrine, international affairs, national development and city and university policies. The girls' English was good, almost perfect as to grammar and syntax with a wide vocabulary and some idiomatic turns of phrase; only in rhythms and inflexions could I tell they had been taught, for the most part, by non-native-speakers. They began their reading course by using anthologies of short extracts from prose and poetry, graduating to the works of Dickens, Thackeray, Galsworthy, Shaw and Shakespeare, with glances at Jane Austen and Charlotte Brontë! Of contemporary literature there was little.

I remember one conversation very clearly, as it removed a misapprehension of mine about the university pattern in China today.

M.R. The university is quite a long way from the city; how do the students get here?

English Student:
I'm sorry, I don't understand.

M.R. Do they come by bus or train?

E.S. I do not know how they come here.

M.R. I mean, what sort of transport morning and evening? Don't tell me they walk!

E.S. They live here all the time; there are the residences over there.

To the Chinese today, university education is resident education and accommodation is provided for both staff and students, Staff live in houses of their own or hostels. Accommodation is very simple indeed, even primitive by our standards. Student residence halls have four or more bunk-beds per small room. We visited several of them, finding girls hard at work, each at her own little table beside her bunk and tiny chest of drawers; there was a common bookcase for them all. (They have to buy 274 text-books but they are cheap and the libraries give good service.) Each girl helped to serve, but not to cook, the meals in the canteen, which seemed about the standard of those I had eaten in the mill canteen. My young friends told me most of them paid for their food, but children of poorer parents received 'stipends' towards the cost of living. I asked two girls where they wanted to work on graduation and both immediately said they would go wherever they were most needed. I asked if they wished to travel overseas and that struck them as quite a new idea; it clearly had never entered their heads before. It was a contrast to English language students whom I had spoken with in the Soviet Union; they were very keen to go to Britain and polish up their English.

My experiences with the students and staff at the Sun Yat-sen University in Canton were very similar to those on my Peking University visit although my visit came seven years later, in 1965. There were the same age-range, subjects, and facilities; the same standard of English and the same enthusiasm for work and country; and the same warm welcome to any foreign visitor.

I had two long sessions with the final-year English class of men and women and a more flatteringly attentive audience I have never had. They listened eagerly to my very ordinary accounts of Australian life in general and universities in particular (they had asked me to talk about this). Not only was every seat in the lecture room full, but groups stood at open windows and in the doorways.

In the course of my talk I told them I had been asked by some Australian schoolboys to speak on the topic, 'Is Red China a threat to the safety of Australia?' They looked astonished, so I explained that many Australians believed their safety threatened by China's 'downward thrust'. After a second's pause, they burst out laughing. I must be joking. Why should they want to come to Australia? They had no wish to take anyone else's territory; it was not part of their thinking at all. They had more than enough land of their own and newly-tapped resources awaiting development. I left them still incredulous.

After my talk, questions came thick and fast. Since this was my third visit to China, I knew they would be social questions and sure enough they were – all of them. Were universities free? Did students in Australia have political freedom? Were there many workers' children at our universities? How much time was given to political education? They looked most surprised when I said none, officially. I explained that interested students formed political clubs which held discussions and where students were free to say exactly what they wanted, even 'Down with the Prime Minister' or 'We want a Republic'.

In short, students could kick the Government and its policies around, or give them full support, according to their inclinations; but many students simply weren't deeply involved, politically. This truly surprised them, and I tried to explain that in an affluent, democratic society the students' position and attitudes were inevitably different from the post-revolution ones in China.

The English Department library was more up to date than I had expected, with works by Hardy, Priestley, C. P. Snow and Steinbeck as well as Galsworthy, Shaw, Dickens and James Aldridge. *Wuthering Heights* was a set book! They took *Time and Tide*, the *Shakespeare Quarterly*, the London *Times*, as well as the *Proceedings of the Modern Language Association*. American books and publications came through Hong Kong.

The students all assured me they liked their manual labour periods, both in the university workshops and the communes; they learned much from living with the people.

Their day was pretty well organized for them. Up at 6 a.m., they did exercises for twenty minutes before breakfast, had lectures in the morning and study until 5.30 p.m. After 5.30 they often read aloud, with or without a teacher, to get practice in verbal English. On several afternoons a week they had athletics or sports; they were especially keen on swimming, since Canton is sub-tropical.

Of the four staff members I met, three had lived in the United States and had returned after Liberation, they told me;

they retained faint, but noticeable, American accents. They asked me if I would record some extracts from their anthology. Time was running out, so I had not much chance to select. Rejecting Anna Louise Strong extracts or passages from Mao Tse-tung, I started on Byron's *To Liberty* and rolled out the fine phrases, wishing mischievously that I could have selected from *Don Juan* instead. I had to avoid the Shaw because it was a less distinguished extract from a play which, Shavian though I am, I had never before read, *Augustus Does His Bit*; it dealt with recruiting for the First World War. Having met *The Gadfly* before, I avoided that too and seized happily upon the opening chapter of *Pride and Prejudice*, which, to my joy, produced ripples of appreciative mirth from my auditors.

I said frankly that I didn't think much of the selection, except for Jane, and even she needed twentieth-century companions; I wished I had long enough to write out, for what they were worth, a few of my ideas on an English anthology for Chinese students. They expressed great interest in this, and after my rash statement I was only too relieved that there was not time for so tricky a task to be set for me!

After the altogether too-enthusiastic applause which greeted the end of my question-and-answer session, I strolled with three students and three teachers back to our car and found them all better informed on world affairs than I had expected and, up to a point, open-minded (although not on the superiority of socialism to capitalism or the need to withstand imperialism and neo-colonialism).

Writing about this visit, I have made the conversation seem ponderous and contentious – like so many of the slogans, headlines and pronouncements of the Propaganda Ministry and the *Peking Review*. Certainly much of our talk was about the students' political activities because that was what interested me most, but there was much laughter and mutual regard and tolerance. For the most part, there was no tension or Communist proselytizing.

PART-WORK, PART-STUDY AGRICULTURAL SCHOOL,
  CANTON

We reached this school* after passing through some of the most crowded suburbs of Canton, with narrow streets and tiny dwellings and, in one part, the largest housing-scheme I had seen in China.

The school buildings were the by now familiar mixture of old and new, for the Chung Kai Agricultural School was founded as a 'universal' school in 1927 with its only agricultural subject the study of silkworms. We had the usual cups of tea in a clean, shabby staff-room where the man Principal and woman Vice-Principal gave us figures and answered questions.

There are now twenty-four classrooms and fourteen laboratories; five hundred and twenty-seven students study agronomy, two hundred and twenty-eight plant protection and two hundred and twenty-two animal husbandry; there are forty-eight teachers and thirty-four assistants. Since 1949 the school had turned out nearly five times as many graduates as it did in the twenty-two years before 1949.

The school, we were told, follows the policy of the Communist Party on study and productive labour, so it has special features. Mental and manual labour are equally important; students usually do turn and turn about of each for two weeks at a time with a month's holiday every year of the three-year course. All the students come from near-by communes and are selected by the commune members, being expected to return after graduation.

Students pay no fees as the school is supported by their labour (though the Government has met the high capital costs of establishing the school and pays some maintenance charges).

To keep the all-important balance between hand and head, teachers work in the fields alongside their classes and lecture on the spot; experienced peasants come to advise teachers and students alike out of their accumulated practical experience.

After seeing the library (an old building due for replacement, we were told) and the laboratories, we tramped cheerfully

* Visited in 1965.

through the school fields to see experimental rice and other crops; to watch some twenty students knee-deep in a stream building a small bridge, and to see others learning how to innoculate chickens against fowl disease. We paused in the warm autumn sunshine to listen to a teacher's introductory talk on, I believe, noxious insects, and then saw the students move off into the paddy to collect their own examples of the creatures.

To a wholly non-agricultural observer like me it all seemed to be offering that wedding of theory and practice, mental and manual work, that China is so vigorously promoting. After their three years, all would return to their villages as agricultural advisers. There are many such schools now all over China and it is clear that they must make an invaluable contribution to the development of the agriculture upon which the welfare of China's millions so much depends.

In education, as in many other things, official pronouncements and Party encyclicals translated into practicalities take more heed of human nature than anyone from the outside looking in would expect. Though Communist principles are never sacrificed, they are often tailored to local, even individual, needs if it seems wiser to do so. The pity, even the tragedy, of the world situation is that outside pressures, Western antagonisms, only serve to strengthen the hand of the more rigid doctrinaire Party men, to over-inflate a legitimate and justified national pride; they make it harder for schools and universities to play the role of impartial critics and for the counsels of more liberal academics to be heeded.

On my last visit I noticed stronger urgings to study the works of Mao, to look to these for guidance on everything from playing ping-pong to selling behind the counter; and more stress on Party loyalty. This was not, I believe, because of increased doubts about that loyalty, but because, as the war on China's southern border escalated, as the USSR'S breach with China has widened and its breach with the United States 279 narrowed, the Chinese, in reaction, have found it necessary to proclaim their own doctrine more vigorously. It is one more illustration of the classical, historical truth that threats from without produce the closing of the ranks and the checking of liberalism within.

SOME BASIC FACTS AND FIGURES

Students and Pupils in Educational Institutions

Year	*Total*	*Kindergarten*	*Primary*	Secondary *Jr 12–15 yrs* *Sr 15–18 yrs*	*Tertiary*
		Age 3–7 yrs	*7–12 yrs*		*18 yrs +*
1949–50	25,384,000	not known	24,000,000	1,229,000	155,000
1958–9	100,760,000	(67,000,000)	90,000,000	9,950,000	810,000

(Leo Orleans. *Professional Manpower and Education in Communist China*, Washington, 1961)

1959–60	104,714,000	—	91,000,000	12,900,000	814,000

(inc. 154,000 in short courses)

(Edgar Snow. *The Other Side of the River*)*

1965–6   111,000,000   (Figure given to author in Peking, 1965)

(Figures for full-time students in tertiary institutions vary from source to source because of confusion between full- and part-time students and ambiguous definitions of 'tertiary instruction'.)

Order of priority of courses is: (1) Engineering (2) Education (3) Health (4) Agriculture (5) Science

TEACHERS

1961   3 million *Full-time*
      275,000 *Part-time* (E. Snow)

PART-TIME STUDENTS

1958–9   Higher Schools   150,000 ⎫
         Secondary ,,   5,000,000 ⎬ 31,150,000
         Primary   ,,   26,000,000 ⎭
                  (Leo Orleans)

---

* These and other figures from *The Other Side of the River* are reprinted by kind permission of Edgar Snow and his publishers, Gollancz.

GRADUATES OF TERTIARY INSTITUTIONS
1912–47   222,000
1949–63   1,110,000

(New China News)

FINANCE
1961   *6,400 million yuan*   = 15–20% National Budget
           47% increase on 1959

(E. Snow)

TYPICAL UNIVERSITY UNDERGRADUATE DAY
    5.30 a.m. or 6 a.m.   Rising Bell
    5.50 a.m. or 6.20 a.m.   Exercises
    Breakfast
    7.30 or 8.0 a.m.–12 noon. Lectures
    12.0–2.30   Lunch break, including siesta
    2.30–5 p.m.   Study Period
    5 p.m.   Sports or cultural activities
    9.50 p.m.   Curfew

TYPICAL MIDDLE SCHOOL, 1965
Canton Middle School No. 1
Size: 28,000 square metres
Numbers: Students – 1,212. (300 resident.) Equal boys and girls.
           Staff   –   80 teachers, 42 administrative and clerical,
                         12 'workers'

Classes: 28 = 17 junior; 11 senior
Laboratories: 3 physics
                2 chemistry
                1 biology
                Plus stores for equipment
Most classes have 24 groups with 2–4 students in each supervised by
one teacher and laboratory assistants
Sports: 4 basket-ball courts
          1 volley-ball court
          1 football (soccer) pitch
          200-metre running track
          1 gymnasium
Labour: Several hours a week in city or school workshops, plus 7–10
    days twice a year in the country   281

School Day : 7.40 a.m.–11.45
  2.30 p.m.–5.30, including study time
  Extra curricular activities in evening and weekends
  Mid-morning exercises for the whole school for 10–15 minutes
Subjects : Biology, Physics, Chemistry, Mathematics, Chinese Language and Literature, Foreign Languages, History, Geography and Political Science
Political Studies : 2 periods a week

TWO TYPICAL GENERAL UNIVERSITIES
Age of admission: 18 or 19 years
Time for political study: 12% to 18%

Sun Yat-sen (Canton)
Size : (Floor space) 120,000 square metres
Numbers : Students – 4,300 (1964) ; 994 (1949)
  Staff – 755 (plus 650 administrative)
Main facilities : Arts, Social Science, Natural Science (5-year course)
Time for manual labour : half a day a week, plus one month a year in the country

Chekiang (Hangchow)
Size : (Grounds) 125 acres
Numbers : Students – 7,000
  Staff – 1,000 (plus 400 administrative)
Main facilities : Science and Engineering, Foreign Languages (5-year course)
Time for manual labour : two weeks a year, plus time in the University's laboratories and factories

BIBLIOGRAPHY
(for the general reader)

ADLER, S. *The Chinese Economy* Routledge & Kegan Paul

CH'EN, J. *Mao Tse-tung and the Chinese Revolution* Oxford University Press

CREEL, H. G. *Chinese Thought* Methuen

CUSACK, D. *Chinese Women Speak* Angus & Robertson (Sydney)

FAURE, EDGAR *The Serpent and the Tortoise* Macmillan

FITZGERALD, C. P. *The Birth of Communist China* Penguin.

FITZGERALD, C. P. *The Chinese View of Their Place in the World* Royal Institute of International Affairs, University Press

FITZGERALD, C. P. *China – A Short Cultural History* Cresset

FLEMING, PETER *Siege at Peking* Arrow Books

GELDER, S. *The Long March to Freedom* Macmillan

GELDER, S. and R. *The Timely Rain* Macmillan

GREENE, FELIX *The Wall Has Two Sides* Cape (Paperback)

GREENE, FELIX *A Curtain of Ignorance* Doubleday

GUILLAIN, R. *The Blue Ants* Secker & Warburg

KUO, P. C. *China: New Age, New Outlook* Penguin

MYRDAL, J. *Report from a Chinese Village* Heinemann

PANNIKAR *The Two Chinas* Allen & Unwin

PURCELL, VICTOR *China* Ernest Benn

REISCHAUER, E. and FAIRBANK, K. *East Asia: the Great Tradition* Allen and Unwin

SNOW, EDGAR *Red Star Over China.* Gollancz (re-issued)

SNOW, EDGAR *The Other Side of the River* Gollancz

STILWELL, GENERAL JOSEPH *The Stilwell Papers* Macdonald

STILWELL, GENERAL JOSEPH, *U. S. Relations with China* Department of State (1949)

SUYIN, HAN *The Crippled Tree* Cape

CHINESE PUBLICATIONS:

History of the Modern Chinese Revolution Ho Kan-Chih. Foreign Languages Press (Peking)

An Outline History of China Ho Kan-Chih. Foreign Languages Press (Peking)

Autobiography of Pu Yi (Last Emperor of China)

MAGAZINES:

Eastern Horizon (Hong Kong monthly)

China Quarterly (London)

Far Eastern Economic Review (Hong Kong monthly)

CHINESE (English Language publications):
Peking Review (weekly)
China Pictorial (monthly)
China Reconstructs (monthly)
Women of China (monthly)

INDEX

Index